PENSIONS
POCKET BOOK
2010

GW00493899

ECONOMIC AND FINANCIAL PUBLISHING

IN ASSOCIATION WITH

PENSIONS POCKET BOOK
2010 EDITION

ISBN–10: 1–84116–217–5
ISBN–13: 978–1–84116–217–1

Produced and published by:

Economic and Financial Publishing Ltd ● Farm Road ● Henley-on-Thames
Oxfordshire RG9 1EJ ● United Kingdom
Tel: (01491) 411000 ● Fax: (01491) 418600

Comments and suggestions for future editions of this pocket book are welcomed. Please contact: Editor, Pensions Pocket Book, Economic and Financial Publishing Ltd at the above address.

Whilst every effort has been made in the preparation of this book to ensure accuracy of the statistical and other contents, the publishers and data suppliers cannot accept any liability in respect of errors or omissions or for any losses or consequential losses arising from such errors or omissions. Readers will appreciate that the data contents are only as up-to-date as their availability and compilation, and printing schedules, will allow and are subject to change during the natural course of events.

Printed in Great Britain by the MPG Books Group,
Bodmin and King's Lynn

NOTES

(i) Symbols used:
 '–' *or* 'n/a' = data not available or not available on a comparable basis.
(ii) Constituent figures in the tables may not add up to the totals, due to rounding.
(iii) For full definitions readers are referred to the sources given at the foot of the tables.
(iv) Some topics are mentioned in more than one place but the information is not necessarily from the same source. Any differences are likely to be due to difference in definition, method of calculation or periods covered.

ACKNOWLEDGEMENTS

The publishers would like to thank all those who have contributed to this compilation of pensions data, in particular Hewitt Associates – co-producers of the book – whose contribution and support have been invaluable.

Other contributors, including government departments, whose help is gratefully acknowledged, include:

Allianz Global Investors AG

AP Information Services, a trading name of Waterlow Legal & Regulatory Ltd

Association of Consulting Actuaries

Barclays Capital

BNY Mellon Asset Servicing

Financial Services Authority (FSA)

General Register Office for Scotland

International Monetary Fund

International Social Security Association

London Business School

The National Association of Pension Funds Ltd

Northern Ireland Statistics and Research Agency

Office for National Statistics (ONS)

The Pension Protection Fund

The Pensions Management Institute

The Pensions Regulator

Population Research Bureau

US Social Security Administration

HEWITT ASSOCIATES

Hewitt Associates (NYSE: HEW) provides leading organisations around the world with expert human resources consulting and outsourcing solutions to help them anticipate and solve their most complex benefits, talent and related financial challenges. Hewitt works with companies to design, implement, communicate and administer a wide range of human resources, retirement, investment management, health care, compensation and talent management strategies. With a history of exceptional client service since 1940, Hewitt has offices in more than 30 countries and employs approximately 23,000 associates who are helping to make the world a better place to work. For more information, please visit *www.hewitt.com*.

ECONOMIC AND FINANCIAL PUBLISHING LIMITED

Economic and Financial Publishing Ltd, formerly known as NTC Publications, is a specialist provider of information to pensions professionals and economists working in industry, government and public bodies, education and research institutions.

FOREWORD

It has been a difficult year for pension schemes and their sponsors. The aftermath of the 'credit crunch' has left many defined benefit schemes in a relatively poor funding position, at a time when sponsors have other significant demands on their financial resources.

Some employers have reacted by proposing changes to the benefits provided for future service for all employees, not just new joiners. This typically involves reducing cost and transferring risk to employees for future service, putting pensions at the centre of the industrial relations battleground by moving from defined benefit to defined contribution.

The impact of financial conditions for employees in defined contribution arrangements has often been all too obvious. Surveys indicate that most people now have no idea when they will be able to afford to retire and the impending review of 'compulsory' retirement at 65, brought forward to 2010, could have far-reaching implications for workforce planning.

On top of this, the Government announced complicated new pension taxation rules for higher earners, just three years after 'simplification' of pensions taxation and with immediate effect. Further significant changes are proposed for 2011.

Dealing with existing pension commitments remains an evolving area. De-risking is the objective for many sponsors. The first contracts for the transfer of longevity risks were agreed in 2009 and the market in these 'longevity swaps' appears likely to expand. However, competition in the traditional buy-out market for pension liabilities has reduced from the heights of 2008.

Looking further ahead, the Personal Accounts legislation continues to progress and appears on target for 2012, or at least for commencing phasing in from 2012. However, the proposed contribution rates still appear too low to provide adequate provision pension for many individuals.

This year's *Pensions Pocket Book* includes additional sections on ceasing accrual and the new special annual allowance charge for higher earners. It has guided people though the changing world of pensions for many years. We are sure you will find this year's edition as helpful as previous editions.

Michael Clare
Leader of the UK Retirement practice, Hewitt Associates

CONTENTS

Section 5: UK SOCIAL SECURITY BENEFITS AND TAX RATES

Section 6: CONTRACTING OUT

Section 7: SCHEME DESIGN AND BENEFITS

Section 8: DEFINED CONTRIBUTION PENSION SCHEMES

Section 12: PENSIONS TAXATION (continued)

Section 13: SPECIAL ANNUAL ALLOWANCE CHARGE

Section 14: EMPLOYER-FINANCED RETIREMENT BENEFIT SCHEMES

Section 15: LEAVING SERVICE BENEFITS

Section 16: TRANSFER VALUES

Section 17: DISCLOSURE OF PENSION SCHEME INFORMATION

Section 22: THE PENSION PROTECTION FUND AND LEVY

Section 23: CEASING ACCRUAL

Section 24: SCHEME CLOSURE AND WIND-UP

Section 25: BUY-OUT

Section 31: SIGNIFICANT PENSION DATES

Section 32: UK PENSIONS CASE LAW

Section 33: INTERNATIONAL

High Level Overview:

> Economy and Government; Labour Relations; Cost of Employment;
> Employment Terms and Conditions; Social Security and other
> Required Benefits; Healthcare System; Taxation of Compensation and
> Benefits; Recent Developments,

for the following countries:

APPENDICES

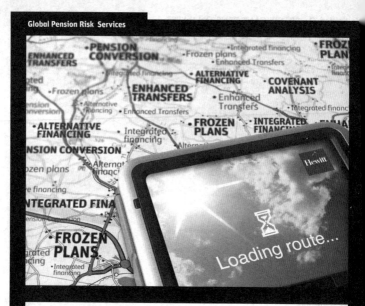

ECONOMICS

THE INTERNAL AND EXTERNAL VALUE OF THE POUND:
1979–2009

	General Index of UK Retail Prices (2000 = 100)		Purchasing power of the £[2] (2000 = 100)	Exchange Rates[1] (Foreign Currency per £ sterling)		
	Index	Yr-on-Yr % Change		US$	Yen	Euro[3]
1979	33.3	13.4	300.6	2.123	465.5	1.479
1980	39.3	18.0	254.8	2.328	525.6	1.624
1981	43.9	11.9	227.7	2.025	444.6	1.785
1982	47.7	8.6	209.7	1.749	435.2	1.767
1983	49.9	4.6	200.5	1.516	359.9	1.706
1984	52.4	5.0	191.0	1.336	316.8	1.697
1985	55.6	6.1	180.0	1.298	307.1	1.710
1986	57.4	3.4	174.1	1.467	246.8	1.482
1987	59.8	4.1	167.1	1.639	236.5	1.404
1988	62.8	4.9	159.3	1.780	228.0	1.499
1989	67.7	7.8	147.8	1.638	225.7	1.469
1990	74.1	9.5	135.0	1.786	257.4	1.373
1991	78.4	5.9	127.5	1.769	237.6	1.400
1992	81.3	3.7	123.0	1.767	223.7	1.333
1993	82.6	1.6	121.0	1.502	166.7	1.262
1994	84.6	2.5	118.2	1.533	156.4	1.272
1995	87.6	3.4	114.2	1.578	148.4	1.191
1996	89.7	2.4	111.5	1.562	170.0	1.210
1997	92.5	3.1	108.1	1.638	198.1	1.449
1998	95.7	3.4	104.5	1.657	216.7	1.489
1999	97.1	1.5	103.0	1.618	184.0	1.519
2000	100.0	3.0	100.0	1.516	163.4	1.642
2001	101.8	1.8	98.3	1.440	174.9	1.609
2002	103.5	1.7	96.6	1.503	187.8	1.591
2003	106.5	2.9	93.9	1.634	189.3	1.445
2004	109.6	3.0	91.2	1.832	198.1	1.474
2005	112.7	2.8	88.7	1.820	200.1	1.463
2006	116.3	3.2	86.0	1.843	214.3	1.467
2007	121.3	4.3	82.4	2.002	235.6	1.462
2008	126.1	4.0	79.3	1.854	192.3	1.258
2009[1,4]	124.8	–1.0	80.1	1.542	146.0	1.129

Notes: [1] Average values over each period. [2] Movements in the purchasing power of the pound are based on movements in the RPI. [3] Prior to January 1999, a synthetic euro has been calculated by geometrically averaging the bilateral exchange rates of the 11 eurozone countries using 'internal weights' based on each country's share of extra-eurozone trade. [4] As to September 2009.

Sources: *Financial Statistics*, National Statistics, © National Statistics website: *www.statistics.gov.uk* Crown copyright material is reproduced with the permission of the Controller of TSO; E&FP.

UK MAIN ECONOMIC INDICATORS, 2002–2008

		2002	2003	2004	2005	2006	2007	2008
Gross Domestic Product[1]								
at current prices	£billion	1,075.6	1,139.7	1,200.6	1,252.5	1,321.9	1,401.0	1,448.1
	% change	5.3	6.0	5.3	4.3	5.5	6.0	3.4
at 2003 prices	£billion	1,108.5	1,139.7	1,171.2	1,195.3	1,229.2	1,266.4	1,222.2
	% change	2.5	2.1	2.8	2.1	2.8	3.0	–3.5
Gross Domestic Product per capita[1]								
at current prices	£	18,131	19,137	20,061	20,793	21,818	22,977	23,590
	% change	4.9	5.6	4.8	3.6	4.9	5.3	2.7
at 2003 prices	£	18,686	19,137	19,570	19,843	20,288	20,769	19,911
	% change	1.7	2.4	2.3	1.4	2.2	2.4	–4.1
Household Final Consumption Expenditure								
at current prices	£billion	681.0	714.6	749.9	784.1	817.0	859.3	891.3
	% change	5.1	4.9	4.9	4.6	4.2	5.2	3.7
at 2003 prices	£billion	720.4	742.8	766.9	784.1	795.6	815.2	822.3
	% change	3.7	3.1	3.2	2.3	1.5	2.5	0.9
Retail Sales Volume	Index	93.0	94.7	99.3	100.0	102.6	106.7	110.1
(2005 = 100)	% change	5.0	1.8	4.9	0.7	2.6	4.0	3.2
Consumer Prices*	Index	103.5	106.5	109.6	112.7	116.3	121.3	126.1
	% change	1.7	2.9	3.0	2.8	3.2	4.3	4.0
Population (Mid-year Est.)	Million	59.3	59.6	59.8	60.2	60.6	61.0	61.4
Average Earnings*	Index	108.2	111.9	116.8	121.5	126.5	131.5	136.1
	% change	3.6	3.4	4.4	4.0	4.1	4.0	3.5
Industrial Production	Index	100.9	100.2	101.3	100.0	100.0	100.3	97.2
(2005 = 100)	% change	–1.6	–0.7	1.1	–1.3	0.0	0.3	–3.1
Unemployment Rate[2]	%	3.1	3.0	2.7	2.7	3.0	2.7	2.8
Interest Rate (Bank Rate)[3]	%	4.00	3.69	4.38	4.65	4.64	5.51	4.59
Gross Fixed Capital Formation								
at 2005 prices	£billion	192.7	194.8	204.8	209.8	223.3	240.6	232.7
	% change	3.6	1.1	5.1	2.4	6.5	7.8	–3.3
Gross Trading Profits[4]								
UK Continental Shelf companies								
at current prices	£billion	18.3	17.9	19.0	23.3	27.6	26.9	37.1
	% change	–3.3	–2.4	6.3	22.6	18.4	–2.7	38.0
Other companies								
at current prices	£billion	160.1	173.6	185.8	190.3	207.7	217.2	218.2
	% change	5.8	8.4	7.1	2.4	9.2	4.5	0.5
at 2000 prices	£billion	154.7	163.1	169.5	168.8	178.6	179.0	173.0
	% change	4.0	5.4	4.0	–0.4	5.8	0.2	–3.4
Balance of Payments								
at current prices	£billion	–18.7	–18.3	–24.9	–32.8	–43.8	–37.7	–23.6

Notes: ONS are rebasing their constant-price data: please note different dates. Indices marked * are 2000 = 100. [1] Gross Domestic Product at market prices, seasonally adjusted. [2] Unemployment rate is the claimant count, seasonally adjusted. Workforce jobs comprise employee jobs, self-employed jobs, HM forces and participants in work-related government supported training. [3] London clearing banks' base rate. [4] Private non-financial corporations.

Sources: *Economic Trends, Mid-2008 population estimates, Economic & Labour Market Review, Financial Statistics* and *Consumer Trends*, National Statistics © Crown Copyright 2009; E&FP.

RETAIL PRICES INDEX

Index based on January 1987 = 100

	Jan.	Feb.	Mar.	Apr.	May	Jun.	Jul.	Aug.	Sep.	Oct.	Nov.	Dec.
1981	70.3	70.9	72.0	74.1	74.6	75.0	75.3	75.9	76.3	77.0	77.8	78.3
1982	78.7	78.8	79.4	81.0	81.6	81.9	81.9	81.9	81.9	82.3	82.7	82.5
1983	82.6	83.0	83.1	84.3	84.6	84.8	85.3	85.7	86.1	86.4	86.7	86.9
1984	86.8	87.2	87.5	88.6	89.0	89.2	89.1	89.9	90.1	90.7	91.0	90.9
1985	91.2	91.9	92.8	94.8	95.2	95.4	95.2	95.5	95.4	95.6	95.9	96.0
1986	96.2	96.6	96.7	97.7	97.8	97.8	97.5	97.8	98.3	98.5	99.3	99.6
1987	100.0	100.4	100.6	101.8	101.9	101.9	101.8	102.1	102.4	102.9	103.4	103.3
1988	103.3	103.7	104.1	105.8	106.2	106.6	106.7	107.9	108.4	109.5	110.0	110.3
1989	111.0	111.8	112.3	114.3	115.0	115.4	115.5	115.8	116.6	117.5	118.5	118.8
1990	119.5	120.2	121.4	125.1	126.2	126.7	126.8	128.1	129.3	130.3	130.0	129.9
1991	130.2	130.9	131.4	133.1	133.5	134.1	133.8	134.1	134.6	135.1	135.6	135.7
1992	135.6	136.3	136.7	138.8	139.3	139.3	138.8	138.9	139.4	139.9	139.7	139.2
1993	137.9	138.8	139.3	140.6	141.1	141.0	140.7	141.3	141.9	141.8	141.6	141.9
1994	141.3	142.1	142.5	144.2	144.7	144.7	144.0	144.7	145.0	145.2	145.3	146.0
1995	146.0	146.9	147.5	149.0	149.6	149.8	149.1	149.9	150.6	149.8	149.8	150.7
1996	150.2	150.9	151.5	152.6	152.9	153.0	152.4	153.1	153.8	153.8	153.9	154.4
1997	154.4	155.0	155.4	156.3	156.9	157.5	157.5	158.5	159.3	159.5	159.6	160.0
1998	159.5	160.3	160.8	162.6	163.5	163.4	163.0	163.7	164.4	164.5	164.4	164.4
1999	163.4	163.7	164.1	165.2	165.6	165.6	165.1	165.5	166.2	166.5	166.7	167.3
2000	166.6	167.5	168.4	170.1	170.7	171.1	170.5	170.5	171.7	171.6	172.1	172.2
2001	171.1	172.0	172.2	173.1	174.2	174.4	173.3	174.0	174.6	174.3	173.6	173.4
2002	173.3	173.8	174.5	175.7	176.2	176.2	175.9	176.4	177.6	177.9	178.2	178.5
2003	178.4	179.3	179.9	181.2	181.5	181.3	181.3	181.6	182.5	182.6	182.7	183.5
2004	183.1	183.8	184.6	185.7	186.5	186.8	186.8	187.4	188.1	188.6	189.0	189.9
2005	188.9	189.6	190.5	191.6	192.0	192.2	192.2	192.6	193.1	193.3	193.6	194.1
2006	193.4	194.2	195.0	196.5	197.7	198.5	198.5	199.2	200.1	200.4	201.1	202.7
2007	201.6	203.1	204.4	205.4	206.2	207.3	206.1	207.3	208.0	208.9	209.7	210.9
2008	209.8	211.4	212.1	214.0	215.1	216.8	216.5	217.2	218.4	217.7	216.0	212.9
2009	210.1	211.4	211.3	211.5	212.8	213.4	213.4	214.4	215.3			

Source: Hewitt, compiled from government information.

RETAIL PRICES INFLATION

Percentage increase in the Retail Prices Index over previous 12 months

	Jan. %	Feb. %	Mar. %	Apr. %	May %	Jun. %	Jul. %	Aug. %	Sep. %	Oct. %	Nov. %	Dec. %
1999	2.4	2.1	2.1	1.6	1.3	1.3	1.3	1.1	1.1	1.2	1.4	1.8
2000	2.0	2.3	2.6	3.0	3.1	3.3	3.3	3.0	3.3	3.1	3.2	2.9
2001	2.7	2.7	2.3	1.8	2.1	1.9	1.6	2.1	1.7	1.6	0.9	0.7
2002	1.3	1.0	1.3	1.5	1.1	1.0	1.5	1.4	1.7	2.1	2.6	2.9
2003	2.9	3.2	3.1	3.1	3.0	2.9	3.1	2.9	2.8	2.6	2.5	2.8
2004	2.6	2.5	2.6	2.5	2.8	3.0	3.0	3.2	3.1	3.3	3.4	3.5
2005	3.2	3.2	3.2	3.2	2.9	2.9	2.9	2.8	2.7	2.5	2.4	2.2
2006	2.4	2.4	2.4	2.6	3.0	3.3	3.3	3.4	3.6	3.7	3.9	4.4
2007	4.2	4.6	4.8	4.5	4.3	4.4	3.8	4.1	3.9	4.2	4.3	4.0
2008	4.1	4.1	3.8	4.2	4.3	4.6	5.0	4.8	5.0	4.2	3.0	0.9
2009	0.1	0.0	−0.4	−1.2	−1.1	−1.6	−1.4	−1.3	−1.4			

Source: Hewitt, compiled from government information.

TRENDS IN AVERAGE EARNINGS PER PERSON
PER WEEK AND THE HOUSEHOLDS' SAVINGS RATIO

	at Current Prices		at Constant 2008 Prices		Households' Savings Ratio (%)
	Average Earnings (£pw)	Annual Change (%)	Average Earnings (£pw)	Annual Change (%)	
1968	24.92	2.3	323.40	−2.3	5.6
1969	26.33	5.7	324.99	0.5	5.7
1970	29.02	10.2	336.26	3.5	6.6
1971	31.43	8.3	333.55	−0.8	5.0
1972	34.26	9.0	338.29	1.4	7.3
1973	37.38	9.1	338.22	0.0	8.2
1974	44.74	19.7	349.17	3.2	8.4
1975	59.04	32.0	371.42	6.4	9.2
1976	64.81	9.8	349.48	−5.9	8.7
1977	70.62	9.0	328.70	−5.9	7.6
1978	79.69	12.8	342.63	4.2	9.4
1979	92.00	15.4	348.78	1.8	10.9
1980	111.15	20.8	357.22	2.4	12.3
1981	125.35	12.8	366.09	0.8	12.0
1982	137.15	9.4	362.80	0.8	10.8
1983	148.77	8.5	376.19	3.7	9.0
1984	157.67	6.0	379.86	1.0	10.2
1985	171.00	8.5	388.35	2.2	9.7
1986	184.80	8.1	405.81	4.5	8.1
1987	198.90	7.6	419.41	3.4	5.4
1988	218.70	10.0	439.58	4.8	3.9
1989	239.80	9.6	447.12	1.7	5.7
1990	263.20	9.8	448.28	0.3	8.1
1991	284.70	8.2	458.08	2.2	10.3
1992	304.80	7.1	472.78	3.2	11.7
1993	317.30	4.1	484.59	2.5	10.8
1994	326.10	2.8	485.99	0.3	9.3
1995	337.60	3.5	486.53	0.1	10.3
1996	351.50	4.1	494.46	1.6	9.4
1997	367.60	4.6	501.40	1.4	9.6
1998	392.50	6.8	517.67	3.2	7.4
1999	407.80	3.9	529.61	2.3	5.2
2000	425.10	4.2	536.38	1.3	4.7
2001	449.70	5.8	557.27	3.9	6.0
2002	472.10	5.0	575.62	3.3	4.8
2003	487.10	3.2	577.09	0.3	5.1
2004	498.20	2.3	573.30	−0.7	3.7
2005	517.00	3.8	578.59	0.9	3.9
2006	534.90	3.5	580.02	0.2	2.9
2007	550.30	2.9	572.27	−1.3	2.2
2008	574.30	4.4	574.30	0.4	1.7

Notes: **Constant 2008 Prices**: Deflated by the Retail Prices Index (2008 = 100). **Earnings**: Wages and salaries of those in employment, excluding those whose pay is affected by absence. Pre-1971 data are derived from average salaries/unit of output; later data from the earnings index of all adults in employment. **Households' Savings Ratio**: Households' saving as % Total Resources; the latter is the sum of Gross Household Disposable Income and the Adjustment for the net equity of the households in pension funds.

Sources: ASHE and *Financial Statistics*, National Statistics, © Crown Copyright 2009; E&FP.

DEMOGRAPHIC & EMPLOYMENT DATA

POPULATION DATA, MID-2008

By Nation

Thousands

	Total	Males	Females
England	51,446	25,319	26,128
Wales	2,993	1,462	1,532
Scotland	5,169	2,500	2,668
Great Britain	**59,608**	**29,281**	**30,328**
Northern Ireland	1,775	871	904
United Kingdom	**61,383**	**30,151**	**31,232**

By Sex and Age, UK

	Total		Males		Females	
Age	*'000s*	*%*	*'000s*	*%*	*'000s*	*%*
0–4	3,700	6.0	1,895	3.1	1,805	2.9
5–9	3,395	5.5	1,737	2.8	1,658	2.7
10–14	3,659	6.0	1,873	3.1	1,785	2.9
15–19	3,988	6.5	2,049	3.3	1,939	3.2
20–24	4,228	6.9	2,166	3.5	2,061	3.4
25–29	4,074	6.6	2,069	3.4	2,006	3.3
30–34	3,826	6.2	1,916	3.1	1,910	3.1
35–39	4,438	7.2	2,197	3.6	2,242	3.7
40–44	4,714	7.7	2,336	3.8	2,377	3.9
45–49	4,353	7.1	2,145	3.5	2,208	3.6
50–54	3,807	6.2	1,882	3.1	1,925	3.1
55–59	3,633	5.9	1,788	2.9	1,845	3.0
60–64	3,639	5.9	1,778	2.9	1,861	3.0
65–69	2,756	4.5	1,324	2.2	1,432	2.3
70–74	2,399	3.9	1,123	1.8	1,275	2.1
75–79	1,985	3.2	873	1.4	1,112	1.8
80–84	1,455	2.4	579	0.9	876	1.4
85–89	918	1.5	313	0.5	605	1.0
90+	417	0.7	108	0.2	309	0.5
Total	**61,383**	**100.0**	**30,151**	**49.1**	**31,232**	**50.9**

Population Projections, UK

Thousands

	2008 (base)	Projections			
		2013	2018	2023	2028
0–14	10,753	11,001	11,550	11,851	11,942
15–44	25,271	7,113	7,614	7,847	7,963
45–64	15,436	16,144	16,735	16,679	16,531
65–74	5,156	5,959	6,471	6,457	7,020
75+	4,776	5,194	5,794	6,951	7,858
Total	**61,393**	**63,498**	**65,645**	**67,816**	**69,832**

Sources: *Mid-2008 Population Estimates*, National Statistics © Crown Copyright 2009; General Register Office for Scotland; Northern Ireland Statistics and Research Agency, Government Actuary's Department.

EXPECTATIONS OF LIFE

Age x	Males Expectation	Females Expectation	Age x	Males Expectation	Females Expectation
0	77.68	81.84			
1	77.10	81.20	51	29.15	32.47
2	76.13	80.23	52	28.27	31.55
3	75.15	79.24	53	27.38	30.64
4	74.16	78.25	54	26.51	29.73
5	73.17	77.26	55	25.65	28.83
6	72.18	76.27	56	24.80	27.94
7	71.19	75.28	57	23.95	27.05
8	70.20	74.28	58	23.11	26.16
9	69.21	73.29	59	22.28	25.28
10	68.22	72.30	60	21.45	24.41
11	67.22	71.30	61	20.63	23.54
12	66.23	70.31	62	19.83	22.69
13	65.24	69.32	63	19.04	21.84
14	64.25	68.32	64	18.26	21.00
15	63.26	67.33	65	17.50	20.17
16	62.27	66.34	66	16.75	19.35
17	61.29	65.35	67	16.01	18.54
18	60.32	64.37	68	15.29	17.73
19	59.36	63.38	69	14.58	16.94
20	58.39	62.40	70	13.88	16.16
21	57.43	61.41	71	13.19	15.40
22	56.47	60.43	72	12.51	14.64
23	55.50	59.45	73	11.86	13.90
24	54.54	58.46	74	11.23	13.18
25	53.58	57.48	75	10.61	12.47
26	52.61	56.49	76	10.01	11.78
27	51.65	55.51	77	9.44	11.11
28	50.69	54.53	78	8.88	10.47
29	49.73	53.55	79	8.35	9.84
30	48.77	52.57	80	7.85	9.24
31	47.82	51.59	81	7.37	8.66
32	46.86	50.61	82	6.91	8.11
33	45.91	49.63	83	6.48	7.57
34	44.95	48.66	84	6.07	7.07
35	44.00	47.68	85	5.70	6.59
36	43.06	46.71	86	5.34	6.14
37	42.11	45.74	87	5.01	5.70
38	41.16	44.77	88	4.66	5.28
39	40.22	43.80	89	4.33	4.89
40	39.28	42.84	90	4.00	4.50
41	38.34	41.88	91	3.71	4.15
42	37.40	40.92	92	3.46	3.84
43	36.47	39.97	93	3.23	3.57
44	35.54	39.02	94	3.01	3.31
45	34.61	38.07	95	2.79	3.08
46	33.69	37.13	96	2.60	2.88
47	32.77	36.18	97	2.43	2.69
48	31.86	35.25	98	2.30	2.50
49	30.95	34.32	99	2.14	2.34
50	30.05	33.39	100	1.97	2.19

Note: The table shows the future expectation of life at various ages of lives subject to the mortality experience of England and Wales in the years 2006 to 2008. The table makes no allowance for improvement in mortality.

Source: 'Interim Life Tables', National Statistics © Crown Copyright 2009.

WORKFORCE JOBS – UNITED KINGDOM*

	June 1989		June 2008		June 2009	
	'000s	%	'000s	%	'000s	%
– Male	12,458	40.6	13,739	42.3	13,257	40.7
– Female	11,694	38.1	13,493	41.5	13,277	40.8
All employee jobs	24,152	78.7	27,232	83.8	26,533	81.5
Self-employed jobs	3,971	12.9	4,181	12.9	4,222	13.0
HM Forces	322	1.0	193	0.6	197	0.6
Government-supported trainees	467	1.5	54	0.2	45	0.1
Workforce jobs	28,912	94.3	31,661	97.4	30,997	95.2
Claimant unemployment	1,762	5.7	843	2.6	1,558	4.8
Total	30,674	100	32,504	100.0	32,555	100.0
Index (June 1989=100)	100.0		106.0		106.1	

Notes: * Seasonally adjusted.
             Employer surveys now measure 'jobs' rather than 'people'. Therefore, figures for the 'total
             working population' are no longer published. (Please refer to the source below for full
             definitions and notes.)

Source: *Economic & Labour Market Review*, National Statistics © Crown Copyright 2009.

UK EMPLOYMENT AND UNEMPLOYMENT

	Total Workers '000s	Employed Labour Force '000s	Employees in Employment '000s	Claimant unemployment	
				'000s	% of Working Population
1989	28,700	26,709	22,577	1,768	6.2
1990	28,775	26,922	22,783	1,648	5.7
1991	28,584	26,365	22,404	2,268	7.9
1992	28,454	25,632	21,634	2,742	9.6
1993	28,181	25,304	21,405	2,877	10.0
1994	28,104	25,505	21,528	2,599	9.2
1995	28,109	25,819	21,865	2,290	8.1
1996	28,147	26,060	22,197	2,087	8.1
1997	28,110	26,526	22,743	1,584	5.6
1998	28,143	26,795	23,182	1,348	4.8
1999	28,415	27,167	23,603	1,248	4.4
2000	28,571	27,483	23,975	1,088	3.8
2001	28,680	27,710	24,183	970	3.4
2002	28,868	27,921	24,386	947	3.3
2003	29,119	28,186	24,427	933	3.2
2004	29,337	28,484	24,645	853	2.9
2005	29,636	28,774	24,928	862	2.9
2006	29,975	29,030	25,098	945	3.2
2007	30,083	29,220	25,186	863	2.9
2008	30,324	29,419	25,411	905	2.7
2009 Jun–Aug	30,534	28,952	24,882	1,582	5.2

Source: *Economic & Labour Market Review*, National Statistics © Crown Copyright 2009.

ANALYSIS BY INDUSTRY OF EMPLOYEES IN EMPLOYMENT – GREAT BRITAIN

	June 1999		June 2009	
Standard Industrial Classification 1992	'000s	%	'000s	%
Agriculture, hunting, forestry & fishing	293	1.2	256	1.0
Mining & quarrying, supply of electricity, gas & water	205	0.8	178	0.7
Food products, beverages & tobacco	505	2.0	403	1.5
Manufacture of clothing, textiles leather & leather products	326	1.3	93	0.4
Wood & wood products	84	0.3	70	0.3
Paper, pulp, printing, publishing & recording media	469	1.9	326	1.2
Chemicals, chemical products & man-made fibres	249	1.0	171	0.6
Rubber & plastic products	244	1.0	162	0.6
Non-metallic mineral products, metal & metal products	674	2.7	430	1.6
Machinery & equipment	373	1.5	252	0.9
Electrical & optical equipment	497	2.0	274	1.0
Transport equipment	399	1.6	285	1.1
Coke, nuclear fuel & other manufacturing	239	1.0	178	0.7
Construction	1,117	4.5	1,297	4.9
Wholesale & retail trade & repairs	4,364	17.4	4,461	16.8
Hotels & restaurants	1,632	6.5	1,772	6.7
Transport & storage	982	3.9	1,085	4.1
Post & telecommunications	482	1.9	446	1.7
Financial intermediation	1,073	4.3	1,004	3.8
Real estate	312	1.2	435	1.6
Renting, research, computer & other business activities	3,278	13.1	4,078	15.4
Public administration & defence; compulsory social security	1,360	5.4	1,469	5.5
Education	1,958	7.8	2,450	9.2
Health & social work activities	2,724	10.9	3,529	13.3
Other community social & personal activities	1,251	5.0	1,424	5.4
All industries & services	25,090	100.0	26,528	100.0

Seasonally adjusted

Source: *Economic & Labour Market Review*, National Statistics © Crown Copyright 2009.

UK ANNUAL INFLATION

UK INVESTMENT YIELDS AND INFLATION

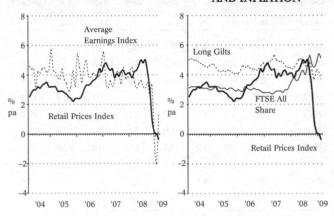

UK INTEREST RATES AND INFLATION

Notes:

[1] Base for Retail Prices Index (RPI) is 1987, and base for Average Earnings Index (AEI) is 2000.

[2] Index for Long Gilts is based on all issues with a term of 15 years.

[3] 3-month Interbank Rate shown is the mid-rate.

Sources:

RPI and AEI data derived from information published by Office for National Statistics. All other figures collated by Hewitt.

UK INVESTMENT HISTORY (1)

One year returns to end of:	Annual Increase[1]:			Corresponding Annual Rate of Return on Investments:				
	RPI[2] %	TPI[3] %	AEI[4] %	Cash Deposits %	Long Gilts %	Index-linked Gilts %	U.K. Equities %	Median Fund[5] %
1999	1.8	1.3	6.3	5.4	−0.4	4.4	24.2	19.8
2000	2.9	2.9	5.1	6.1	8.0	4.3	−5.9	−0.9
2001	0.7	−0.8	2.1	5.0	−0.9	−0.5	−13.3	−9.8
2002	2.9	3.1	3.2	4.0	9.9	8.2	−22.7	−17.0
2003	2.8	3.6	3.1	3.7	1.2	6.6	20.9	19.0
2004	3.5	3.5	4.2	4.6	8.4	8.5	12.8	11.3
2005	2.2	2.0	4.2	4.7	11.0	9.0	22.0	21.5
2006	4.4	4.4	3.9	4.8	0.0	2.9	16.8	11.8
2007	4.0	4.0	3.8	6.0	2.7	8.5	5.3	8.6
2008	0.9	−0.3	3.3	5.5	13.6	3.7	−29.9	−18.6

Average annual increases and rates of return for periods to end of 2008 (number of years in brackets):

1999 (10)	2.6	2.4	3.9	5.0	5.2	5.5	1.2	3.5
2000 (9)	2.7	2.5	3.7	4.9	5.9	5.6	−1.1	1.9
2001 (8)	2.7	2.4	3.5	4.8	5.6	5.8	−0.5	2.2
2002 (7)	3.0	2.9	3.7	4.7	6.6	6.7	1.5	4.0
2003 (6)	3.0	2.9	3.7	4.9	6.0	6.5	6.2	8.0
2004 (5)	3.0	2.7	3.9	5.1	7.0	6.5	3.5	6.0
2005 (4)	2.9	2.5	3.8	5.2	6.7	6.0	1.3	4.7
2006 (3)	3.1	2.7	3.7	5.4	5.3	5.0	−4.8	−0.4
2007 (2)	2.5	1.8	3.6	5.7	8.0	6.1	−14.1	−6.0

Notes: [1] The increase shown is measured over the calendar year(s) from December to December.

[2] Retail Prices Index.   [3] Tax and Prices Index.

[4] Average Earnings Index, whole economy, not seasonally adjusted, including bonus.

[5] The median fund represents the total fund return, as at 31 December, taken from BNY Mellon Asset Servicing's CAPS Universe.

Source: Annual increases in indices and annual rates of return collated, and averages calculated, by Hewitt.

UK INVESTMENT HISTORY (2)

Historic Yields and Returns (% p.a.)

5 Years to end of:	Retail Prices Index	UK Assets: Real Rates of Return		
		Equities	Government Bonds	Treasury Bills
1963	2.2	11.6	–	–
1968	3.8	10.3	–2.9	1.7
1973	7.5	–6.6	–4.6	–0.7
1978	16.1	–0.3	–2.1	–4.6
1983	11.2	11.0	6.0	2.2
1988	4.7	13.9	5.7	5.4
1993	5.6	11.9	9.5	5.9
1998	3.0	10.2	7.9	3.5
2003	2.2	–3.3	1.3	2.7
2008	3.4	0.2	3.5	2.0
10 Years to end of:				
1963	–	12.2	–1.7	–
1968	3.0	11.0	–1.4	–
1973	5.6	1.5	–3.7	0.5
1978	11.7	–3.5	–3.3	–2.7
1983	13.6	5.2	1.9	–1.3
1988	7.9	12.4	5.8	3.8
1993	5.2	12.9	7.6	5.7
1998	4.3	11.1	8.7	4.7
2003	2.6	3.2	4.6	3.1
2008	2.8	–1.5	2.4	2.4

Sources: Office for National Statistics and Barclays Capital Equity Gilt Study.

UK INVESTMENT RETURNS AND INFLATION

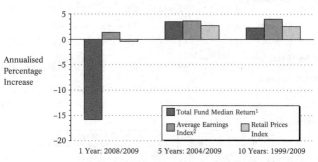

Notes:
[1] The median fund return represents the median return achieved by all pension funds participating in the Mellon Analytical Solutions performance measurement service.
[2] Average Earnings Index data represents the whole economy, not seasonally adjusted, including bonus. Returns shown are to March 2009.

Sources: BNY Mellon Asset Servicing pension fund information service, data to 31 March 2009. Hewitt, compiled from government information.

INDEX RETURNS FOR YEARS TO 31 MARCH

	2000 %	2001 %	2002 %	2003 %	2004 %	2005 %	2006 %	2007 %	2008 %	2009 %
FTSE All-Share	9.9	–10.8	–3.2	–29.8	31.0	15.6	28.0	11.1	–7.7	–29.3
FTSE-AW All-World excl. UK[1]	26.2	–14.8	–3.4	–31.4	25.4	7.3	31.9	2.4	–1.0	–19.8
CAPS Consensus Overseas (incl. Emerging Mkts)	28.1	–16.2	–6.0	–30.2	35.2	10.7	36.3	5.5	0.1	–22.6
FTSE USA	19.6	–12.9	–0.6	–32.4	15.9	3.8	23.0	–1.0	–6.2	–13.4
FTSE W Europe excl. UK	23.0	–11.4	–7.4	–34.4	36.4	18.2	35.5	12.0	2.4	–31.4
FTSE-AW Japan	56.3	–28.0	–20.8	–25.6	46.4	–4.3	48.1	–10.0	–15.5	–10.8
FTSE-AW Dev. Asia Pacific excl. Japan[2]	23.4	–9.8	5.8	–19.1	33.4	18.5	33.8	**19.9**	8.6	–22.4
incl. Japan[2]	49.5	–24.9	–15.1	–23.7	42.5	1.9	44.0	–2.0	–7.6	–15.3
FTSE-AW Canada	**57.8**	–16.1	3.1	–19.6	31.8	**20.0**	47.5	0.6	17.3	–22.1
MSCI Emerging Markets Free	53.4	–28.2	**14.6**	–28.6	**56.2**	13.4	**60.6**	6.7	**19.7**	–26.6
FTSE Actuaries										
All Stocks Gilts	1.3	7.4	1.6	11.3	2.3	5.0	7.4	0.6	7.6	10.3
ILG[3] (All Stocks)	2.7	1.2	3.3	10.4	6.2	5.4	8.4	3.0	13.1	–1.3
ML Sterling Non-gilt	0.7	10.0	5.4	10.9	5.0	6.4	7.8	1.2	–0.8	–5.9
JP Morgan Traded WXUK	0.3	**11.4**	0.3	**12.5**	–2.8	2.3	3.7	–5.1	19.1	**36.7**
CAPS UK Cash	5.0	5.7	4.4	3.7	3.5	4.5	4.5	4.8	5.6	3.6
CAPS Property	15.1	10.8	4.4	7.1	9.3	18.4	21.9	17.6	–11.3	–27.4
CAPS Discretionary excl. Property	11.1	–8.1	–2.7	–23.0	26.2	12.2	27.3	7.4	–2.2	–19.2
CAPS Discretionary incl. Property	11.2	–7.6	–2.5	–22.2	25.6	12.2	27.2	7.6	–2.2	–19.2
Retail Prices Index	2.6	2.3	1.3	3.1	2.6	3.2	2.4	4.8	3.8	–0.4
Earnings Index	5.6	4.3	3.0	4.7	4.6	4.3	4.5	3.5	4.5	1.4

Notes:
[1] FTSE-W World excl. UK to 30 Sep. 2000; FTSE-AW All-World excl. UK thereafter.

[2] FTSE-W Asia Pacific to 30 Sep. 2000; FTSE-AW Developed Asia Pacific thereafter. This applies to both indices (i.e. excluding and including Japan).

[3] UK index-linked gilts.

This table details the returns achieved on representative indices in the individual years during the ten-year period ending 31 March 2009 and highlights (in **bold**) the best index in each year. Increases in the Retail Prices Index and the Average Earnings Index are also shown for comparison, with the latter representing not-seasonally-adjusted data for the whole economy, including bonus.

Sources: BNY Mellon Asset Servicing's Index Returns to 31 March 2009, and Office for National Statistics.

INDEX RETURNS OVER CUMULATIVE PERIODS ENDING 31 MARCH 2009

Annualised Returns	Last 12 Months %	Last 3 Years %	Last 5 Years %	Last 10 Years %
UK Equities	−29.3	−10.2	1.4	−0.7
UK Smaller Companies	−40.4	−19.3	−5.5	−0.6
Overseas Equities	−19.8	−6.7	2.9	0.3
North American	−14.0	−6.7	1.0	−1.3
European (excl. UK)	−31.1	−7.5	4.8	1.3
Pan-European	−30.2	−8.1	3.9	0.8
Japanese	−10.8	−12.1	−0.8	−0.7
Pacific Basin (excl. Japan)	−22.4	0.3	9.9	7.4
Emerging Markets	−26.4	−1.8	**11.7**	**9.4**
UK Bonds (Standard)	10.3	6.1	6.1	5.4
UK Bonds (Long Term)	8.6	4.1	5.7	4.9
International Bonds	**36.7**	**15.6**	10.4	7.2
Index-linked Gilts	−1.3	4.8	5.6	5.2
Sterling Cash	3.9	4.8	4.7	4.6
Property Assets	−27.4	−8.8	1.8	5.5

Note: The best performing sector over each period is highlighted in **bold** typeface.
Source: BNY Mellon Asset Servicing.

PENSION FUND INVESTMENT PERFORMANCE FOR YEARS TO 31 MARCH

Table 1: Total Fund

Per cent

	9th Decile	Lower Quartile	Median	Upper Quartile	1st Decile
1999/2000	8.5	11.1	13.5	16.4	19.1
2000/01	−11.8	−9.6	−7.6	−5.3	−1.7
2001/02	−3.6	−2.4	−1.5	−0.5	0.6
2002/03	−26.2	−23.1	−20.9	−16.2	−10.1
2003/04	16.0	20.0	23.3	25.7	28.1
2004/05	8.6	9.6	10.6	11.7	13.0
2005/06	18.1	20.3	23.1	25.4	28.1
2006/07	3.1	4.3	5.7	6.8	8.1
2007/08	−5.0	−3.1	−1.5	0.6	3.1
2008/09	−21.9	−19.3	−15.8	−11.8	−7.1

Table 2: Total Fund excluding Property

Per cent

	9th Decile	Lower Quartile	Median	Upper Quartile	1st Decile
1999/2000	8.3	11.1	13.5	16.4	19.1
2000/01	−11.9	−9.9	−7.8	−5.5	−2.1
2001/02	−3.6	−2.6	−1.6	−0.6	0.4
2002/03	−26.6	−23.7	−21.4	−16.8	−10.4
2003/04	16.0	20.1	23.6	26.0	28.5
2004/05	8.6	9.5	10.5	11.6	12.9
2005/06	18.0	20.3	23.1	25.5	28.1
2006/07	3.0	4.0	5.4	6.6	7.7
2007/08	−4.7	−2.8	−1.2	0.7	3.9
2008/09	−21.8	−19.3	−15.6	−11.2	−6.6

(Continued overleaf)

Table 3: UK Equities   Per cent

	9th Decile	Lower Quartile	Median	Upper Quartile	1st Decile
1999/2000	6.4	8.6	10.7	13.8	17.0
2000/01	−12.6	−10.9	−9.3	−6.9	−3.1
2001/02	−5.0	−3.5	−2.4	−1.3	0.2
2002/03	−31.5	−30.6	−29.8	−29.0	−28.3
2003/04	28.9	30.3	31.5	33.3	35.2
2004/05	13.6	14.5	15.2	15.8	17.2
2005/06	24.6	26.2	27.8	29.3	31.1
2006/07	8.4	9.7	11.1	11.9	13.3
2007/08	−12.1	−9.2	−7.8	−6.2	−2.8
2008/09	−33.7	−30.3	−29.1	−27.2	−23.7

Table 4: Overseas Equities   Per cent

	9th Decile	Lower Quartile	Median	Upper Quartile	1st Decile
1999/2000	24.7	29.9	37.0	39.1	44.9
2000/01	−22.6	−21.4	−18.2	−15.5	−10.2
2001/02	−6.9	−5.6	−4.5	−3.1	−1.5
2002/03	−32.8	−31.9	−30.9	−29.7	−28.5
2003/04	26.6	29.6	32.0	33.9	35.9
2004/05	6.0	7.9	9.4	10.6	12.2
2005/06	31.0	33.0	35.0	37.5	39.9
2006/07	0.1	1.8	3.6	5.5	8.4
2007/08	−8.0	−5.6	−3.3	−0.9	2.1
2008/09	−33.5	−28.0	−22.3	−19.7	−17.7

Table 5: US Equities   Per cent

	9th Decile	Lower Quartile	Median	Upper Quartile	1st Decile
1999/2000	10.1	11.7	16.7	22.1	26.6
2000/01	−22.1	−20.8	−17.9	−12.5	−5.8
2001/02	−5.8	−4.7	−2.8	−0.6	3.2
2002/03	−39.1	−34.4	−32.4	−30.8	−29.9
2003/04	12.6	13.4	15.8	16.6	22.2
2004/05	−3.1	3.3	4.2	5.8	9.3
2005/06	19.6	21.8	23.5	26.2	30.1
2006/07	−7.4	−4.0	−2.0	−0.6	3.2
2007/08	−18.5	−13.6	−8.0	−5.0	1.5
2008/09	−37.1	−28.6	−15.9	−13.2	−9.8

Table 6: European (excluding UK) Equities   Per cent

	9th Decile	Lower Quartile	Median	Upper Quartile	1st Decile
1999/2000	20.3	24.6	32.0	37.5	40.5
2000/01	−19.2	−14.8	−12.8	−11.0	−6.6
2001/02	−7.4	−6.8	−5.3	−4.0	−2.2
2002/03	−36.7	−35.3	−34.5	−33.3	−31.4
2003/04	31.8	33.4	35.1	36.6	38.2
2004/05	14.8	17.1	18.5	20.1	21.9
2005/06	34.3	35.3	36.0	38.1	41.1
2006/07	7.6	9.6	11.8	12.7	14.7
2007/08	−7.1	−1.9	2.1	3.0	4.3
2008/09	−37.1	−33.0	−30.8	−27.9	−23.3

Table 7: Japanese Equities

Per cent

	9th Decile	Lower Quartile	Median	Upper Quartile	1st Decile
1999/2000	45.1	56.0	62.0	71.0	85.0
2000/01	−34.4	−33.6	−29.9	−26.8	−23.7
2001/02	−22.8	−21.1	−20.4	−18.1	−12.9
2002/03	−28.8	−27.4	−25.5	−25.1	−22.9
2003/04	33.0	35.8	43.8	48.0	52.6
2004/05	−6.3	−4.8	−4.2	−2.7	−1.5
2005/06	43.2	47.5	49.3	51.9	55.2
2006/07	−16.3	−12.7	−10.1	−8.3	−4.3
2007/08	−22.3	−18.6	−16.2	−15.0	−13.1
2008/09	−29.1	−21.4	−14.3	−10.6	−9.5

Table 8: Pacific Basin (excluding Japan) Equities

Per cent

	9th Decile	Lower Quartile	Median	Upper Quartile	1st Decile
1999/2000	20.4	26.3	38.3	43.5	52.6
2000/01	−26.6	−20.6	−11.7	−8.3	−3.8
2001/02	3.1	6.3	7.4	10.8	14.6
2002/03	−29.1	−25.8	−22.1	−19.6	−18.9
2003/04	31.8	33.5	35.4	40.2	43.6
2004/05	8.8	12.9	17.8	19.1	21.2
2005/06	29.0	33.6	35.2	38.5	43.7
2006/07	11.3	16.1	19.9	21.4	25.5
2007/08	3.1	6.1	9.1	11.5	15.5
2008/09	−29.3	−24.4	−21.9	−20.8	−17.9

Table 9: Overseas Bonds

Per cent

	9th Decile	Lower Quartile	Median	Upper Quartile	1st Decile
1999/2000	−6.2	−5.0	−2.8	−1.8	−0.3
2000/01	11.0	12.3	13.6	15.4	17.8
2001/02	−1.9	−0.8	0.6	2.2	3.9
2002/03	8.0	11.0	13.5	21.0	29.9
2003/04	−4.4	−3.0	−1.0	2.1	3.9
2004/05	1.9	3.2	5.4	8.3	14.3
2005/06	3.5	4.5	6.4	9.7	16.3
2006/07	−14.0	−6.0	−4.6	−2.9	2.4
2007/08	−0.5	4.5	11.7	15.2	18.5
2008/09	−21.2	−11.6	15.0	27.6	37.0

Table 10: UK Bonds

Per cent

	9th Decile	Lower Quartile	Median	Upper Quartile	1st Decile
1999/2000	−0.2	0.1	0.5	1.3	2.7
2000/01	4.3	6.3	7.7	8.7	9.5
2001/02	−1.0	0.7	2.0	2.7	3.9
2002/03	10.1	11.1	12.0	12.8	13.4
2003/04	2.5	3.0	3.6	4.4	5.2
2004/05	5.3	5.7	6.1	6.4	6.9
2005/06	7.3	7.8	9.1	10.2	10.7
2006/07	−1.0	−0.5	0.3	0.9	1.4
2007/08	−3.1	−0.1	1.6	3.6	5.6
2008/09	−6.4	−3.5	0.5	2.8	7.6

(Continued overleaf)

Table 11: UK Index-linked Gilts   Per cent

	9th Decile	Lower Quartile	Median	Upper Quartile	1st Decile
1999/2000	1.8	2.5	2.7	3.0	3.5
2000/01	−0.2	0.0	0.7	1.3	2.1
2001/02	2.5	2.8	3.2	3.6	4.0
2002/03	10.1	10.4	10.8	11.0	11.2
2003/04	5.9	6.3	6.6	6.7	7.1
2004/05	5.4	5.6	5.7	5.9	6.4
2005/06	7.8	8.4	8.9	9.0	9.5
2006/07	2.4	2.6	2.7	3.0	3.2
2007/08	11.6	13.1	13.5	13.6	13.9
2008/09	−4.8	−2.9	−2.7	−1.6	−1.2

Table 12: Property   Per cent

	9th Decile	Lower Quartile	Median	Upper Quartile	1st Decile
1999/2000	12.7	14.7	16.5	20.1	21.5
2000/01	6.8	10.0	12.7	15.7	16.6
2001/02	3.2	4.7	5.6	7.5	9.6
2002/03	6.5	8.7	9.1	11.0	12.0
2003/04	8.7	9.4	12.2	13.8	15.6
2004/05	14.8	16.7	18.6	19.9	21.2
2005/06	18.7	20.4	22.2	23.3	24.0
2006/07	12.9	14.5	16.6	19.9	21.6
2007/08	−13.2	−11.9	−10.8	−9.4	−4.2
2008/09	−35.2	−25.2	−20.2	−11.6	

Notes:	The figures show the range of returns in each year since 1999 obtained by funds participating in the CAPS investment performance measurement service.
Source:	BNY Mellon Asset Servicing's pension fund information service, data to 31 March 2009.

PENSION FUND ASSET DISTRIBUTION

This table shows the average distribution of pension fund assets between the major market sectors at 31 March each year between 2000 and 2009, based on proportions of overall market values. Percentages are rounded to add up to 100% for each year.

	UK Equities	Overseas Equities	Overseas Bonds	UK Bonds	Global Index-linked Gilts	Cash	Property	Other
	%	%	%	%	%	%	%	%
31.3.2000	53	23	4	11	4	3	2	–
31.3.2001	50	23	4	13	5	3	2	–
31.3.2002	47	26	2	15	6	2	2	–
31.3.2003	42	25	2	19	8	2	2	–
31.3.2004	40	27	1	20	8	2	2	–
31.3.2005	38	28	1	21	8	2	2	–
31.3.2006	36	29	1	22	8	2	2	–
31.3.2007	33	28	1	23	8	3	3	1
31.3.2008	27	25	2	26	11	4	3	2
31.3.2009	24	24	1	30	13	4	3	1

Source: BNY Mellon Asset Servicing's pension fund information service, data to 31 March 2009.

POOLED PENSION FUND PERFORMANCE

This table sets out the median returns achieved on a net-of-fees basis by the UK Pooled Pension Funds participating in the CAPS Survey over cumulative periods ending 31 March 2009.

Annualised Returns	Last 12 Months %	Last 3 Years %	Last 5 Years %	Last 10 Years %
Balanced	−20.5	−6.6	3.2	1.4
UK Smaller Companies	−38.4	−14.6	−0.1	3.7
UK Equity (Standard)	−29.4	−10.1	0.9	−0.7
Overseas	−20.1	−7.3	3.3	1.2
Global Equity	−24.4	−8.4	2.4	0.3
North America	−13.5	−7.6	0.3	−2.5
Europe (excl. UK)	−28.1	−7.6	4.8	2.4
Pan-European*	–	–	–	–
Japan	−13.7	−14.9	−2.3	−1.4
Pacific Basin (excl. Japan)	−21.5	0.1	9.3	8.8
Emerging Markets	−29.1	−4.6	10.5	8.6
UK Bonds (Standard)	−2.9	−0.3	2.6	4.3
UK Bonds (Long Term)	−4.0	−2.3	2.3	4.5
International Bond	32.6	13.5	9.4	6.7
Index-linked	−2.5	4.0	5.2	4.9
Cash	4.0	4.7	4.6	4.6
Property	−22.8	−7.2	1.9	6.2

Note: * Insufficient funds in this index to produce a median return at the time of publication.

Source: CAPS Pooled Pension Fund Update (Quarter ended 31 March 2009).

CHANGES TO STRATEGIC ASSET ALLOCATION

This table sets out the proportion of schemes that have changed within the last 12 months.

	Reduced (%)	Increased (%)
Equities	50	3
Bonds/fixed interest securities	11	32
Alternatives (hedge funds, commodities, venture capital, etc)	4	24
Property	10	12
Other	2	25

Source: NAPF Annual Survey, 2008.

PENSION STATISTICS

NOTES ON SOURCES USED

This Section provides a snapshot of selected features of occupational pension schemes in the UK. The charts and tables on pages 19 to 26 are based on data from the following sources:

- **Occupational Pension Schemes Survey, 2007**: this survey, produced by National Statistics, covers 1,500 private and public sector schemes registered in the UK. The survey covers a range of topics, including scheme membership, DB benefits and contribution rates.

- **The NAPF Annual Survey, 2008**: this survey is based on responses from over 300 NAPF fund members (private sector schemes).

- **The Association of Consulting Actuaries' (ACA) 2009 Pension trend survey**: this survey covers over 300 employers of all sizes.

- **The Pensions Regulator's Annual Report and Accounts, 2008–2009**: summarises membership data for occupational private and public sector schemes taken from the Regulator's Score database.

- **Pension Funds and their Advisers, 2009**: an annual directory showing details of 2,700 major UK pension funds. The directory covers companies and organisations with 100 or more employees and certain smaller schemes where assets exceed £1 million.

- **General Household Survey, 2007**: a survey through field work which started in 1971 and is normally carried out annually.

- **The Purple Book 2008, DB pensions universe risk profile**: a joint study by the Pensions Regulator and the Pension Protection Fund focusing mainly on private sector defined benefit schemes. Most of the analysis is based on a sample of almost 7,000 schemes, with much of the basic information coming from scheme returns provided to the Pensions Regulator.

It should be noted that, as some of the questions were multiple-response, percentages shown in some tables may total more than 100% and so care is needed in interpreting the figures.

Percentages throughout have been rounded.

NORMAL PENSION AGE
% Private sector schemes

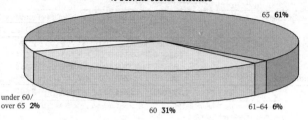

65 **61%**

under 60/
over 65 **2%**

60 **31%**

61–64 **6%**

Source: Based on data from the National Statistics *Occupational Pension Schemes Survey, 2007.*
(*See note on page 18 concerning this source.*)

ACCRUAL RATES

Accrual rate used in private sector defined benefit schemes (% schemes)

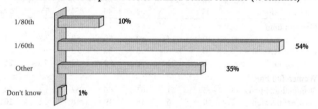

1/80th **10%**

1/60th **54%**

Other **35%**

Don't know **1%**

Note: 'Other' includes 1/60th or 1/80th depending on factors such as seniority or member contribution; in some cases members are given a choice of accrual rates; other rates such as 1/50th or 1/70th are also included.

Source: Based on data from the NAPF *Annual Survey, 2008.* (*See note on page 18 concerning this source.*)

CONTRIBUTION RATES

Average contributions paid into pension schemes (% total earnings)

% by benefit type	Member contributions	Employer contributions
Defined Benefit schemes	6.3	23.2
Defined Contribution schemes	4.3	6.7
Group Personal Pension	3.9	6.0
Stakeholder (see note)	4.0	4.5

Note: Stakeholder figures exclude nil employer contributions, which is the level for 22% of stakeholder schemes.

Source: Data from the Association of Consulting Actuaries' *2009 Pension trend survey.*
(*See note on page 18 concerning this source.*)

PENSION SCHEME MEMBERSHIP BY BENEFIT TYPE
Private sector schemes

Status of scheme	Number of members		Number of schemes	
	DC	DB and Hybrid	DC	DB and Hybrid
Open	1,151,000	8,128,000	41,775	2,276
Closed	203,000	6,342,000	3,263	3,654
Paid up	95,000	509,000	6,092	1,482
Winding up	90,000	245,000	2,567	1,195
Total	**1,539,000**	**15,224,000**	**53,697**	**8,607**

Source: Data taken from the Pensions Regulator's Annual Report and Accounts, 2008–2009.
(See note on page 18 concerning this source.)

PENSION SCHEME MEMBERSHIP BY AGE AND SEX, 2007

	Percentage of employees who are members, by age group						
Scheme members in Great Britain	16– 17	18– 24	25– 34	35– 44	45– 54	55+	**Total**
Men full time							
Occupational pension[1]	0	17	50	59	67	58	**53**
Personal pension	0	6	16	28	28	31	**23**
Any pension	0	21	58	72	77	73	**64**
Women full time							
Occupational pension[1]	3	31	61	60	67	61	**58**
Personal pension	0	6	16	19	18	21	**16**
Any pension	3	33	68	68	73	70	**64**
Women part time							
Occupational pension[1]	0	8	44	50	45	36	**39**
Personal pension	1	0	11	16	16	8	**11**
Any pension	1	7	47	56	50	39	**43**

Notes: [1] The data include a few people who were not sure if they were in a scheme.

Source: General Household Survey, 2007. *(See note on page 18 concerning this source.)*

THE LARGER UK PENSION FUNDS
Pension funds estimated to be in excess of £1,200m

£ million	£ million
40,430 Scottish Public Pensions Agency (NHS and Teachers)	22,527 Electricity Pensions Services Ltd Pension Scheme
31,187 BT Pension Scheme	20,400 Railways Pension Scheme
29,030 Universities Superannuation Scheme Ltd	17,895 Royal Bank of Scotland Group Pension Fund
23,688 Royal Mail Pension Plan	14,797 BP plc Pension Fund

THE LARGER UK PENSION FUNDS (cont.)

Pension funds estimated to be in excess of £1,200m

£ million		£ million	
13,102	The Shell Contributory Pension Fund	4,300	Merseyside Pension Fund
13,017	Mineworkers' Pension Scheme	3,931	Tesco plc Pension Scheme
12,769	National Grid UK Pension Scheme	3,895	Invensys Pension Scheme
11,996	British Coal Staff Superannuation Scheme	3,890	Rolls-Royce Pension Fund
		3,776	BMW (UK) Holdings Ltd Operations Pension Scheme
11,749	BAe Systems Pension Scheme	3,720	South Yorkshire Pension Fund
9,821	British Steel Pension Scheme	3,683	Tyne & Wear Pension Fund
9,686	Strathclyde Pension Fund	3,670	Lancashire County Council Pension Fund
9,553	Barclays Bank plc UK Retirement Fund	3,631	Boots Pension Scheme
9,445	Lloyds TSB Group Pension Scheme No 1	3,597	London Pensions Fund Authority Pension Fund
9,287	Greater Manchester Pension Fund	3,545	The Pensions Trust
8,131	BBC Pension Trust Ltd	3,537	Diageo plc Pension Scheme
7,406	West Midlands Metropolitan Authorities	3,531	RWE npower Group Defined Benefit Scheme
7,367	New (British) Airways Pension Scheme	3,340	TRW Pension Scheme
		3,329	J. Sainsbury Pension & Death Benefit Scheme
7,286	West Yorkshire Pension Fund	3,277	Zurich Financial Services UK Pension Scheme
7,120	ICI Pension Fund		
6,780	HBOS plc Final Salary Pension Scheme	3,225	City of Edinburgh Council Lothian Pension Fund
6,674	British Airways Airways Pension Scheme	3,115	The Northern Ireland Local Government Officers' Superannuation Committee
6,603	IBM Pension Plan/IBM IT Solutions Pension Scheme	3,100	AstraZeneca UK Ltd Pension Fund
6,204	AVIVA Staff Pension Scheme	3,032	MMC UK Final Salary Scheme
5,850	HSBC Bank (UK) Pension Scheme	3,016	Network Rail Section of the Railways Pension Scheme
5,491	Co-operative Group Pension (Average Career Earnings) Scheme	2,992	Civil Aviation Authority National Air Traffic Section
5,216	Marks & Spencer Group plc Defined Benefit Scheme	2,952	Hampshire County Council Pension Fund
5,101	E.On UK plc Electricity Supply Pension Scheme	2,927	Essex County Council Pension Fund
5,061	Unilever plc UK Pension Fund	2,837	Royal & SunAlliance Insurance Group plc SAL Pension Scheme
4,791	Prudential plc Defined Benefit Scheme	2,738	Imperial Tobacco Pension Fund
4,682	Transport for London Pension Fund	2,650	Nestlé UK Ltd Pension Fund
4,657	Lloyds TSB Group Pension Scheme No 2		

continued...

THE LARGER UK PENSION FUNDS (cont.)
Pension funds estimated to be in excess of £1,200m

£ million		£ million	
2,646	British Energy Generation Group of Electricity Supply Pension Scheme	2,080	Leicestershire County Council Pension Fund
2,600	AXA UK plc Group Pension Scheme	2,077	Derbyshire County Council Pension Fund
2,517	ITV plc Pension Scheme	2,050	Ford Motor Company Ltd Hourly Paid Contributory Pension Fund
2,500	FirstGroup plc Pension Schemes		
2,489	Kent County Council Superannuation Fund	2,048	Teesside Pension Fund
2,481	The Telent Pension Office GEC 1972 Plan	2,042	Civil Aviation Authority Section
		2,025	Scottish Power Pension Scheme
2,446	Nottinghamshire County Council Pension Fund	2,015	The RHM Pension Scheme
		2,013	East Riding of Yorkshire Council Pension Fund
2,324	EDF Energy Group of the Electricity Supply Pension Scheme	2,000	BOC Pension Scheme
		1,968	Akzo Nobel Defined Benefit Scheme
2,293	Cheshire Pension Fund		
2,265	Ford Motor Company Ltd Salaried Pension Fund	1,900	Fujitsu Services Ltd ICL Group Pension Plan
2,238	Associated British Foods DB Section	1,900	Total UK Pension Plan
		1,847	Nationwide Building Society Pension Fund
2,216	Bank of England Pension Fund		
2,189	Staffordshire County Council Pension Fund	1,843	Norfolk County Council Pension Fund
2,178	Avon Pension Fund	1,842	Pearl Group Ltd Staff Pensions
2,158	Devon County Council Pension Fund	1,827	MNOPF Trustees Ltd New Section
2,146	Hertfordshire County Council Superannuation Fund	1,817	Royal London Group Pension Scheme
2,146	Reed Elsevier (UK) Ltd Pension Scheme	1,807	Royal Insurance Group Pension Scheme
2,131	GKN plc Group Pension Scheme	1,803	Xerox Ltd Final Salary Scheme
2,129	Lafarge UK Pension Plan	1,796	Balfour Beatty plc Pension Fund
2,113	Philips Electronics UK Ltd Final Salary Section	1,773	Exel plc Retirement Plan
		1,770	Aberdeen City Council Pension Fund
2,113	Cable & Wireless plc Superannuation Fund		
		1,760	Social Housing Pension Scheme
2,106	Vauxhall Motors Ltd Common Investment Pool	1,744	Pearson plc Group Pension Plan
		1,730	Abbey National plc Amalgamated Pension Fund
2,099	Siemens Global Shared Services Ltd Defined Benefit Scheme		
		1,723	Surrey County Council Pension Fund
2,094	Scottish & Newcastle plc Pension Fund		
		1,700	John Lewis Partnership plc Trust for Pensions
2,087	BAA plc Pension Scheme		

THE LARGER UK PENSION FUNDS (cont.)
Pension funds estimated to be in excess of £1,200m

£ million		£ million	
1,679	East Sussex County Council Pension Fund	1,411	TI Group Pension Scheme
1,663	Jaguar Pension Plan	1,408	Kingfisher plc Pension Fund Final Salary Section
1,661	British American Tobacco Defined Benefit Section	1,400	General Electric GE Pension Plan
1,657	Nortel Networks UK Ltd UK Pension Plan	1,400	ALSTOM Pension Scheme
1,655	Whitbread plc Group Pension Fund	1,399	Alliance & Leicester Pension Scheme
1,633	VT Nuclear Services Ltd Pension Scheme	1,366	Whitbread plc DB
1,628	Daily Mail & General Trust plc Defined Benefit Scheme	1,350	Michelin Tyre plc Pension & Life Assurance Plan
1,611	GlaxoSmithKline plc GSK Pension Scheme	1,350	Rhondda, Cynon, Taff CBC Superannuation Funds
1,609	United Utilities Pension Scheme	1,348	Pilkington Group Ltd Superannuation Scheme
1,592	Safeway Pension Scheme	1,343	Dorset County Council Pension Scheme
1,591	Tayside Superannuation Funds		
1,588	Mars UK Ltd Pension Plan	1,339	UBS Defined Benefit Scheme
1,586	Saint-Gobain UK Pension Scheme	1,339	National Grid Co Group of Electricity Supply Pension Scheme
1,551	Metal Box Pension Scheme	1,310	Greater Gwent (Torfaen) Pension Fund
1,527	The Pensions Trust Social Housing Pension Scheme	1,305	Suffolk County Council Pension Fund
1,522	West Sussex County Council Pension Fund	1,301	Trafalgar House Pensions Trust
1,500	The Environment Agency Active Pension Fund	1,300	Thales UK Pension Scheme
		1,274	The Willis Pension Scheme
1,497	Land Rover Pension Plan	1,266	Superannuation Arrangements of the University of London
1,488	Royal County of Berkshire Pension Fund	1,261	Vauxhall Motors Pension Plan
1,482	Coats plc Pension Plan	1,223	North Yorkshire County Council Pension Fund
1,477	The Shipbuilding Industries Pension Scheme	1,220	The AA Pension Scheme
1,432	Smiths Industries Pension Scheme	1,210	Buckinghamshire County Council Pension Fund
1,428	Durham County Council Superannuation Fund	1,207	Western Power Distribution Electricity Supply Pension Scheme
1,421	MNOPF Trustees Ltd Old Section		
1,421	Pfizer Ltd Group Pension Scheme	1,200	Hanson Industrial Pension Scheme

Notes: 1. Certain figures relate to the total of several funds within a group.

2. Certain figures are estimates not necessarily supplied by the fund.

Source: Based on information derived from *Pension Funds and their Advisers, 2009,* AP Information Services Ltd, a trading name of Waterlow Legal & Regulatory Ltd. (*See note on page 18 concerning this source.*)

NUMBER OF PENSION FUNDS WITH CAPITAL VALUES OF VARIOUS SIZES, ANALYSED BY REGION & SIZE OF FUNDS

Region	Estimated size of fund, £ million								
	0–4.9	5–9.9	10–19.9	20–49.9	50–99.9	100–249.9	250–999.9	1,000+	Total
London	224	21	38	55	38	49	74	39	**538**
South East	225	14	27	49	53	43	66	42	**519**
South West	65	5	13	15	13	7	23	16	**157**
Eastern	98	10	11	27	21	19	27	15	**228**
E. Midlands	58	3	12	11	13	11	7	8	**123**
W. Midlands	106	5	10	19	15	17	28	18	**218**
N.E., Yorks. & The Humber	115	3	13	23	25	26	21	15	**241**
N.W. & Merseyside	105	7	19	24	15	13	11	15	**209**
Wales	17	2	0	8	4	1	6	4	**42**
N. Ireland	17	2	4	3	1	1	4	1	**33**
Scotland	71	4	9	21	10	9	18	17	**159**
Total	**1,101**	**76**	**156**	**255**	**208**	**196**	**285**	**190**	**2,467**

Source: Pension Funds and their Advisers, 2009, AP Information Services Ltd, a trading name of Waterlow Legal & Regulatory Ltd. (See note on page 18 concerning this source.)

VALUE OF TOTAL PENSION FUND ASSETS ANALYSED BY REGION AND SIZE OF FUNDS

Region	Estimated size of fund, £ million								
	0–4.9	5–9.9	10–19.9	20–49.9	50–99.9	100–249.9	250–999.9	1,000+	Total
London	29	146	573	1,845	2,638	7,678	38,090	225,955	**276,954**
South East	19	107	390	1,692	3,838	6,830	32,408	122,205	**167,489**
South West	9	35	196	434	954	1,040	10,983	49,371	**63,022**
Eastern	17	72	173	844	1,524	2,867	13,056	31,025	**49,579**
E. Midlands	11	21	178	354	896	1,669	2,981	14,808	**20,918**
W. Midlands	20	41	154	642	1,035	2,558	16,173	57,343	**77,967**
N.E., Yorks. & The Humber	17	27	187	733	1,706	3,889	10,853	67,769	**85,180**
N.W. & Merseyside	15	55	281	726	1,068	2,120	5,146	70,011	**79,421**
Wales	0	13	0	308	240	217	4,113	7,681	**12,572**
N. Ireland	2	14	49	114	74	126	2,421	3,115	**5,915**
Scotland	12	29	132	640	694	1,691	9,873	93,804	**106,874**
Total	**151**	**558**	**2,315**	**8,331**	**14,666**	**30,685**	**146,097**	**743,089**	**945,891**

Note: Due to rounding, figures may not add up to totals shown.
Source: Pension Funds and their Advisers, 2009, AP Information Services Ltd, a trading name of Waterlow Legal & Regulatory Ltd. (See note on page 18 concerning this source.)

NUMBER OF ORGANISATIONS ANALYSED BY
REGION AND NUMBER OF EMPLOYEES

	Number of employees per organisation								
Region	0–499	500–999	1,000–1,999	2,000–4,999	5,000–9,999	10,000–24,999	25,000–99,999	100,000+	Total
London	264	65	66	65	36	25	9	2	**532**
South East	250	54	68	67	43	23	12	1	**518**
South West	74	20	18	21	9	10	4	0	**156**
Eastern	114	26	26	28	14	14	4	2	**228**
E. Midlands	54	23	12	20	7	6	1	0	**123**
W. Midlands	97	30	28	34	15	9	5	0	**218**
N.E.,Yorks. & The Humber	98	40	38	39	14	4	5	3	**241**
N.W. & Merseyside	114	31	20	21	10	7	6	0	**209**
Wales	16	10	2	3	7	3	0	1	**42**
N. Ireland	21	6	1	3	1	0	1	0	**33**
Scotland	65	30	19	21	14	7	3	0	**159**
Total	**1,167**	**335**	**298**	**322**	**170**	**108**	**50**	**9**	**2,459**

Source: *Pension Funds and their Advisers, 2009*, AP Information Services, a trading name of Waterlow Legal & Regulatory Ltd. (*See note on page 18 concerning this source.*)

SUMMARY OF INVESTMENTS BY SIZE OF PENSION FUND
(all figures are in percentages)

	Pension fund size, £ million								
Type of Investment	0–4.9	5–9.9	10–19.9	20–49.9	50–99.9	100–249.9	250–999.9	1,000+	Av.
Equities									
UK	40.0	46.6	44.9	43.0	40.4	40.2	34.6	26.0	**28.6**
Overseas	23.4	16.7	18.8	22.1	23.5	23.9	25.8	25.7	**25.6**
Fixed Interest									
UK	13.9	16.6	13.6	16.0	15.3	14.9	14.6	15.6	**15.4**
Overseas	0.9	0.7	1.0	1.9	1.4	1.4	2.3	2.3	**2.3**
Index-Linked Gilts	8.6	3.5	8.8	6.6	8.3	8.6	9.7	10.4	**10.1**
Property									
UK	3.5	3.4	3.2	2.8	1.9	2.9	3.8	6.8	**5.9**
Overseas	0.0	0.0	0.1	0.0	0.0	0.2	0.1	0.2	**0.2**
Cash and Deposits	3.4	4.0	6.0	3.4	2.9	2.8	2.8	3.5	**3.3**
Others	6.4	8.7	3.6	4.2	6.4	5.2	6.3	9.5	**8.5**

Note: Due to rounding, figures may not add up to 100%.

Source: *Pension Funds and their Advisers, 2009*, AP Information Services, a trading name of Waterlow Legal & Regulatory Ltd. (*See note on page 18 concerning this source.*)

OVERALL FUNDING LEVELS

	Section 179 (£bn)	FRS17 (£bn)	Full buy-out (£bn)
Total assets	837.2	837.2	837.2
Total liabilities	842.3	850.2	1,356.0
Total balance	−5.1	−13.1	−518.6
Total balance (for schemes in deficit)	−67.7	−64.8	−520.4
Total balance (for schemes in surplus)	62.6	51.8	1.6

Note: Shows estimated figures for a total of 6,897 schemes as at 31 March 2008.
Source: *The Purple Book, DB pensions universe risk profile*, the Pensions Regulator, 2008.
          (See note on page 18 concerning this source.)

SECTION 179 FUNDING LEVELS BY SCHEME SIZE

Scheme membership	Schemes in sample	Market value of assets (£bn)	Total s179 liabilities (£bn)	Weighted average funding level (%)	Simple average funding level (%)
5–99	2,468	9.9	9.7	102	101
100–999	3,132	73.0	79.5	92	88
1,000–4,999	884	122.8	133.4	92	89
5,000–9,999	191	89.6	94.9	94	93
10,000+	222	542.0	524.8	103	100
Total	**6,897**	**837.2**	**842.3**	**99**	**94**

Note: Data as at 31 March 2008.
Source: *The Purple Book, DB pensions universe risk profile*, the Pensions Regulator, 2008.
          (See note on page 18 concerning this source.)

SECTION 179 FUNDING LEVELS BY SCHEME MATURITY

Pensions in payment as % liabilities	Schemes in sample	Market value of assets (£bn)	Total s179 liabilities (£bn)	Weighted average funding level (%)	Simple average funding level (%)
25% and less	3,161	127.6	154.1	83	86
26%–50%	2,725	455.7	462.9	98	95
51%–75%	835	231.3	206.7	112	111
76%–100%	176	22.6	18.5	122	132
Total	**6,897**	**837.2**	**842.3**	**99**	**94**

Note: Data as at 31 March 2008.
Source: *The Purple Book, DB pensions universe risk profile*, the Pensions Regulator, 2008.
          (See note on page 18 concerning this source.)

UK SOCIAL SECURITY BENEFITS AND TAX RATES

INTRODUCTION

The main Social Security benefits and tax allowances and rates are outlined in this section.

SOCIAL SECURITY BENEFIT RATES AND ELIGIBILITY RULES

This table gives the rates for 2009/2010 and 2010/2011 and sets out the main eligibility rules. Receipt of some benefits affects entitlement to other benefits. **Eligibility conditions are not necessarily comprehensive and may also be subject to change.** Further information on benefits can be found at *www.direct.gov.uk*. Information is correct as at 14 December 2009, at which date the Government had not announced certain benefit rates for 2010/2011. Spaces have been provided for these figures, which will be published at *www.hewitt.com/ppbstats*.

All rates are weekly unless otherwise specified

Benefit	Rates, 2009/2010	2010/2011	Eligibility
CHILDREN			
Child Benefit	Eldest child for whom benefit is payable: £20.00 Each subsequent child: £13.20 *tax free*	£20.30 £13.40	Responsible for a child who is: (i) under the age of 16 *or* (ii) aged 16–19 in full-time, but not advanced, education *or* (iii) aged 16 or 17 and registered for work or training. Usually paid to the mother.
Guardian's Allowance	Each eligible child: £14.10 *tax free*	£14.30	Must look after a child who is orphaned and be entitled to **Child Benefit** for that child. Need not be the child's legal guardian. Same rate for all children.
DISABILITY			
Disability Living Allowance	Care component: lowest: £18.65 middle: £47.10 highest: £70.35 Mobility component: lower: £18.65 higher: £49.10 *tax free*	£18.95 £47.80 £71.40 £18.95 £49.85	Under 65; *and* (i) has needed help with personal care or walking for previous 3 months and likely to need help for a further 6 months *or* (ii) is disabled and not expected to live more than 6 months. <div align="right">continued ...</div>

All rates are weekly unless otherwise specified

Benefit	Rates, 2009/2010	2010/2011	Eligibility

DISABILITY (continued)

Benefit	Rates, 2009/2010	2010/2011	Eligibility
Attendance Allowance	Lower: £47.10 Higher: £70.35 *tax free*	£47.80 £71.40	(i) Aged 65 or over *and* (ii) has needed help with personal care for 6 months.
Severe Disablement Allowance (see **Employment and Support Allowance** for new claims from 27 October 2008)	Basic rate: £57.45 Addition if age first unable to work was: Under 40 £15.65 40–49 £9.10 50–59 £5.35 *tax free*	£59.45 £15.00 £8.40 £5.45	(i) Aged 16–64 *and* (ii) receiving allowance before April 2001, having been incapable of work for a continuous period of 196 days *and* (iii) assessed as at least 80% disabled.
Carer's Allowance	Allowance: £53.10 *(Earnings limit £95.00)* *taxable*	£53.90 *(£95.00)*	(i) Caring (for 35+ hours per week) for a person receiving **Attendance Allowance**, or certain categories of **Disability Living Allowance** or **Constant Attendance Allowance** *and* (ii) aged 16 or over at date of claim.

INDUSTRIAL INJURIES & DISEASE

Benefit	Rates, 2009/2010	2010/2011	Eligibility
Industrial Injuries Disablement Benefit	100% assessment: £143.60 (person aged over 18) *tax free*	£145.80	Disabled on or after 5 July 1948 because of accident at work.
Reduced Earnings Allowance	Maximum: £57.44 *tax free*	£58.32	(i) Accident happened or disease started before October 1990 *and* (ii) ability to do regular job is is affected by industrial injury or disease.
Retirement Allowance	25% of **Reduced Earnings Allowance**, subject to a maximum rate of: £14.36 *tax free*	£14.58	Replaces **Reduced Earnings Allowance** when claimant reaches State Pension Age (SPA) and ceases employment.

All rates are weekly unless otherwise specified

Benefit	Rates, 2009/2010	2010/2011	Eligibility

INDUSTRIAL INJURIES & DISEASE (continued)

Benefit	Rates, 2009/2010	2010/2011	Eligibility
Constant Attendance Allowance	Part-time rate: £28.75 Normal maximum: £57.50 Intermediate rate: £86.25 Exceptional rate: £115.00 *tax free*	£29.20 £58.40 £87.60 £116.80	Receiving **Industrial Injuries Disablement Benefit** and needs constant care and attention.
Exceptionally Severe Disablement Allowance	Standard: £57.50 *tax free*	£58.40	(i) Exceptionally severely disabled *and* (ii) entitled to **Constant Attendance Allowance** at one of the two higher rates *and* (iii) needs permanent attendance.

LOW INCOME

Benefit	Rates, 2009/2010	2010/2011	Eligibility
Housing Benefit	Up to full eligible rent. *tax free*		(i) Low income *and* (ii) paying rent *and* (iii) capital less than £16,000.
Income Support (from 27 October 2008 replaced by **Employment and Support Allowance** for claims relating to illness or disability)	Personal allowances vary with age, marital status, or dependent children. Basic rate for a single person aged 25 or over: £64.30 A couple, both aged 18 or over: £100.95 A lone parent aged 18 or over: £64.30 *tax free*	£65.45 £102.75 £65.45	(i) Aged 16–59 *and* (ii) works less than 16 hours per week *and* (iii) joint capital less than £16,000 *and* (iv) not in receipt of **Jobseeker's Allowance**. *means tested*
Pension Credit (formerly **Minimum Income Guarantee**)	Single pensioner £130.00 (minimum) Married couple £198.45 (minimum) *minimum after-tax income*	£132.60 £202.40	Aged over 60. Lower capital limit £10,000 (from 2 November 2009) *means tested*
Council Tax Benefit	Maximum benefit is 100% of Council Tax. *tax free*		(i) Paying council tax *and* (ii) capital less than £16,000.

All rates are weekly unless otherwise specified

Benefit	Rates, 2009/2010	2010/2011	Eligibility

MATERNITY

Benefit	Rates, 2009/2010	2010/2011	Eligibility
Maternity Allowance	Standard rate: Lesser of (a) 90% of average earnings, *and* (b) £123.06. *tax free*	Lesser of (a) 90% of average earnings, *and* (b) £124.88	(i) Not eligible for **Statutory Maternity Pay** *and* (ii) employed/self-employed *and* (iii) must have been employed/self-employed for at least 26 of the 66 weeks before baby is due, and average earnings at least £30.00 per week (the Maternity Allowance Threshold).
Statutory Maternity Pay	First 6 weeks: 90% of average earnings After 6 weeks, and up to week 39: Lesser of: (a) 90% of average earnings, *and* (b) £123.06. *taxable subject to NICs*	90% of average earnings Lesser of (a) 90% of average earnings, *and* (b) £124.88	(i) Employed with same employer for at least 26 weeks, 15 weeks before the baby is due *and* (ii) earning above Lower Earnings Limit.
Statutory Paternity Pay	For up to 2 weeks: Lesser of: (a) 90% of average earnings, *and* (b) £123.06. *taxable subject to NICs*	Lesser of (a) 90% of average earnings, *and* (b) £124.88	As for **Statutory Maternity Pay**.
Statutory Adoption Pay	For up to 39 weeks: Amount as for **Statutory Paternity Pay**. *taxable subject to NICs*	Amount as for **Statutory Paternity Pay**.	(i) Employed with same employer for at least 26 weeks, 15 weeks before adoption agency informed matched with child *and* (ii) earning above Lower Earnings Limit.

All rates are weekly unless otherwise specified

Benefit	Rates, 2009/2010	2010/2011	Eligibility

RETIREMENT BENEFITS

Benefit	Rates, 2009/2010	2010/2011	Eligibility
Basic State Pension	Based on own or late spouse's NICs: £95.25 Based on spouse's NICs: £57.05	£97.65 £58.50	(i) Reached State Pension Age *and* (ii) NIC record sufficient.
	Over 80s pension: £57.05 Over 80s addition £0.25 *taxable*	£58.50 £0.25	The Over 80s pension is non-contributory and subject to residence conditions. Payable to individuals who receive little/no other State pension.
Additional Pension	SERPS/State Second Pension (S2P) – *see page 38.* *taxable*		(i) Reached State Pension Age *and* (ii) paid Class 1 NICs and/or received credits.
Graduated Retirement Benefit	Per unit: 11.53p Employees may have been contracted-out and receive EPBs instead. *taxable*	11.53p	Based on NICs paid between April 1961 and April 1975.

SICKNESS

Benefit	Rates, 2009/2010	2010/2011	Eligibility
Employment and Support Allowance	**Assessment Phase:** (first 13 weeks of claim) Under 25, up to: £50.95 25 or over, up to: £64.30 **Main Phase:** (from week 14 of claim) In the Work-Related Activity Group, up to: £89.80 In the Support Group: £95.15	£51.85 £65.45 £91.40 £96.85	Have an illness or disability that affects ability to work, and be over 16 and under State Pension Age; *and* (i) not or no longer receiving **Statutory Sick Pay** *or* (ii) self-employed or unemployed *or* (iii) have been receiving **Statutory Maternity Pay** but not gone back to work due to illness or disability. Must pass a 'Work Capability Assessment' for benefit to continue to be paid from 13th week. continued ...

All rates are weekly unless otherwise specified

Benefit	Rates, 2009/2010	2010/2011	Eligibility

SICKNESS (continued)

Benefit	Rates, 2009/2010	2010/2011	Eligibility
Incapacity Benefit (from 27 October 2008 replaced by **Employment and Support Allowance** for new claimants)	**Short Term** Under State Pension Age: lower rate (up to 28 weeks): £67.75 adult dependant: £41.35 higher rate (29–52 weeks): £80.15 adult dependant: £41.35 Over State Pension Age: lower rate (up to 28 weeks): £86.20 higher rate (29–52 weeks): £89.80 adult dependant: £51.10	£68.95 £41.35 £81.60 £41.35 £87.75 £91.40 £51.10	NIC record sufficient. First 28 weeks: (i) employees excluded from **Statutory Sick Pay** and others who meet contribution conditions *and* (ii) unable to work for at least 4 consecutive working days because of sickness or disability. From 29th week, must pass a 'Personal Capability Assessment'.
	Long Term Under State Pension Age: basic rate (after 52 weeks): £89.80 adult dependant: £53.10	£91.40 £53.10	Above State Pension Age, Long-Term Incapacity Benefit ceases.
	Child Dependency Increases *first child*: £8.20 *each other child*: £11.35 Age additions: incapacity began aged under 35 £15.65 aged 35–44 £6.55	£8.10 £11.35 £15.00 £5.80	Child Dependency increases are payable, if before 6 April 2003, the claimant was in receipt of **Long-Term Incapacity Benefit**, **Short-Term Incapacity Benefit** at the higher rate, or **Short-Term Incapacity Benefit** at the lower rate and over State Pension Age.
	Invalidity Allowance (transitional) lower: £5.35 middle: £9.10 higher: £15.65 *taxable (unless previously on Invalidity Benefit), except for benefits paid in first 28 weeks.*	£5.45 £8.40 £15.00	For existing claimants of **Invalidity Benefit** a transitional Invalidity Allowance is paid in addition. The level depends on age on the first day of incapacity.
Statutory Sick Pay	Standard rate: £79.15 *taxable subject to NICs*	£79.15	(i) Earnings at least equal to Lower Earnings Limit *and* (ii) has been sick for at least four consecutive days.

Social Fund payments are one-off or annual

Benefit	Rates, 2009/2010	2010/2011	Eligibility

SOCIAL FUND

Benefit	Rates, 2009/2010	2010/2011	Eligibility
'Sure Start' Maternity Grant	Lump sum: £500 Non-repayable Paid for each baby. *tax free*	£_____*	(i) Receiving **Income Support, Income-based Jobseeker's Allowance, Employment and Support Allowance** or certain **Tax Credits** *and* (ii) having a baby or adopting one not more than 12 months old.
Funeral Payments	Necessary fees, other specified expenses *and up to* £700 for any funeral expenses. *tax free*	£_____*	(i) Specified relationship with deceased *and* (ii) is in receipt of **Income Support, Income-based Jobseeker's Allowance, Employment and Support Allowance**, certain **Tax Credits, Housing Benefit** or **Council Tax Benefit.**
Budgeting/ Crisis Loans & Community Care Grant	Varies. *tax free*		Depends on merits of case and the district Social Fund budget.
Cold Weather Payment	Payment: £25.00 for each qualifying week *tax free*	£_____*	Receiving **Pension Credit** or certain other benefits.
Winter Fuel Payment	Payment: Full rate £250.00 Reduced rate £125.00 Aged 80 or over: Full rate £400.00 *tax free*	£_____* £_____* £_____*	Aged 60 or over. (The qualifying age will rise gradually from 60 to 65 between 2010 and 2020 in line with changes to the State Pension Age for women; *see page 38.*)

All rates are weekly unless otherwise specified

Benefit	Rates, 2009/2010	2010/2011	Eligibility

UNEMPLOYMENT

Benefit	Rates, 2009/2010	2010/2011	Eligibility
Jobseeker's Allowance	Single person aged 25 or over: £64.30 Couple both aged 18 or over: £100.95 Benefits reduced if earnings or pension over specified limits. *taxable NIC credits*	£65.45 £102.75	(i) Out of work or working less than 16 hours a week *and* (ii) available for and actively seeking work *and* (iii) between 18 and State Pension Age.

WIDOW'S/WIDOWER'S BENEFITS

Benefit	Rates, 2009/2010	2010/2011	Eligibility
Widow's Pension (replaced by **Bereavement Allowance** from 9 April 2001)	Standard rate: £95.25 Plus SERPS pension. Lower rates where widow under age 55 on benefit becoming payable. *taxable*	£97.65	Woman widowed before 9 April 2001 and husband's NIC record sufficient, *and either*: (i) 45 or over when husband died and **Widowed Mother's Allowance** is not payable *or* (ii) 45 or over when **Widowed Mother's Allowance** ceased.
Widowed Mother's Allowance (replaced by **Widowed Parent's Allowance** from 9 April 2001)	Allowance: £95.25 Additional child allowance: *first child*: £8.20 *each other child*: £11.35 Plus SERPS pension. *taxable but children's allowance tax free*	£97.65 £8.10 £11.35	(i) Woman widowed before 9 April 2001 *and* (ii) has dependent child for whom she receives **Child Benefit** *and* (iii) husband's NIC record sufficient.
Bereavement Payment	Lump sum: £2,000 *tax free*	£2,000	Husband's, wife's or civil partner's NIC record sufficient *and either*: (i) he or she was not entitled to **Retirement Pension** *or* (ii) claimant was under State Pension Age when husband, wife or civil partner died.

All rates are weekly unless otherwise specified

Benefit	Rates, 2009/2010	2010/2011	Eligibility

WIDOW'S/WIDOWER'S BENEFITS (continued)

Benefit	Rates, 2009/2010	2010/2011	Eligibility
Bereavement Allowance	Standard rate: £95.25 Lower rate where widow, widower or surviving civil partner was under age 55 when benefit became payable *taxable*	£97.65	Husband's, wife's or civil partner's NIC record sufficient *and*: (i) claimant was 45 or over but under State Pension Age when husband, wife or civil partner died *and* (ii) **Widowed Parent's Allowance** is not payable.

Widowed Parent's Allowance	Allowance: £95.25
	
	Additional Child Allowance:
	  first child: £8.20
	  each other child: £11.35
	
	Plus SERPS/S2P pension.
	
	taxable but children's allowance tax free
		£97.65
		
		£8.10
		£11.35
			(i) Has child for whom entitled to **Child Benefit**
			and:
			(ii) husband's, wife's or civil partner's NIC record sufficient.

Note: * As at 11 December 2009 the Government had not announced certain benefit rates for 2010/2011. These figures can be found at *www.hewitt.com/ppbstats*.

BASIC STATE RETIREMENT PENSIONS

From		Single person		Married couple	
		£ per week	£ per year	£ per week	£ per year
1948	(July)	1.30	67.60	2.10	109.20
1951	(October)	1.50	78.00	2.50	130.00
1952	(September)	1.62½	84.50	2.70	140.40
1955	(April)	2.00	104.00	3.25	169.00
1958	(January)	2.50	130.00	4.00	208.00
1961	(April)	2.87½	149.50	4.62½	240.50
1963	(May)	3.37½	175.50	5.45	283.40
1965	(March)	4.00	208.00	6.50	338.00
1967	(October)	4.50	234.00	7.30	379.60
1969	(November)	5.00	260.00	8.10	421.20
1971	(September)	6.00	312.00	9.70	504.40
1972	(October)	6.75	351.00	10.90	566.80
1973	(October)	7.75	403.00	12.50	650.00
1974	(July)	10.00	520.00	16.00	832.00
1975	(April)	11.60	603.20	18.50	962.00
1975	(November)	13.30	691.60	21.20	1,102.40
1976	(November)	15.30	795.60	24.50	1,274.00
1977	(November)	17.50	910.00	28.00	1,456.00
1978	(November)	19.50	1,014.00	31.20	1,622.40
1979	(November)	23.30	1,211.60	37.30	1,939.60
1980	(November)	27.15	1,411.80	43.45	2,259.40
1981	(November)	29.60	1,539.20	47.35	2,462.20
1982	(November)	32.85	1,708.20	52.55	2,732.60
1983	(November)	34.05	1,770.60	54.50	2,834.00
1984	(November)	35.80	1,861.60	57.30	2,979.60
1985	(November)	38.30	1,991.60	61.30	3,187.60
1986	(July)	38.70	2,012.40	61.95	3,221.40
1987	(April)	39.50	2,054.00	63.25	3,289.00
1988	(April)	41.15	2,139.80	65.90	3,426.80
1989	(April)	43.60	2,267.20	69.80	3,629.60
1990	(April)	46.90	2,438.80	75.10	3,905.20
1991	(April)	52.00	2,704.00	83.25	4,329.00
1992	(April)	54.15	2,815.80	86.70	4,508.40
1993	(April)	56.10	2,917.20	89.80	4,669.60
1994	(April)	57.60	2,995.20	92.10	4,789.20
1995	(April)	58.85	3,060.20	94.10	4,893.20
1996	(April)	61.15	3,179.80	97.75	5,083.00
1997	(April)	62.45	3,247.40	99.80	5,189.60
1998	(April)	64.70	3,364.40	103.40	5,376.80
1999	(April)	66.75	3,471.00	106.70	5,548.40
2000	(April)	67.50	3,510.00	107.90	5,610.80
2001	(April)	72.50	3,770.00	115.90	6,026.80
2002	(April)	75.50	3,926.00	120.70	6,276.40
2003	(April)	77.45	4,027.40	123.80	6,437.60
2004	(April)	79.60	4,139.20	127.25	6,617.00
2005	(April)	82.05	4,266.60	131.20	6,822.40
2006	(April)	84.25	4,381.00	134.75	7,007.00
2007	(April)	87.30	4,539.60	139.60	7,259.20
2008	(April)	90.70	4,716.40	145.05	7,542.60
2009	(April)	95.25	4,953.00	152.30	7,919.60
2010	(July)	97.65	5,077.80	156.15	8,119.80

NATIONAL INSURANCE CONTRIBUTION RATES AND STATE SCHEME EARNINGS LIMITS

Earnings Per Week by Tax Year	National Insurance Contribution Rates					National Insurance Earnings Limits				State Scheme Limits	
	Employer			Employee		LEL		UEL		LET	UAP
	Contracted-Out COSRS (%)	COMPS (%)	Not Contr'd-Out (%)	Contr'd-Out (%)	Not Contr'd-Out (%)	Per Week (£)	Per Annum (£)	Per Week (£)	Per Annum (£)	Per Annum (£)	Per Annum (£)
2007/2008											
Under LEL	0.00	0.00	0.00	0.00	0.00	87.00	4,524	670.00	34,840	13,000	–
LEL – £100.00	0.00	0.00 *	0.00	0.00 *	0.00						
£100.01 – UEL	9.10	11.40	12.80	9.40	11.00						
Above UEL	12.80	12.80	12.80	1.00	1.00						
2008/2009											
Under LEL	0.00	0.00	0.00	0.00	0.00	90.00	4,680	770.00	40,040	13,500	–
LEL – £105.00	0.00	0.00 *	0.00	0.00 *	0.00						
£105.01 – UEL	9.10	11.40	12.80	9.40	11.00						
Above UEL	12.80	12.80	12.80	1.00	1.00						
2009/2010											
Under LEL	0.00	0.00	0.00	0.00	0.00	95.00	4,940	844.00	43,888	13,900	40,040
LEL – £110.00	0.00	0.00 *	0.00	0.00 *	0.00						
£110.01 – UEL	9.10	11.40	12.80	9.40	11.00						
Above UEL	12.80	12.80	12.80	1.00	1.00						
2010/2011											
Under LEL	0.00	0.00	0.00	0.00	0.00	97.00	5,044	844.00	45,888	Not known at time of going to press	40,040
LEL – £110.00	0.00	0.00 *	0.00	0.00 *	0.00						
£110.01 – UEL	9.10	11.40	12.80	9.40	11.00						
Above UEL	12.80	12.80	12.80	1.00	1.00						

Notes: From 2011/12, employee and employer National Insurance contribution rates will increase by 1%. The primary threshold (£110 per week in 2010/11) will be increased so employees earning under £20,000 per year will pay lower contributions. Contributions are based on each separate tranche of earnings. An asterisk indicates that there is a negative contracted-out contribution rate, which for employees is 1.6% and for employers 3.7% for a COSRS or 1.4% for a COMPS. The lower limit for SERPS/S2P is the LEL. The upper limit was the UEL prior to 2009/2010 and is the UAP from 2009/10. **COSRS**: Contracted-Out Salary Related Scheme. **COMPS**: Contracted-Out Money Purchase Scheme. **UAP**: Upper Accrual Point.

THE STATE PENSION SCHEMES

There are currently two tiers of state pension provision: the Basic State Pension (BSP) and the State Second Pension (S2P), which replaced the State Earnings Related Pension (SERPS) from April 2002.

State Pension Age

State Pension Age (SPA) is currently 65 for men and 60 for women. SPA for women will be gradually increased from 60 to 65 over the ten years from April 2010. The Pensions Act 2007 increases SPA from 65 to 68, for both men and women, between 2024 and 2046.

Basic State Pension

This is a flat-rate pension that is payable to any individual that has paid, or been credited as having paid, sufficient National Insurance contributions. Currently, in order to receive the full BSP an individual must have paid NI contributions for at least 90% of their working life (defined as the period between age 16 and SPA). Individuals without a sufficient NI record receive a proportion of the full amount of the BSP. The BSP is increased in April each year, in line with the increase in the Retail Prices Index (RPI) over the year, and is currently subject to a minimum increase of 2.5%.

Under changes being made by the Pensions Act 2007, the BSP will increase in line with average earnings from 2012 or shortly thereafter, and from 6 April 2010 the number of contributory years needed for a full BSP is 30 for both men and women.

SERPS

SERPS accrued between 1978 and 2002 and is paid in addition to the BSP. It is based on a person's earnings throughout their career. When it was replaced in 2002, SERPS was targeting a pension of approximately 20% of the employee's Middle Band Earnings (i.e. earnings between the Lower and Upper Earnings Limits) at SPA.

The State Second Pension

The State Second Pension (S2P) came into effect on 6 April 2002 and is currently an earnings-related scheme like SERPS, which it replaced. Any SERPS entitlement earned up until April 2002 will remain. S2P has 3 salary bands which build up benefits at different rates *(see below)*. Certain non-earners (or low earners), such as those caring for the sick or disabled, also build up a S2P entitlement.

The salary bands used to calculate S2P take into account the Low Earnings Threshold (LET) and a figure which approximates to $3 \times$ LET $- 2 \times$ Lower Earnings Limit (LEL). This figure is referred to below as the Middle Earnings Threshold (MET).

There are currently three bands:

Band 1 – LEL to LET:	Target pension is 40% of earnings
Band 2 – LET to MET:	Target pension is 10% of earnings
Band 3 – MET to UAP:	Target pension is 20% of earnings

From around 2030, S2P will become a flat-rate top-up to the BSP. Accrual on Band 1 will be replaced with a flat-rate accrual. Bands 2 and 3 will be merged from 6 April 2010 and accrue pension at a rate of 10%; the UAP was frozen from 6 April 2009 for this purpose so that this band gradually disappears.

TAX ALLOWANCES AND RATES 2009/2010

Income Tax		Tax Bands and Rates	
Personal Allowances		**Taxable income**	Rate
Single Person[1]	£6,475	0–£37,400	20%
	(previously set at £6,035)	(2010/11: 0–£37,400)	
	(2010/11: £6,475)[2]	Above £37,400	40%
Married couple where one	£6,965	(2010/11: above £37,400)[5]	
aged over 75[3]	(2010/11: £6,965)	For savings income, the rates are 10%[6] for taxable income below £2,440; 20% for taxable	
Married couple's allowance	£2,670	income between £2,441 and £37,400; and 40% for taxable income above £37,400	
minimum amount[4]	(2010/11: £2,670)		
		For dividends, the rates are 10% for taxable income up to £37,400 and 32.5% for taxable income above £37,800	
Capital Gains Tax		**Exempt Amount** £10,100	
		(2010/11: To be confirmed)	
		A flat rate of 18%, with no taper relief.[7]	
Inheritance Tax		**Nil Rate Band** £325,000[8] (or £650,000 for couples)	
		(2010/11: £325,000 – or £650,000 for couples)	
		Rate is 40% on excess over Nil Rate Band (tapering relief on gifts within 7 years of death)	

Notes: [1] Higher allowances apply for those aged over 65 (and below an income threshold).

[2] From 2010/11, the personal allowance will be reduced by £1 for every £2 above an income of £100,000.

[3] Tax relief restricted to 10%, and amount of allowance reduces for income above a threshold.

[4] Applicable only where at least one of the couple was aged 65 before 6 April 2000.

[5] From 2010/11, an 'additional rate' of 50% will apply for those with taxable income over £150,000.

[6] If an individual's non-savings taxable income exceeds £2,440, the 10% starting rate for savings income will not be available.

[7] 'Entrepreneurs' Relief' is available for gains made on the disposal of all or part of a business, or on assets following the cessation of a business, by certain individuals.

[8] A transfer of unused nil-rate band from a deceased spouse or civil partner may be made to the estate of their surviving spouse or civil partner who dies on or after 9 October 2007.

TAX ALLOWANCES AND RATES 2009/2010 (continued)

Corporation Tax	Full rate is 28%
Value Added Tax (VAT)	Registration level is £68,000; rate is 15% (reduced from 17.5%, effective until 31 December 2009).
Insurance Premium Tax (IPT)	Standard rate is 5% of gross premium; a higher rate of 17.5% applies to travel insurance, breakdown insurance and insurance sold in relation to goods subject to VAT.

TAX ON PENSION SCHEMES

(See Sections 12 and 13 for further details)

Registered Pension Schemes

Tax Charge	Tax Rate
Lifetime allowance charge	25% if benefits taken as pension 55% if benefits taken as lump sum
Annual allowance charge	40%
Special annual allowance charge[1]	20%
Unauthorised payments charge	40%
Unauthorised payments surcharge	15%
Scheme sanction charge	40%, but may be reduced to as low as 15% where the unauthorised payments charge has been paid
Authorised surplus payments charge	35%
Short service refund lump sum charge[2]	20% on first £10,800 40% on balance
Charge on trivial commutation and winding-up lump sums	25% of uncrystallised rights tax free, balance taxed at member's marginal rate
Special lump sum death benefits charge[3]	35%

Note: [1] For 2010/11, the special annual allowance charge will be between 20% and 30% depending on total taxable income.

[2] From 2010/11, the short service refund lump sum charge will be 20% on the first £20,000 and 50% on the balance.

[3] This applies to pension protection lump sum death benefits, annuity protection lump sum death benefits and unsecured pension fund lump sum death benefits.

CONTRACTING OUT

The ability to contract out of the additional State pension was introduced alongside SERPS *(see Section 5)* in 1978. Initially only defined benefit schemes were able to contract out, although this was extended to most types of money purchase scheme in 1988 to tie in with the introduction of personal pension schemes.

The system of contracting out has changed a number of times over the years, building up various layers of complexity. This complexity, coupled with changes to the contracted-out rebates (which are generally held not to make contracting-out a financially advantageous option) have resulted in a situation where those in contracted-out employment are generally in this situation as a result of decisions made some time in the past.

With a reducing population of those in contracted-out employment, contracting out may not be regarded as a burning issue. However, it is an issue that many schemes will need to live with well into the future. Subject to certain changes in the pipeline, even where a scheme is no longer actively contracting out, it will need to continue to satisfy the legal requirements relating to those rights. Indeed, COSR schemes are unlikely to revisit a decision to contract out unless benefits are redesigned as it is generally expected that such schemes will continue to satisfy the reference scheme test.

In consequence, where a new scheme is being established, or a significant redesign exercise undertaken, contracting out is quite unlikely to be considered as an attractive option.

What does contracting out involve?

When an earner is contracted out, his State additional pension (SERPS between April 1978 and April 2002; State Second Pension (S2P) thereafter – *see Section 5*) becomes subject to a contracted-out deduction in respect of his period of contracted-out service. In return, depending on the type of contracted-out scheme *(see below)*:

- the employee and employer pay reduced rates of National Insurance (NI) contributions (Contracted-out Salary-Related scheme, or COSR), *or*

- the HMRC National Insurance Contributions Office (NICO) makes payments directly to the scheme in respect of its contracted-out members (Appropriate Personal Pension, or APP), *or*

- a combination of both the above (Contracted-out Money Purchase scheme, or COMP): reduced rates of NI contributions are paid and the employer pays the level contracting-out rebates into the scheme with top-up age-related payments made to the scheme by NICO.

In order to protect contracted-out members' pensions, extra requirements and restrictions apply to such schemes. With various exceptions in relation to stakeholder schemes, NICO has responsibility for contracting-out procedures and supervision, with some aspects being handled by the HMRC Audit and Pension Schemes Services office.

Contracted-out deductions from State additional pension

Where an employee was contracted out prior to 6 April 1997, the accrual of SERPS pension up to that date is subject to a contracted-out deduction equal to the guaranteed minimum pension (GMP) (or the 'notional' GMP in the case of a member of a contracted-out scheme other than a COSR).

Between April 1997 and April 2002, the contracted-out deduction for members of all types of contracted-out scheme was equal to the full SERPS pension, and so they accrued no SERPS benefit. Following the introduction of S2P in April 2002, members of contracted-out occupational schemes continue to have a contracted-out deduction based on the SERPS level of benefit with earnings limits changed as for S2P *(see Section 5)*. A top-up pension, payable by the State, accrues to such members, equal to the amount (if any) by which the member's S2P would have exceeded the SERPS level of benefit adjusted as for S2P *(see Section 5)*. In contrast, the contracted-out deduction for members of APPs is equal to the full S2P and so they do not accrue a top-up pension from the State (except for members earning below the Low Earnings Threshold – *see Section 5*). These differences are reflected in the rebates available from April 2002 *(see page 49)*.

BASIS OF CONTRACTING OUT

Contracted-out Salary Related scheme (COSR)

Guaranteed Minimum Pensions (GMPs)

Before 6 April 1997, COSRs had to promise to pay at least a minimum pension (the GMP) to each participating employee; this reduced the employee's SERPS pension from the State and, in return, both the employer and the employee paid lower-rate NI contributions. COSRs still need to provide GMPs accrued before 6 April 1997.

These are subject to strict regulatory requirements, including revaluation for early leavers, as described in *Section 15*. Tables of revaluation rates are included *on pages 48 and 49*.

The total NI rebates for contracted-out schemes are split between employee and employer. The split has varied over time, *and components can be found on page 49*.

New legislation that allows schemes the option of converting GMPs to 'normal' scheme benefits of equal value came into effect on 6 April 2009. To use this option, trustees must have employer consent and have consulted affected members.

The Reference Scheme Test (RST)

From 6 April 1997, no further GMPs accrued and, in order to contract out, the scheme has to pass a 'Reference Scheme Test'.

The scheme's actuary is required to certify that the pensions provided by the scheme are 'broadly equivalent to' or 'better than' the pensions under a Reference Scheme which is specified in legislation. The test is applied 'collectively' for employees and separately for their widows, widowers or surviving civil partners 'considered as a whole'. The RST is failed if benefits for more than 10% of individual employees or their survivors are not broadly equivalent to, or better than, pensions under the Reference Scheme.

The RST must be carried out separately for each separate benefit scale (if relevant) within a scheme, which must satisfy the test in its own right before the members to whom it applies can be contracted out on a salary-related basis. If separate contracting-out certificates are required for individual employers participating in a scheme, then the test must be carried out separately for each employer.

The main features of the Reference Scheme from 6 April 2009 are:

Pension age	65
Pension accrual rate	1/80
Pensionable salary	average qualifying earnings in the last three tax years
Qualifying earnings	90% of earnings between the Lower Earnings Limit (x52) and the Upper Accrual Point (x53)
Service	if limited to a maximum, this must not be less than 40 years
Spouse's or surviving civil partner's pension	50% of the member's pension (based on completed service for members who die before age 65)

Frequency of testing

Guidance requires the actuary to consider, at least every three years, whether there are any changes in the scheme's membership profile that might prevent the scheme from continuing to satisfy the test. A scheme's ability to pass the test must also be reconsidered whenever the actuary is informed of any changes which might affect that ability, such as:

- a change to the terms of the scheme (e.g. the definition of pensionable pay), *or*
- a significant change to the scheme's active membership profile, including remuneration patterns.

Money purchase contracting out

Abolition of money purchase contracting out

From a date to be decided, probably April 2012, contracting out on a money purchase basis (*as set out below*) will be abolished. Contracting-out certificates will automatically be cancelled and all affected schemes automatically contracted back in.

Contracted-out rights (known as 'Protected Rights' – *see below*) will cease to exist and will be treated in exactly the same way as any other money purchase benefits under the scheme. This applies to contingent spouses' rights as well as to members' rights.

Contracted-out Money Purchase scheme (COMP)

Occupational money purchase schemes can contract out if contributions equal to the flat-rate contracted-out rebates are paid to the scheme by the employer. Part of this is recoverable from the employee, *as discussed below*.

Prior to April 1997, COMP NI rebates were flat-rate, but since then they have been age-related. The age-related rebates, which are calculated on a unisex basis with no allowance for marital status, are based on the cost of providing the level of benefit given up and incorporate an expense allowance, but are capped at 7.4% of Upper Band Earnings which, from 6 April 2009, has been earnings between the Lower Earnings Limit and the Upper Accrual Point, for this purpose *(see table on page 46)*. The underlying assumptions have been revised from time to time.

The flat-rate part of the rebate (currently 3%) is paid by the employer to the trustees. Of this, 1.6% is attributed to, and may be recovered from, the employee. For members whose age-related rebate exceeds the flat-rate part, the balance is paid to the trustees in the following tax year by NICO. All rebates paid into the COMP, and any investment return on them, are known as Protected Rights and have to be used to provide benefits as set out in legislation.

Appropriate Personal Pension (APP)

Employees may take out an APP contract in order to contract out. Employers and employees continue to pay full-rate NI contributions and, following the end of the tax year, NICO then rebates part of these NI contributions by making so-called 'minimum contributions' directly into the APP. A basic rate 'tax rebate' on that part of these minimum contributions deemed to be in respect of employee NI contributions is also paid into the scheme by NICO. These payments, and any investment return on them, are Protected Rights under an APP.

Since April 1997, minimum contributions have been age-related *(see the table on page 47)*. The rebates have been revised from time to time to allow for changes in underlying assumptions. For the purpose of calculating the contracting-out rebates available from April 2002, earnings between the Lower Earnings Limit and Upper Earnings Limit (or, from 6 April 2009, the Upper Accrual Point) are divided into three bands representing different components of a member's earnings (as for S2P – *see Section 5*). Different rebate rates then apply to the portions of a member's earnings falling within each band. The table *on page 47* shows the rebate rates applicable to the top band. For the lower and middle bands, the rates shown should be multiplied by 2 and by ½ respectively.

Stakeholder schemes

In order to satisfy the stakeholder requirement to accept transfer payments (which may include contracted-out rights), all stakeholder pension schemes must be able to accept contracted-out rights. Most stakeholder schemes are established as personal pensions, and will be contracted out on the same basis as an APP *(see above)* and subject to the same changes when money purchase contracting-out is abolished.

Contracted-out Mixed Benefit scheme (COMB)

With effect from 6 April 1997, COSRs were permitted to retain GMP liabilities whilst contracting out on a money purchase basis for service after that date. Furthermore, from that date, two sections of a single scheme have been permitted to contract out concurrently on the two different bases.

STATE SCHEME PREMIUMS

Before 6 April 1997, contracted-out schemes were able to buy their members back into SERPS by payment of a State scheme premium in a number of circumstances, thereby extinguishing the scheme's liability to provide the member with contracted-out benefits. Only the Contributions Equivalent Premium (CEP) now remains, which COSRs may opt to pay in respect of members with less than two years' qualifying service when either scheme membership ceases or the scheme ceases to contract out. The options for discharging Protected Rights prior to pension commencement are very limited for schemes not in wind-up.

CONTRACTING BACK IN

A contracted-out scheme can decide to cease to contract-out (and must do so in certain circumstances). In order to do so the trustees or managers must notify the Audit and Pension Schemes Services and will, in turn, receive a notice from them setting out the date from which the contracting-out certificate is cancelled. From this date all affected members will be contracted back in and the trustees or managers will then have two years to either discharge the rights or determine to preserve them within the scheme, in which case the scheme will need to continue to comply with the relevant requirements. (If no action is taken HMRC may issue a notice giving the scheme six months to discharge the liabilities outside the scheme.) The following methods may be used to secure the liabilities:

- transfer to another contracted-out scheme *(see Section 16)* – member consent will be required unless this is part of a bulk transfer exercise and prescribed conditions are met

- the purchase of an annuity or deferred annuity contract, *or*

- provision of benefits within the scheme that satisfy HMRC requirements.

The scheme does not need to use the same method for all members.

COMPs: AGE-RELATED REBATES

Percentage of Upper Band Earnings

	Rebates for COMPs:[1]									
Age[2]	2002–2003	2003–2004	2004–2005	2005–2006	2006–2007	2007–2008	2008–2009	2009–2010	2010–2011	2011–2012
15	2.6	2.6	2.6	2.6	2.6	3.0	3.0	3.0	3.0	3.0
16	2.6	2.6	2.6	2.6	2.6	3.0	3.0	3.0	3.0	3.0
17	2.7	2.7	2.7	2.7	2.7	3.1	3.1	3.1	3.1	3.1
18	2.7	2.7	2.7	2.7	2.7	3.2	3.2	3.2	3.2	3.2
19	2.8	2.8	2.8	2.8	2.8	3.3	3.3	3.3	3.3	3.3
20	2.8	2.8	2.8	2.8	2.8	3.4	3.4	3.4	3.4	3.4
21	2.9	2.9	2.9	2.9	2.9	3.4	3.4	3.4	3.4	3.4
22	2.9	2.9	2.9	2.9	3.0	3.5	3.5	3.5	3.5	3.5
23	3.0	3.0	3.0	3.0	3.0	3.6	3.6	3.6	3.6	3.6
24	3.1	3.1	3.1	3.1	3.1	3.7	3.7	3.7	3.7	3.7
25	3.1	3.1	3.1	3.1	3.1	3.8	3.8	3.8	3.8	3.8
26	3.2	3.2	3.2	3.2	3.2	3.9	3.9	3.9	3.9	3.9
27	3.2	3.2	3.2	3.2	3.2	4.0	4.0	4.0	4.0	4.0
28	3.3	3.3	3.3	3.3	3.3	4.1	4.1	4.1	4.1	4.1
29	3.4	3.4	3.4	3.4	3.4	4.1	4.2	4.2	4.2	4.2
30	3.4	3.4	3.4	3.4	3.4	4.2	4.3	4.3	4.3	4.3
31	3.6	3.6	3.6	3.6	3.6	4.3	4.4	4.4	4.4	4.4
32	3.6	3.6	3.6	3.6	3.6	4.5	4.5	4.5	4.5	4.5
33	3.7	3.7	3.7	3.7	3.7	4.6	4.6	4.6	4.6	4.6
34	3.8	3.8	3.8	3.8	3.8	4.7	4.7	4.7	4.7	4.7
35	3.8	3.8	3.8	3.8	3.8	4.8	4.8	4.8	4.8	4.8
36	3.9	3.9	3.9	3.9	3.9	5.0	5.0	5.0	5.0	5.0
37	4.0	4.0	4.0	4.0	4.0	5.1	5.1	5.1	5.1	5.2
38	4.1	4.1	4.1	4.1	4.1	5.3	5.3	5.3	5.3	5.3
39	4.1	4.1	4.1	4.1	4.1	5.5	5.5	5.5	5.5	5.5
40	4.3	4.2	4.2	4.2	4.2	5.6	5.6	5.6	5.6	5.6
41	4.4	4.4	4.3	4.3	4.3	5.8	5.8	5.8	5.8	5.8
42	4.6	4.5	4.4	4.4	4.4	5.9	5.9	6.0	6.0	6.0
43	4.8	4.7	4.6	4.5	4.4	6.1	6.1	6.1	6.1	6.1
44	5.0	4.9	4.8	4.7	4.6	6.3	6.3	6.3	6.3	6.3
45	5.3	5.1	5.0	4.9	4.8	6.6	6.4	6.4	6.5	6.5
46	5.5	5.4	5.3	5.1	5.0	6.9	6.7	6.6	6.6	6.6
47	6.0	5.6	5.5	5.4	5.3	7.2	7.1	6.9	6.8	6.8
48	6.8	6.1	5.7	5.6	5.5	7.4	7.4	7.2	7.1	7.0
49	7.8	6.9	6.2	5.8	5.7	7.4	7.4	7.4	7.4	7.3
50	9.0	7.9	7.1	6.4	5.9	↑	↑	↑	↑	↑
51	10.3	9.1	8.1	7.2	6.5					
52	10.5	10.5	9.3	8.2	7.4					
53	10.5	10.5	10.5	9.5	8.4					
54	10.5	10.5	10.5	10.5	9.7					
55	10.5	10.5	10.5	10.5	10.5					
56	10.5	10.5	10.5	10.5	10.5	7.4	7.4	7.4	7.4	7.4
57	10.5	10.5	10.5	10.5	10.5					
58	10.5	10.5	10.5	10.5	10.5					
59	10.5	10.5	10.1	9.7	9.3					
60	10.5	10.5	10.5	10.3	9.9					
61	10.5	10.5	10.5	10.5	10.5					
62	10.5	10.5	10.5	10.5	10.5					
63	10.5	10.5	10.5	10.5	10.5	↓	↓	↓	↓	↓

Notes: [1] Including flat-rate rebate.   [2] Age on last day of preceding tax year.
Source: Hewitt, compiled from government information.

APPs: AGE-RELATED REBATES

Percentage of Upper Band Earnings

Age[2]	Rebates for APPs:[1]									
	2002–2003	2003–2004	2004–2005	2005–2006	2006–2007	2007–2008	2008–2009	2009–2010	2010–2011	2011–2012
15	4.2	4.2	4.2	4.2	4.2	4.7	4.7	4.7	4.7	4.7
16	4.2	4.2	4.2	4.2	4.2	4.7	4.7	4.7	4.7	4.7
17	4.2	4.2	4.2	4.2	4.2	4.8	4.8	4.8	4.8	4.8
18	4.3	4.3	4.3	4.3	4.3	4.9	4.9	4.9	4.9	4.9
19	4.3	4.3	4.3	4.3	4.3	4.9	4.9	4.9	4.9	5.0
20	4.4	4.4	4.4	4.4	4.4	5.0	5.0	5.0	5.0	5.0
21	4.4	4.4	4.4	4.4	4.4	5.1	5.1	5.1	5.1	5.1
22	4.5	4.5	4.5	4.5	4.5	5.2	5.2	5.2	5.2	5.2
23	4.5	4.5	4.5	4.5	4.5	5.2	5.2	5.2	5.2	5.2
24	4.5	4.5	4.5	4.5	4.5	5.3	5.3	5.3	5.3	5.3
25	4.6	4.6	4.6	4.6	4.6	5.4	5.4	5.4	5.4	5.4
26	4.6	4.6	4.6	4.6	4.6	5.5	5.5	5.5	5.5	5.5
27	4.7	4.7	4.7	4.7	4.7	5.5	5.5	5.6	5.6	5.6
28	4.7	4.7	4.7	4.7	4.7	5.6	5.6	5.6	5.6	5.6
29	4.8	4.8	4.8	4.8	4.8	5.7	5.7	5.7	5.7	5.7
30	4.8	4.8	4.8	4.8	4.8	5.8	5.8	5.8	5.8	5.8
31	4.9	4.9	4.9	4.9	4.9	5.9	5.9	5.9	5.9	5.9
32	4.9	4.9	4.9	4.9	4.9	6.0	6.0	6.0	6.0	6.0
33	5.0	5.0	5.0	5.0	5.0	6.0	6.0	6.0	6.1	6.1
34	5.0	5.0	5.0	5.0	5.0	6.1	6.1	6.1	6.1	6.1
35	5.0	5.0	5.1	5.1	5.1	6.3	6.3	6.3	6.3	6.3
36	5.1	5.1	5.1	5.1	5.1	6.4	6.4	6.4	6.4	6.4
37	5.1	5.1	5.1	5.2	5.2	6.5	6.6	6.6	6.6	6.6
38	5.2	5.2	5.2	5.2	5.2	6.7	6.7	6.7	6.7	6.7
39	5.2	5.2	5.2	5.2	5.3	6.8	6.8	6.8	6.8	6.9
40	5.4	5.3	5.3	5.3	5.3	7.0	7.0	7.0	7.0	7.0
41	5.6	5.5	5.3	5.3	5.4	7.1	7.1	7.1	7.1	7.1
42	5.7	5.6	5.5	5.4	5.4	7.2	7.2	7.2	7.3	7.3
43	5.9	5.8	5.7	5.6	5.5	7.4	7.4	7.4	7.4	7.4
44	6.1	6.0	5.9	5.7	5.6	↑	↑	↑	↑	↑
45	6.3	6.2	6.0	5.9	5.8					
46	6.5	6.4	6.2	6.1	6.0					
47	7.0	6.6	6.4	6.3	6.2					
48	7.8	7.1	6.6	6.5	6.4					
49	8.8	7.9	7.2	6.7	6.6					
50	9.9	8.9	8.0	7.3	6.8					
51	10.5	10.0	9.0	8.0	7.3					
52	10.5	10.5	10.1	9.0	8.1					
53	10.5	10.5	10.5	10.2	9.1	7.4	7.4	7.4	7.4	7.4
54	10.5	10.5	10.5	10.5	10.3					
55	10.5	10.5	10.5	10.5	10.5					
56	10.5	10.5	10.5	10.5	10.5					
57	10.5	10.5	10.5	10.5	10.5					
58	10.5	10.5	10.5	10.5	10.5					
59	10.5	10.5	10.5	10.2	9.8					
60	10.5	10.5	10.5	10.5	10.3					
61	10.5	10.5	10.5	10.5	10.5					
62	10.5	10.5	10.5	10.5	10.5					
63	10.5	10.5	10.5	10.5	10.5	↓	↓	↓	↓	↓

Notes: [1] The rebates shown (which, until 5 April 2010, apply to earnings in the highest of the three S2P earnings bands) must be multiplied by 2 and by ½ for earnings in the lowest and middle bands respectively *(see page 44)*. It is expected that the rebates for the highest band will also be multiplied by ½ for 2010/11 and 2011/12.
[2] Age on last day of preceding tax year.

Source: Hewitt, compiled from government information.

FIXED RATE GMP REVALUATION FACTORS

Number of Years	8.5%	7.5%	7.0%	6.25%	4.5%	4.0%
1	1.085	1.075	1.070	1.0625	1.045	1.040
2	1.177	1.156	1.145	1.1289	1.092	1.082
3	1.277	1.242	1.225	1.1995	1.141	1.125
4	1.386	1.335	1.311	1.2744	1.193	1.170
5	1.504	1.436	1.403	1.3541	1.246	1.217
6	1.631	1.543	1.501	1.4387	1.302	1.265
7	1.770	1.659	1.606	1.5286	1.361	1.316
8	1.921	1.783	1.718	1.6242	1.422	1.369
9	2.084	1.917	1.838	1.7257	1.486	1.423
10	2.261	2.061	1.967	1.8335	1.553	1.480
11	2.453	2.216	2.105	1.9481	1.623	1.539
12	2.662	2.382	2.252	2.0699	1.696	1.601
13	2.888	2.560	2.410	2.1993	1.772	1.665
14	3.133	2.752	2.579	2.3367	1.852	1.732
15	3.400	2.959	2.759	2.4828	1.935	1.801
16	3.689	3.181	2.952	2.6379	2.022	1.873
17	4.002	3.419	3.159	2.8028	2.113	1.948
18	4.342	3.676	3.380	2.9780	2.208	2.026
19	4.712	3.951	3.617	3.1641	2.308	2.107
20	5.112	4.248	3.870	3.3619	2.412	2.191
21	5.547	4.566	4.141	3.5720	2.520	2.279
22	6.018	4.909	4.430	3.7952	2.634	2.370
23	6.530	5.277	4.741	4.0324	2.752	2.465
24	7.085	5.673	5.072	4.2844	2.876	2.563
25	7.687	6.098	5.427	4.5522	3.005	2.666
26	8.340	6.556	5.807	4.8367	3.141	2.772
27	9.049	7.047	6.214	5.1390	3.282	2.883
28	9.818	7.576	6.649	5.4602	3.430	2.999
29	10.653	8.144	7.114	5.8015	3.584	3.119
30	11.558	8.755	7.612	6.1641	3.745	3.243
31	12.541	9.412	8.145	6.5493	3.914	3.373
32	13.607	10.117	8.715	6.9587	4.090	3.508
33	14.763	10.876	9.325	7.3936	4.274	3.648
34	16.018	11.692	9.978	7.8557	4.466	3.794
35	17.380	12.569	10.677	8.3467	4.667	3.946
36	18.857	13.512	11.424	8.8683	4.877	4.104
37	20.460	14.525	12.224	9.4226	5.097	4.268
38	22.199	15.614	13.079	10.0115	5.326	4.439
39	24.086	16.785	13.995	10.6372	5.566	4.616
40	26.133	18.044	14.974	11.3021	5.816	4.801
41	28.354	19.398	16.023	12.0084	6.078	4.993
42	30.764	20.852	17.144	12.7590	6.352	5.193
43	33.379	22.416	18.344	13.5564	6.637	5.400
44	36.217	24.098	19.628	14.4037	6.936	5.617
45	39.295	25.905	21.002	15.3039	7.248	5.841
46	42.635	27.848	22.473	16.2604	7.574	6.075
47	46.259	29.936	24.046	17.2767	7.915	6.318
48	50.191	32.182	25.729	18.3565	8.271	6.571

Note: The revaluation rate of 4.0% applies for leavers on or after 6 April 2007.

Source: Hewitt.

SECTION 148 ORDERS:
REVALUATION OF EARNINGS FACTORS

				Tax Year of Termination				
Tax Year of Earnings	2009/10 (%)	2008/09 (%)	2007/08 (%)	2006/07 (%)	2005/06 (%)	2004/05 (%)	2003/04 (%)	2002/03 (%)	2001/02 (%)
1978/79	677.6	654.2	623.8	595.3	572.4	545.9	522.3	500.7	475.9
1979/80	586.3	565.7	538.8	513.7	493.5	470.1	449.2	430.2	408.3
1980/81	473.3	456.1	433.7	412.7	395.8	376.3	358.8	342.9	324.6
1981/82	380.2	365.7	347.0	329.4	315.3	298.9	284.3	270.9	255.6
1982/83	336.1	323.0	306.0	290.0	277.2	262.3	249.0	236.9	223.0
1983/84	305.0	292.8	276.9	262.1	250.2	236.4	224.1	212.8	199.9
1984/85	275.0	263.7	249.0	235.3	224.3	211.5	200.1	189.7	177.7
1985/86	251.7	241.2	227.4	214.5	204.2	192.2	181.5	171.7	160.5
1986/87	223.0	213.3	200.7	188.8	179.3	168.3	158.5	149.5	139.2
1987/88	200.7	191.7	179.9	168.9	160.1	149.8	140.7	132.3	122.7
1988/89	176.7	168.4	157.5	147.4	139.3	129.8	121.4	113.7	104.9
1989/90	149.7	142.2	132.4	123.3	115.9	107.4	99.8	92.9	84.9
1990/91	132.7	125.7	116.6	108.1	101.2	93.3	86.2	79.8	72.4
1991/92	111.4	105.0	96.7	89.0	82.8	75.6	69.2	63.3	56.5
1992/93	98.5	92.5	84.7	77.5	71.6	64.9	58.8	53.3	47.0
1993/94	89.0	83.3	75.9	69.0	63.5	57.0	51.3	46.0	40.0
1994/95	83.3	77.8	70.7	63.9	58.5	52.3	46.7	41.6	35.8
1995/96	75.6	70.3	63.5	57.0	51.9	45.9	40.5	35.7	30.1
1996/97	70.8	65.7	59.0	52.7	47.7	41.9	36.7	32.0	26.5
1997/98	62.7	57.8	51.4	45.5	40.7	35.1	30.2	25.7	20.5
1998/99	55.5	50.9	44.8	39.1	34.5	29.2	24.5	20.1	15.2
1999/00	49.3	44.8	38.9	33.5	29.1	24.0	19.5	15.3	10.6
2000/01	40.4	36.2	30.7	25.6	21.4	16.6	12.4	8.5	4.0
2001/02	35.0	31.0	25.7	20.7	16.8	12.2	8.1	4.3	
2002/03	29.5	25.6	20.5	15.8	11.9	7.5	3.6		
2003/04	25.0	21.2	16.3	11.7	8.1	3.8			
2004/05	20.4	16.8	12.1	7.6	4.1				
2005/06	15.6	12.2	7.6	3.4					
2006/07	11.8	8.5	4.1						
2007/08	7.4	4.2							
2008/09	3.1								

Source: Hewitt, compiled from government information.

CONTRACTING-OUT REBATES

	Employee	Employer	
		COSR	COMP (See Note)
Tax Years	(%)	(%)	(%)
2002/03 to 2006/07	1.60	3.50	1.00
2007/08 to 2011/12	1.60	3.70	1.40

Note: For COMPs, in addition to the flat-rate rebates shown in the table, a further age-related payment is due from NICO. The total age-related rebate (flat-rate rebate plus age-related payment) is specified for each tax year up to 2011/12 (*see page 46*).

Source: Hewitt, compiled from government information.

SCHEME DESIGN AND BENEFITS

This section gives a brief explanation of the different types of benefit commonly provided by occupational pension schemes in the UK, and some of the factors that affect the design of those benefits.

Over the past ten years or so, many employers have closed traditional final salary pension schemes because of the significant risks, and associated costs, that they have to bear. In many cases employers have replaced these with defined contribution schemes where individual members bear most of the risks. However, employers are also looking for other solutions that fall somewhere between these two extremes, retaining the risks they want to manage, whilst providing benefits which are still attractive to employees from a recruitment and retention perspective.

TYPES OF PENSION BENEFIT

Pension schemes are often classified as defined benefit or defined contribution. However, many of the newer designs incorporate features of both types. Further, hybrid schemes also exist which provide different types of benefit in different circumstances. The key characteristics of the various scheme designs are covered below.

Defined Contribution

Defined contribution (DC) schemes provide benefits which depend on the amount of the contributions paid into the scheme, the investment return credited to those contributions, any expenses deducted and the financial conditions at the time benefits are converted into a future retirement income. *The types of arrangement that are based on defined contribution are described in Section 8.* Personal accounts, *which are discussed in Section 9*, will also provide DC benefits.

Final Salary

A traditional form of defined benefit scheme is the final salary scheme, under which the pension paid is equal to the number of years worked, multiplied by the member's salary at or near to retirement, multiplied by a factor known as the accrual rate (commonly 1/80 or 1/60). After a career of 40 years, this would give a pension of one-half or two-thirds of the member's 'final salary'. Members can usually choose to give up some of their pension in return for a lump sum (currently tax free), although some schemes provide a lump sum as a separate benefit.

Members generally pay a fixed rate of contributions (or no contributions in some cases), with the employer funding the 'balance of cost'.

CARE

Career Average Revalued Earnings schemes are defined benefit in nature, but are a variation of the traditional final salary design. Rather than the pension at retirement being based on earnings close to retirement, it is based on the average earnings throughout the member's entire career. These earnings are usually revalued in line with some index, commonly the Retail Prices Index (RPI).

If the revaluation rate turns out to be lower than the average earnings increases received by the member (which is generally the case), then the pension at retirement will be less than for an otherwise identical final salary scheme. From an employer's perspective, this means that CARE schemes usually cost less to fund.

Retirement Balance

Under retirement balance arrangements, members build up lump sum benefits on either a final salary or a CARE basis. For example, the lump sum accrual rate could be 20% of salary per annum, giving a lump sum after 40 years of eight times either final or career average earnings. Up to this point the scheme is considered as defined benefit.

At retirement, part of the lump sum can be taken as cash with the balance turned into pension. The conversion to pension is usually carried out by purchasing an annuity with an insurance company, in the same way as for a defined contribution scheme. However, in some cases preferential conversion terms are offered through the scheme itself.

Cash Balance

Cash balance schemes can be thought of as defined contribution schemes with defined investment returns. Employer and employee contributions are invested on behalf of each member and the investment return is guaranteed at the outset. For example, the return could be defined as the increase in RPI plus 2% p.a.

As with retirement balance schemes, the lump sum at retirement can be taken partly as cash, with the balance converted to pension.

Hybrid schemes

There are many forms of hybrid scheme which incorporate features of the above designs. The two most common types are:

- a 'better of' two (or more) different types of benefit, for example a defined contribution scheme with a minimum level of benefit calculated on a defined benefit basis, *and*
- a combination of different types of benefit, for example benefits might accrue on a final salary basis up to a certain level of earnings, but on a defined contribution basis above that level.

Risk sharing

In June 2008 the Government launched a consultation on risk-sharing pension arrangements, looking at various options for sharing risk between employers and employees and how risk sharing is dealt with internationally. In December 2008, it published its response to this consultation. The Government has indicated it will look further at the potential for:

- collective defined contribution schemes – based on fixed contribution rates, benefits are calculated as in a defined benefit scheme, but revaluation in deferment and indexation in payment can be withheld if underfunded; if the scheme remains underfunded, basic benefit levels can be reduced or the normal pension age increased

- removal of mandatory indexation for pensions from cash balance schemes
- sharing longevity risks between members and employers, *and*
- reducing the burdens imposed by the current arrangements for contracting out.

The Government has stated that mandatory indexation of pensions in payment for defined benefit schemes will not be removed and 'conditional indexation' will not be considered further at this time, which had been other proposals included in its consultation.

OTHER ISSUES AFFECTING SCHEME DESIGN

Registered Pension Schemes

To obtain tax concessions, the majority of UK pension schemes are 'registered' with HMRC. Registered schemes are subject to requirements that impact on the type and size of benefits that they can provide. *These requirements are described in Section 12. Section 14 describes arrangements outside the tax-privileged environment.*

Interaction with State Benefits

Many schemes are designed to target an overall level of pension at retirement, including state pensions. Schemes can also contract out of the State Second Pension (S2P), and previously SERPS. *For information on contracting out, see Section 6.*

AVCs

From 6 April 1988, all occupational pension schemes had to allow members to make Additional Voluntary Contributions (AVCs). Free-standing Additional Voluntary Contributions (FSAVCs) were introduced from 26 October 1987 to allow members greater flexibility in investment choice and portability should they leave service *(see Section 8).*

With effect from 6 April 2006, the Pensions Act 2004 removed the requirement that trustees must provide members with access to an AVC arrangement. However, this does not stop such a facility being offered. Furthermore, under the current tax regime the concept of AVCs and FSAVCs has disappeared. They have simply become part of the range of pension arrangements, and both contributions to and benefits from AVC arrangements are now subject to the tax legislation in the same way as any other pension arrangement.

Pension increases in payment

The Pensions Act 1995 made it compulsory for approved occupational pension schemes to provide at least Limited Price Indexation (LPI) of pensions accrued after 5 April 1997 once in payment. However, the scope of this requirement was reduced from 6 April 2005 when the Pensions Act 2004 removed it for pensions arising from money purchase benefits coming into payment on or after that date.

For pensions that remain subject to the LPI requirement, the minimum annual increase required is the lower of the RPI increase and 5% for service between 6 April 1997 and 5 April 2005, and the lower of the RPI increase and 2.5% for service after 5 April 2005.

Scheme modifications

With effect from 6 April 2006, the Pensions Act 2004 replaced the modification provisions under section 67 of the Pensions Act 1995. Essentially, modifications of an occupational pension scheme are 'voidable' unless for each member or survivor:

- *either* 'informed consent' has been given in writing by the member or survivor *or* (where permitted) the actuarial equivalence requirements, involving certification by the scheme actuary, have been met, *and*

- the trustees have formally determined to make (or have consented to) the modification and, before it takes effect, have notified the affected members and survivors.

Informed consent is always required in relation to a special category of major changes called 'protected modifications'. Members must be given a reasonable opportunity to make representations, and the modification must take effect within a 'reasonable period' of the consent being given.

The Regulator may make an order declaring the modification void if the requirements have not been met. It also has the power to levy fines on trustees and others exercising a power to modify a scheme, where 'voidable' modifications have been made or the requirements specified in an order by the Regulator have not been met. The Regulator has issued a Code of Practice to help trustees comply with the legislation and to provide guidance on what the Regulator considers to be 'reasonable periods' for the various stages of the process.

Consultation by employers

The Information and Consultation of Employees Regulations 2004 took effect on 6 April 2005. These regulations apply to businesses that employ 50 or more staff.

The regulations give employees the right – in certain circumstances – to be informed and consulted about the business they work for, including:

- the prospects for employment, *and*

- substantial changes in work organisation (e.g. proposed redundancies or changes in working hours) or contractual relationships.

The requirement for employers to have an agreement to inform and consult is not automatic but can be triggered in various ways, for example by a formal request from a minimum number of members. If an employer fails to initiate negotiations for an agreement to inform and consult employees when required to do so, or when negotiations fail, 'standard provisions' apply.

In addition, from 6 April 2006, the Pensions Act 2004 introduced provisions that require employers to consult with members before they can make certain 'listed changes' to a pension scheme. The associated regulations operate alongside the Information and Consultation Regulations, which are amended so that the employer only need comply with the specific pensions regulations (as long as the employer notifies the relevant parties that he is doing so) where a listed change is being made. Listed changes include closing a scheme, changing from defined benefit to defined contribution, ceasing or reducing defined benefit accrual or reducing an employer's contribution to a defined contribution scheme.

Inalienability of occupational pension

With certain exceptions (e.g. where a scheme member has defrauded his employer), entitlements or rights under occupational pension schemes may not be forfeited, assigned, surrendered, subjected to a charge or lien, or set off, and an agreement to do any of these things is unenforceable. The legislation was amended with effect from 6 April 2005 to permit trustees to reduce future benefits to recover a previous payment made in error.

Salary sacrifice

A 'salary sacrifice' is an arrangement whereby an employee waives his entitlement to part of his salary (or bonus), in exchange for his employer paying a pension contribution of an equivalent amount.

Prior to 6 April 2006, salary sacrifice could be used to overcome the 15% ceiling on employee pension contributions and, hence, was an effective way of enhancing a member's benefits. Under the current pensions tax regime, this ceiling has disappeared. However a particular advantage of salary sacrifice remains, whereby savings in National Insurance contributions (NICs) can be generated. Employee contributions are paid out of salary which is subject to NICs (both employer and employee), whereas employer contributions are not.

In the past, salary sacrifice was used almost exclusively by higher earners. However the concept is now more commonplace through the growth of 'flexible remuneration' plans, under which an employee has a 'flexfund' which can be used to purchase selected benefits from those on offer, with the remaining money being paid like a normal salary.

Cross-border activities

The Pensions Act 2004 introduced a number of provisions relating to cross-border activities under the EU Pensions Directive. A UK scheme that wishes to accept contributions from employers elsewhere in the EU (which employ members of the scheme who work elsewhere in the EU) must first receive a general authorisation from the Pensions Regulator. It must then apply for and receive approval from the Regulator in respect of each EU employer. Based on information passed on about the social and labour laws of the 'host' member state (i.e. the other EU country), the UK scheme has the responsibility for ensuring compliance, with the Regulator being able to monitor such compliance and impose sanctions for non-compliance.

Where the cross-border activity is the other way round (i.e. the UK is the 'host' state and the scheme is established elsewhere), the Regulator has the role of notifying the other country's authority of relevant UK law and monitoring compliance with it.

The EU Directive requires that non-money purchase cross-border schemes are 'fully funded' at all times. UK law interprets this as meeting the statutory funding objective introduced by the Pensions Act 2004 *(see Section 20)*. In addition, in order to be authorised, cross-border schemes must obtain annual actuarial valuations, with any deficit against the statutory funding objective being removed within 24 months of the valuation's effective date.

DEFINED CONTRIBUTION PENSION SCHEMES

Defined contribution (DC) schemes provide benefits which depend on the amount of the contributions paid into the scheme, the investment return credited to those contributions, any expenses deducted and the financial conditions at the time benefits are converted into a future retirement income. There are various types of arrangement that may be used to provide DC benefits (also known as money purchase benefits) which are considered below. Personal accounts will also provide DC benefits *and are discussed in Section 9*.

TYPES OF DC PENSION SCHEME

Trust-based occupational pension scheme

Employer-sponsored occupational DC pension schemes are operated as a trust. Many occupational pension schemes are now DC. The switch from defined benefit (DB) schemes to DC schemes for employees has accelerated in recent years. Many schemes now have separate DC and DB sections. Most schemes offer additional voluntary contributions on a DC basis and many that accept transfers into the scheme will offer DC benefits in respect of the transfer payment received even if the other benefits are accruing on a DB basis.

Personal pensions and retirement annuity contracts

Personal pensions in their present form have been available since July 1988. They were introduced with the intention of extending pension choice and encouraging individuals not in occupational schemes to save for retirement. All personal pensions are DC and are provided as a contract with an insurer or other provider, rather than trust-based. Personal pensions replaced retirement annuity contracts (RACs), often referred to as s226 contracts after the section of the Taxes Act 1970 which set out their provisions. RACs were available to the self-employed and to employees in non-pensionable employment. Those who already had RACs prior to July 1988 were allowed to continue to contribute to them. Prior to 6 April 2006, contributions to personal pensions were generally restricted to a maximum percentage of earnings, which varied by age. These limits were replaced with a single annual limit from 6 April 2006, when the provisions of the Finance Act 2004 came into force. A personal pension scheme that is used for the purpose of contracting out of S2P (SERPS prior to 6 April 2002) is known as an 'Appropriate Personal Pension' (APP).

Group personal pensions

Group personal pensions (GPPs) are personal pensions arranged by an employer for the benefit of its employees. These are often seen as a low-cost (to the employer) alternative to a DC trust-based occupational pension scheme, as most administration is handled by the insurance company running the GPP.

Self-invested personal pensions

A self-invested personal pension (SIPP) is an arrangement under a personal pension scheme which allows the member to choose the investments. From 6 April 2006, SIPPs became subject to the tax regime introduced under the Finance Act 2004. As the members may select its investments, SIPPs are classed as 'investment-regulated pension schemes'. As such, SIPPs are subject to prohibitive tax charges if they invest in residential property or most tangible moveable assets.

Small self-administered schemes

Small self-administered schemes (SSAS) are a particular type of trust-based occupational pension scheme and were introduced for company controlling directors in 1973. Due to the close relationship between the employer, the trustees and the members of these schemes, often all being the same people, HMRC imposed particular restrictions on SSASs. Since 6 April 2006, these restrictions have been removed and SSASs are now subject to the tax regime introduced under the Finance Act 2004. Most SSASs are 'investment-regulated pension schemes' and are, therefore, subject to prohibitive tax charges if they invest in residential property or most tangible moveable assets.

Free-standing AVC schemes

Free-standing AVC schemes (FSAVCs) are insurance contracts to which employees can contribute as an alternative to an AVC arrangement within an occupational pension scheme. Under the pre-6 April 2006 tax regime members of occupational pension schemes could only pay limited contributions (if any) to a personal pension at the same time as accruing benefits under the occupational scheme. Since 6 April 2006 these contracts are virtually indistinguishable from personal pensions and many have been closed and rolled into personal pension arrangements.

Stakeholder pensions

Stakeholder pension schemes were introduced by the Government in 2001 as a way of encouraging more private pension provision. They became available for members from 6 April 2001. Stakeholder schemes can only provide money purchase benefits. Various special requirements and restrictions apply to stakeholder schemes, including that the scheme must:

- be formally registered as a stakeholder scheme with the Pensions Regulator, *and*
- meet certain 'minimum standards', including in relation to the level of charges, flexibility of contribution payments, acceptance of transfer payments, and provision of information.

A stakeholder scheme must be contracted out, although individual members will usually be able to decide whether or not to be contracted out or contracted in.

Employer access requirements

Since October 2001, 'employer access requirements' mean that an employer must 'designate' a stakeholder scheme and publicise this to employees. For any employee who requests it, the employer must deduct contributions from the employee's remuneration and pay them within stated time limits to the designated scheme. There is, though, no requirement for the employer to contribute anything to the scheme himself.

Exemptions from these access requirements mean that many employers will not need to provide 'stakeholder access' to many or any of their employees. The most significant exemptions cover small employers (fewer than five employees), and employers who already offer a suitable pension scheme.

When the Personal Accounts Scheme is introduced in 2012 *(see Section 9)*, the employer access requirements will be removed.

Minimum standards

With a few exceptions *(see below)*, the maximum expense charge that can be levied on a member of a stakeholder scheme is equivalent to an annual charge of 1.5% of the value of the member's fund for the first ten years of membership, reducing to 1% thereafter. However, where the member joined the scheme before 6 April 2005, the maximum is 1% throughout. No extra charges can be imposed on ceasing contributions or transferring out of the scheme.

The exceptions include costs incurred in buying an annuity or administering income drawdown, stamp duty and other dealing costs incurred in buying or selling investments, market value adjustments on with-profits funds, maintenance costs on property, and costs associated with pension sharing activity or complying with an earmarking order on divorce.

Life assurance or waiver of contribution benefit, or financial advice, must be included within the above charge unless it is offered under a separate, optional contract with the extra charges explained.

The highest minimum contribution level which a stakeholder scheme can impose is £20 (net of basic rate tax relief), both for regular and one-off contributions.

Stakeholder schemes must accept any transfer payments from other pension schemes and, accordingly, must be contracted out.

Stakeholder schemes must meet wider requirements than other schemes concerning the provision of information to members. In particular, a lot of extra detail is required on the annual member's statement.

All stakeholder schemes must produce an annual declaration confirming compliance with the various stakeholder requirements, including those relating to maximum charges. The scheme's 'reporting accountant' must give a statement as to the reasonableness of this declaration.

Investments

A stakeholder scheme must not require members to make a choice about how their money is invested. A default option must be provided, although alternative investment options can also be offered. The Government introduced a requirement from 6 April 2005 for default funds to be 'lifestyled', whereby assets in the fund are gradually moved from equities towards fixed income as retirement nears.

Subject to certain conditions, stakeholder-only with-profits funds may be offered. Money invested in deposit funds must earn a return (net of charges) of at least base rate minus 2%. Trustees or managers may not invest in collective investment schemes which contain a bid/offer spread.

BENEFITS

Under the tax legislation, DC arrangements may provide the same types of benefit as other registered schemes, *which are described in Section 12*. DC schemes have greater flexibility when it comes to the form of pension benefits, which may be paid as a lifetime annuity, an unsecured pension (up to age 75), an alternatively secured pension (from age 75), or a scheme pension. If a scheme pension is provided, the member must also have the option to purchase a lifetime annuity contract on the open market.

Funds that have been designated to provide unsecured pension may be used to purchase short-term annuities or provide pension via income withdrawal. Alternatively secured pension funds must be used to provide income withdrawal. There are limits on the maximum and minimum pension that may be drawn each year, which are determined with reference to a 'basis amount'. The basis amount must be calculated annually for alternatively secured pensions and at least every five years for unsecured pensions, and is assessed using tables published by the Government Actuary's Department. For unsecured pension, annual income must not exceed 120% of the basis amount. For alternatively secured pension, income drawn each year must be between 55% and 90% of the basis amount.

CONTRACTING OUT

Occupational money purchase schemes, personal pension schemes and stakeholder schemes may be used to contract out of S2P (SERPS prior to 6 April 2002). *See Section 6 for details on contracting out.* It is planned that, from 2012, contracting out on a money purchase basis will be abolished and members of affected schemes will be automatically contracted back in for future service.

Prior to 1 October 2007, most SIPPs were unable to hold contracted-out benefits.

REGULATION OF DC SCHEMES

The Pensions Regulator (TPR) has a statutory responsibility for work-based DC schemes. A work-based pension scheme is any scheme that an employer makes available to employees. This includes all occupational DC schemes, and any stakeholder and personal pension schemes where employees have direct payment arrangements. Its objectives include protecting members' benefits and improving the understanding of good administration.

TPR issued a series of good practice guidance on the running of DC schemes for trustees and employers in 2008. These cover member retirement options, communicating with members and a guide for members on investment options. *See Section 10 for more details on these guides.*

The Financial Services Authority (FSA) authorises and regulates firms that operate or provide advice on personal pension schemes. They also regulate the sale and marketing of personal pension schemes. As a result, TPR and FSA have joint responsibility to regulate workplace group personal pension schemes.

DISCLOSURE

The disclosure requirements for occupational DC schemes are discussed *in Section 17*. The requirements for other types of DC scheme are generally the same. In addition, DC schemes provided by an insurer – such as stakeholder and personal pension products – must comply with additional disclosure requirements imposed by the FSA.

PERSONAL ACCOUNTS

The Government first announced in 2006 that it intended to introduce a system of automatic pension scheme enrolment for all employees, with combined contributions totalling 8% by employer and employee. The Pensions Act 2008 implemented the framework for the 'Personal Accounts' regime. During 2009, a number of consultations by the Government and the Personal Accounts Delivery Authority *(see below)* have provided more detailed proposals and we have assumed that these will be implemented *in the summary below*.

AUTOMATIC ENROLMENT

An employer will be required to automatically enrol its workers in the Personal Accounts Scheme, or its own qualifying auto-enrolment scheme, if they are at least 22 but younger than State pension age, earn over £5,035 per annum and are based in Great Britain. (Similar legislation is expected to be introduced for Northern Ireland.)

The requirement to enrol the worker in the pension scheme will normally apply from the first day the worker is employed, reaches age 22 or earns above the qualifying earnings level.

Opting out

An individual worker who has been auto-enrolled can subsequently opt out by giving notice within a limited period, in which case any member and employer contributions paid would be returned. The individual could usually then give notice to opt back in again. Employees who opt out will usually be automatically re-enrolled on the subsequent third anniversary of the employer's 'staging date' *(see below)* unless they have opted out within the previous 12 months.

The Pensions Regulator will have powers to issue a compliance notice to any employer who offers employees an inducement, the main purpose of which is to encourage employees to opt out of, or not join, an occupational pension scheme or a personal pension that exempts them from enrolment into the Personal Accounts Scheme.

Opting in

Workers who are not subject to the auto-enrolment arrangements can give notice requiring the employer to arrange for them to be enrolled in the automatic enrolment scheme. The employer then has a requirement to provide the minimum contributions or benefits on that employee's behalf (unless the employee earns below the qualifying earnings level, in which case the employer must provide access to a registered pension scheme).

CONTRIBUTION REQUIREMENTS

The contributions required to the Personal Accounts Scheme are a total of 8% of qualifying earnings, with the employer paying at least 3% and the employee making up any shortfall. The 'relief at source' method will provide basic rate tax relief, with the tax relief paid directly into the scheme and counting towards the 8%. Higher-rate tax-payers will need to claim additional relief directly from HMRC. The employer will have the authority to deduct contributions from workers' remuneration and pay them to the Scheme.

For this purpose, qualifying earnings are gross earnings, including sick pay, statutory maternity pay and paternity and adoption pay, between £5,035 and £33,540 per annum (in 2006/07 values). This qualifying earnings band will be reviewed annually in line with increases in average earnings (s 148 Orders – *see Section 6*).

TRANSITIONAL ARRANGEMENTS

The Government intends to phase in the requirement for automatic enrolment. This will occur over a three-year 'staging' period between 1 October 2012 and 1 October 2015. Larger employers will become subject to the requirements over the first year, and small employers over the following 18 months to two years. Each employer will therefore have its own 'staging date'.

The transitional arrangements will vary according to the type of pension scheme. For money purchase arrangements and the Personal Accounts Scheme, phasing-in will be in three steps:

From	Employer minimum contribution	Total minimum contribution (including tax relief)
October 2012	1%	2%
October 2015	2%	5%
October 2016	3%	8%

Employers providing defined benefit and hybrid schemes will be able to defer automatic enrolment until October 2015, provided jobholders can opt in during the period between the employer's 'staging date' and October 2015.

EXEMPTIONS FOR EMPLOYERS PROVIDING THEIR OWN QUALIFYING SCHEMES

To be exempt from the requirement to auto-enrol employees in the Personal Accounts Scheme, the employer will have to provide its own automatic enrolment scheme for workers. An automatic enrolment scheme is an occupational pension scheme which meets the *qualifying scheme test* and does not require the worker to express a choice or provide any information in order to remain an active member – for example, a money purchase scheme must have a default investment option.

There was originally much concern that a personal pension scheme would not be eligible to be an automatic enrolment scheme, because the employee's written consent is needed to join. However, the Government announced that automatic enrolment will be extended to insurance-based workplace pensions, following confirmation by the European Commission that this would not be a breach of EU legislation.

A *qualifying scheme* is an occupational scheme or personal pension scheme that satisfies the quality requirement for that jobholder *(see below)*, and is registered under Finance Act 2004. Regulations may prevent a scheme from being a qualifying scheme – for example, if the required level of contributions is too high.

Type of scheme	The quality requirement
Occupational money purchase schemes	Provides minimum total contributions of 8%, including a minimum 3% employer contribution, on the jobholder's qualifying earnings.
Personal pension schemes	The employer must operate direct payment arrangements. The minimum levels of contribution are the same as for occupational money purchase schemes. The basic rate tax relief claimed from HMRC will count towards the 8%.
Contracted-out member of a defined benefits or hybrid scheme	The quality requirement is met automatically if the scheme has a contracting-out certificate in force.
Contracted-in member of a defined benefits scheme	The 'test scheme standard' requires members to be entitled to a pension of 1/120 of qualifying earnings (averaged over the last three tax years) for each year of pensionable service (up to a maximum of 40) payable from 65. The pensions of no more than 10% of relevant members can be less than broadly equivalent to these test scheme benefits.
Contracted-in member of a hybrid scheme	The test scheme standard is modified in respect of hybrid schemes, which are sub-divided by type, to which different rules apply. For example, a scheme providing concurrent defined benefit and money purchase accrual, for individual members, must either satisfy the defined benefit or money purchase test alone, or provide percentages of the minimum accrual under each test which sum to at least 100% and meet the other requirements of both tests.

THE PERSONAL ACCOUNTS SCHEME

A Personal Accounts Scheme is to be established by the Government into which all employers can auto-enrol their workers and make required contributions.

Maximum contributions

A maximum annual contribution limit to the Personal Accounts Scheme has been allowed for, apparently to ensure that the Scheme remains focused on low-to-moderate earners, although the limit has not yet been specified. The Government proposed £3,600 (based on 2005 earnings levels) in its response to consultation.

In order to minimise 'market disturbance' and avoid the need for complex decisions, there will be a general ban on transfer payments to or from the Personal Accounts Scheme. However, the Scheme will accept cash transfer sums, in respect of leavers with less than two years' service *(see Section 15)*, and transfers out will be allowed for members who wish to consolidate their pension savings before an annuity purchase.

Charges

The Government intends to delegate the responsibility for setting the appropriate charges for the Personal Accounts Scheme to the Trustee Corporation *(see below)*. It states that the Trustee Corporation is best placed to make decisions relating to the charging structure, the level of charges and any additional charges for particular services. In particular, trust law will provide an incentive for the Trustee Corporation to set a charging structure that is fair and to keep charges down.

The Government's intention is that the Scheme will be self-financing through member charges 'in the long term' and that state support should not provide the Scheme with an unfair competitive advantage.

The stated aim is to provide 'a low-cost, good value way to save'. The Pensions Commission originally suggested that an annual management charge of 0.3% was achievable. The Government agrees that this is achievable in the long term but that in the short term the charges may be slightly higher (perhaps 0.5%) to take account of start-up costs, including establishing a compliance regime. No detail on the level of fees or proposed fee structure has yet been legislated for.

Investment options

The Government proposed that members will be offered a limited choice of investment funds:

- default fund
- small number of bulk-bought funds at low charges, *and*
- wider range of funds to include social, environmental, ethical and branded funds (likely to be at additional cost to the member).

The Personal Account Delivery Authority *(see below)* issued a discussion paper on designing an investment approach, but this did not include detailed information on the investment options. The Trustee Corporation will ultimately be responsible for investment decisions.

FINANCIAL ADVICE AND PROVISION OF INFORMATION

The Government has stated that it will be working closely with the Personal Accounts Delivery Authority *(see below)*, as well as the FSA, TPAS and organisations in the voluntary sector, to identify the information requirements of the new scheme and develop strategy in this area. Otto Thoresen's final report on delivering a national approach to generic financial advice, published on 3 March 2008, is likely to influence the model adopted. It sets out his recommendations for making 'money guidance' available to enable people in the UK to make informed financial decisions.

GOVERNANCE OF THE PERSONAL ACCOUNTS SCHEME

The Personal Accounts Scheme will be run as a trust-based occupational pension scheme:

- a trustee board, called the Trustee Corporation, will be the governing body, with wide-ranging powers to manage the scheme in the interests of its members

- contributions made and benefits paid will be subject to the same taxation arrangements and limitations as other registered pension schemes under Finance Act 2004 *(see Section 12)*, and

- regulations may require the Trustee Corporation to comply with general pensions legislation.

The trustee will take the key strategic decisions, but will delegate all executive and operational functions to a management board. The first members and their 'chair' will be appointed by the Government but, after the initial period, appointments will be made by the Corporation itself. Appointments will be for no more than four years. A Members' Panel will be created to be consulted by the trustee on key decisions. There will also be an Employers' Panel. It is possible that a modified version of the member-nominated directors requirements of the Pensions Act 2004 could be applied in future.

In April 2009, the Government published the draft scheme order that will establish the Personal Accounts Scheme and its rules. Scheme orders may only be made with the consent of the trustee, after it has consulted the members' and employers' panels. Further provisions about the Scheme may be made by rules. Any proposed rules must be published in draft for comment by interested persons, and the members' and employers' panels must be consulted. Rules cannot be made by the Secretary of State without trustee consent and consultation.

The Trustee Corporation will have a broad power to invest, allowing it to do anything it needs to in connection with investment in line with existing pension and trust law.

The Personal Accounts Delivery Authority

The Personal Accounts Delivery Authority (PADA) is a separate body overseeing the Personal Accounts Scheme. Its role is to assist with the establishment and ongoing operation of the Scheme, and compliance with and enforcement of the auto-enrolment requirements.

In carrying out its functions, PADA must have regard to the following principles:

- encourage and facilitate participation in qualifying schemes
- minimise burdens on employers
- minimise the adverse effects on qualifying schemes and their members of the establishment of the Personal Accounts Scheme
- minimise the cost of membership of the Personal Accounts Scheme
- take account of members' preferences regarding investment choice, as far as practicable, *and*
- respect diversity of members.

COMPLIANCE BY EMPLOYERS

The monitoring of employers' compliance with the auto-enrolment and contribution requirements will be a function of the Pensions Regulator. Employers will have to keep records and provide the Regulator with certain information for this purpose.

A penalty regime for employers who do not comply with the requirements will be administered by the Pensions Regulator, who will be able to issue compliance notices, which require remedial action, to employers who contravene the auto-enrolment requirements and impose fines where things are not put right. In particular, workers may have to be put in the same position as if the contravention had not occurred.

An employer who fails to comply with the requirement for automatic enrolment, re-enrolment or workers' requests to opt in commits a criminal offence which could lead to up to two years' imprisonment and/or a fine. The Regulator will consider criminal prosecution for the most serious or persistent offenders.

Protection of employment rights

The Pensions Act 2008 includes provision to protect employees who do not opt out after automatic enrolment from suffering detrimental treatment by employers compared with those who do opt out. It includes statutory rights, building on the existing framework of employment rights, so that those individuals who wish to save should be protected from being unfairly dismissed and from other detrimental treatment (including in relation to recruitment).

TRUSTEES AND SCHEME GOVERNANCE

This section deals with the role of trustees within the legal framework governing pensions in the UK and with scheme governance in general. References to the legal system are to the system which in general applies in the UK. However, some differences exist under Scottish law. The existing legal framework includes trust law, tax law, social security law (in particular, specific DWP pensions legislation), financial services legislation and European Union law.

Trust law, which is at the heart of pensions law, is considered in more detail below. Tax law is dealt with in *Section 12*. Various aspects of DWP pensions legislation (including provisions which transpose EU requirements into UK law) are also discussed in this and other sections. The Financial Services and Markets Act 2000 is dealt with in more detail in *Section 28*.

TRUSTS AND TRUSTEES

Trust law

The principles of trust law have mainly been established, over the years, by court precedents. However, over time some of these principles have been incorporated in legislation, for example in the Trustee Act 2000.

What is a trust?

One definition is that 'a trust is an equitable obligation binding a person (who is called a trustee) to deal with property over which he has control (which is called the trust property) for the benefit of persons (who are called the beneficiaries) of whom he may himself be one, and any of whom may enforce the obligation'.

In the case of a pension scheme, the trustees hold the pension fund assets for the benefit of the members, and their first duty is to them – not to their employer, their trade union, or any outside body. 'Members' for this purpose includes not just those currently employed and paying into the scheme, but also people with deferred pensions, those who are drawing benefits and those who are potentially eligible for benefits, such as spouses and other dependants.

Why use a trust?

The vast majority of UK occupational pension schemes are set up under trust. The three main reasons why trusts have been used are:

- to provide security for the members by keeping the scheme's assets separate from those of the employer

- to ensure third-party beneficiaries, such as spouses and dependants of members, have legal rights, *and*

- (historically) to enable the scheme to be approved by the Revenue as an 'exempt approved' scheme, and thereby qualify for valuable tax reliefs on contributions, investment income and some of the benefits paid.

Note that, whilst no longer a Revenue requirement, the Pensions Act 2004 requires funded occupational schemes to be established under irrevocable trusts and to have effective written rules specifying the benefits and the conditions on which they are payable. This reflects the requirements of the EU Pensions Directive.

Who can be a trustee?

The trustees of a scheme can be either individuals (so long as they are over 18 and not insane) or corporations, or a combination of both.

Neither the scheme actuary nor the scheme auditor can be a trustee, and certain people are automatically disqualified (e.g. undischarged bankrupts or people who have been convicted of an offence involving dishonesty). The Pensions Regulator has power to prohibit a person from acting as trustee of a particular scheme, a particular type of scheme, or schemes in general, where it is satisfied that he or she is not a fit and proper person to be a trustee. It may suspend a person from acting as a trustee where the outcome of legal proceedings is awaited. It may also appoint an independent trustee where an employer becomes insolvent or where it believes the appointment is in the best interest of the members *(see* Conflicts of Interest, *below)*.

The Pensions Act 1995 (as amended by the Pensions Act 2004) requires all schemes to have a minimum proportion of 'member-nominated trustees'. Such trustees must be 'nominated' as the result of a process involving (as a minimum) all the active and pensioner members of the scheme (or organisations representing them), and then 'selected' as a result of a further process. The 'minimum proportion' is initially one-third, but the Government has given itself the power to increase this to one-half at some time in the future. The Pensions Regulator has issued a 'code of practice' on this requirement.

The trust deed and rules

A scheme's definitive documentation usually has two main parts: the trust deed and the rules. The trust deed defines the powers and duties of the trustees and employer, and the duties of trustees to the members.

The rules state who is eligible to be a scheme member and cover details of the benefits promised, the areas where the trustees have discretion, the arrangements for determining the employer's contributions, and the level of members' contributions.

The trust documents govern the trustees' actions. Generally speaking, only when the deed and rules do not deal with a point is it necessary to apply the principles of trust law. However, it should be noted that Acts of Parliament can 'override' provisions contained in trust deeds, for example the Civil Partnership Act 2005.

Scheme documentation can be altered in various ways: for example, a supplemental deed extends the definitive documentation, perhaps by introducing new powers. An amending deed changes it. Trustees may have to refer to several different documents, if amendments have not been incorporated into the main deed. It is therefore good practice to try to keep a single consolidated deed which is amended as necessary. Many Trustees will now have a 'working copy' of their rules, which whilst not a formally signed set of rules incorporates changes into a single document.

Duties, responsibilities and rights of a Trustee

The fundamental duty of a trustee is to give effect to the provisions of the trust deed. A trustee who fails to do this is in breach of trust. Other duties are many and varied, and include:

- paying out the right benefits at the right time
- keeping accurate records of members and their dependants
- keeping proper accounts, *and*
- ensuring that scheme assets are properly and prudently invested.

Under the provisions of the Employment Rights Act 1996, employee trustees (or employee directors of trustee companies) of an occupational scheme of their employer have statutory rights to time off work for the performance of their trustee duties and training, payment for this time off and rights not to suffer detriment or dismissal related principally to the performance of their trustee functions.

Legislation (for example the Pensions Acts 1995 and 2004) places a number of particular responsibilities on trustees. Exceptions apply in certain cases but, in general, these responsibilities include:

Appointment of professional advisers

The trustees must appoint an individual actuary (except for pure money purchase schemes) and an auditor (known respectively as the 'scheme actuary' and the 'scheme auditor') and, where investments covered by the Financial Services and Markets Act 2000 are held, a fund manager, to carry out certain specified functions. Another actuary may also be appointed to provide actuarial advice which is not required to be given by the scheme actuary. Any person having custody of scheme assets must be appointed by the trustees, except where they are sub-custodians appointed by a main custodian or other adviser who has been specifically authorised by the trustees. A legal adviser must also be appointed by the trustees if such advice is required.

Investment of the scheme's assets

Trustees have complete power to invest scheme assets as if they were their own, subject to their duty of care, the taking of 'proper advice' from qualified advisers, any scheme restrictions (except that any requirement for the direct or indirect consent of the employer is void) and the statutory restriction that not more than five per cent of the market value of the resources of a scheme may at any time be invested in employer-related investments. Their decision-making powers may be delegated to an external fund manager. The trustees remain responsible for any actions taken, but they are not liable for the fund manager's actions so long as they have taken steps to ensure that he has appropriate knowledge and experience, and is acting competently and in accordance with the written 'statement of investment principles' *(see below)*.

Regulations introduced from late 2005 to comply with the EU Pensions Directive require the trustees (amongst other things) to invest predominantly in regulated markets and to ensure proper diversification.

Statement of investment principles
The trustees must prepare (and maintain) this statement, after taking advice from an experienced investment adviser and after consulting the employer. Amongst other things it must cover:

- the kinds of investment to be held and the balance between them
- risk and expected return
- realisation of assets, *and*
- the trustees' policy (if any) on socially responsible investment, including the exercise of voting rights.

The statement must be reviewed at least every three years and immediately after any significant change in investment policy.

Compliance with scheme funding legislation
Scheme-specific funding was introduced under the Pensions Act 2004 (replacing the previous Minimum Funding Requirement). Under this regime, trustees are responsible for setting the funding strategy as well as monitoring the funding level and payment of contributions. *See Section 20 for further details.*

Disclosure of pension scheme information
Under UK pensions law, scheme trustees are required to make a substantial range of information available to scheme members and others. *See Section 17 for further details.*

Compliance with the Data Protection Act 1998
For the purposes of the Data Protection Act 1998, pension scheme trustees are generally classified as 'data controllers'. As such, they are required to ensure the adequacy of their own data security arrangements and of those who process data on their behalf; for example the scheme administrators. They are responsible for keeping the Information Commissioner up to date with details of their security measures. Trustees must obtain explicit member consent before holding or processing sensitive data, such as data relating to physical/mental health or sexual life. They must also ensure they have suitable procedures in place for complying with requests by scheme members exercising their statutory right to see a copy of personal data held about them within 40 days.

Whistle-blowing and Notifiable Events
Under the Pensions Act 2004, responsibility for reporting breaches ('whistle-blowing') was extended to scheme trustees (and others). In addition, a new requirement was introduced for trustees to notify the Regulator of certain events. *See Section 11 for further details.*

Scheme governance

Scheme governance encompasses the different aspects of operating a pension scheme. Trustees' core responsibilities include safeguarding and investing scheme assets, monitoring funding levels, ensuring members receive the correct benefits when they fall due, and ensuring compliance with the law and the scheme's own trust deed and rules. Meeting these responsibilities requires carefully developed procedures covering aspects such as:

- the constitution of the trustee body, appointment and removal of trustees, formation of sub-committees, the process of decision taking
- skills assessment, induction, training and performance evaluation
- risk assessment and management, and internal controls *(see below)*
- dealing with (potential) conflicts of interest *(see below), and*
- relations with the sponsoring employer, exchange of information (and confidentiality agreements, where appropriate) and mutual understanding of objectives.

Internal controls

A formal requirement (imposed by the EU Pensions Directive) for schemes to establish internal controls to ensure compliance with the law and their own rules was introduced into UK law by the Pensions Act 2004. The Pensions Regulator's code of practice (and accompanying guidance) stresses the need for trustees to set up internal controls to enable them to react to significant operational, financial, funding, regulatory and compliance risks. These controls should be proportionate, based on an assessment of the risks to which the scheme is exposed, having regard to its particular circumstances and to their likelihood of materialising and potential impact. Internal controls should be reviewed at least annually and more frequently if substantial changes take place or inadequacies are revealed. It is suggested that a statement confirming that key risks have been considered and effective controls established could be incorporated in the scheme's annual report to demonstrate good practice.

Where trustees delegate their responsibilities (e.g. to third-party administrators or investment managers and custodians), they should take care to examine the internal control assurance reports produced by their agents.

The code of practice was issued in November 2006 and in November 2008 the Pensions Regulator commenced a review of the code and guidance as part of its commitment to ensuring that materials available for trustees, employers and professionals remain fit for purpose.

Conflicts of Interest

Conflicts of interest can pose a serious risk to good governance and, as such, are subject to some very complex legal considerations. In 2008, the Pensions Regulator published guidance relating to conflicts of interest. The guidance covers five broad principles, which are: understanding the importance of conflicts of interest; identifying conflicts of interest; evaluation, management or avoidance of conflicts; managing adviser conflicts; and conflicts of interest policy. The principles are supported by practical guidance on matters relating to the governance of each. A determination by the Ombudsman in January 2009 confirmed that conflicts of interest do not invalidate trustees' decisions, so long as they are properly managed.

The Pensions Regulator has also published guidance on *Relations with Advisers*. The guidance sets out some key issues for trustees to consider in their relations with advisers and covers general issues as well as those specific to the scheme actuary, scheme auditor, legal adviser, scheme administrator, independent financial adviser and benefit consultant. The guidance also raises issues and provides hints on questions that trustees should be asking their advisers.

The importance of being able to control potential conflicts of interest was highlighted in the *Telent* case. In November 2007, Pensions Corporation bought Telent. The trustees of the Telent pension scheme asked the Pensions Regulator to intervene; it temporarily put in place three independent trustee directors with sole power over the scheme, as it was felt that a clear conflict of interest had arisen which had not been managed appropriately. In April 2008, Pensions Corporation and the Regulator came to an agreement on the future governance of the scheme – the three independent trustee directors would remain on the trustee board, comprising nine trustee directors, and measures would be put in place to identify and manage conflicts of interest on the board.

Defined contribution schemes and good practice guidance
In 2008, the Pensions Regulator published guidance in three specific areas relating to the regulation of defined contribution (DC) schemes.

The first covered member retirement options. This was intended to help employers and trustees ensure that effective processes are in place and help members make retirement income decisions.

It then published guidance on effective member communication which was designed to help schemes assess their communication policy. This guidance identified four events where communication is key:

- at or prior to joining a pension arrangement
- approaching retirement
- scheme design changes or changes in fund choice, *and*
- ongoing ad hoc communications through notices, the employer's intranet, etc.

The Regulator also published investment guidance. This was designed to provide individuals with basic knowledge about investment funds whilst stressing the need to obtain financial advice.

The various types of guidance apply to all registered schemes that offer benefits on a DC basis (including AVCs).

Wednesbury Principles
These define the process by which trustees should approach decision making in order to minimise the risk of legal challenge:

- the trustees must ask themselves the correct questions
- they must direct themselves correctly in law; in particular, they must adopt a correct construction of the trust deed and rules
- they must not arrive at a perverse decision, i.e. a decision at which no reasonable body of trustees would have arrived, *and*
- they must take into account all relevant and no irrelevant facts.

If the trustees can demonstrate that they followed this process when exercising discretionary powers, it is unlikely that their decision will be overturned by the Pensions Ombudsman or the courts. Recent Ombudsman determinations have highlighted the need for scheme minutes to include a clear record of the steps taken in reaching a decision. However, care should be taken if reasons are given, as these could be challenged.

Internal Dispute Resolution Procedure

Under the Pensions Act 1995, trustees are required to put in place, and disclose via the scheme's explanatory booklet, an internal scheme dispute resolution procedure under which scheme members may bring written complaints. This was initially set up as a two-stage procedure with an individual appointed by the trustees to rule in the first stage. If dissatisfied with the decision the complainant could then appeal to the trustees as a second stage. The Pensions Act 2007 (with effect from 6 April 2008) gives schemes the option of replacing the two-stage procedure with a single stage process under which all decisions would be taken by the trustees. In addition the prescribed time limits are replaced to make a decision within a 'reasonable period'. Having exhausted the scheme's internal dispute resolution procedure, a complainant may take his complaint to the Pensions Ombudsman.

Trustee Knowledge and Understanding

Following recommendations in the Myners Report *(see below)*, the Pensions Act 2004 introduced a formal requirement for trustees to have knowledge and understanding about the law relating to pensions and trusts and the principles of funding and investment. In addition, they are required to be conversant with the scheme's trust deed and rules, statements of investment and (where applicable) funding principles and other relevant scheme documents.

The Pensions Regulator has issued a code of practice and scope guidance on these requirements. The level of knowledge and understanding expected is that necessary for the individual concerned to exercise his or her own trustee function (so more is expected of the chair of the trustee board, or a significant sub-committee). Trustees should carry out a review of their training needs at least annually and when required in response to internal and external scheme changes or new responsibilities. Records should be kept of learning activities undertaken.

The requirements came into effect on 6 April 2006. Newly appointed trustees will generally have a six-month period of grace before the requirements apply to them. An updated Code of Practice came into effect in October 2009. The code and accompanying scope documents have been restructured and extended to cover areas that have become more prominent since the originals were published in 2006. These include matters such as employer covenant, wind-up, buy-out and personal accounts. A new (much reduced) scope document for trustees of small insured DC schemes has also been published.

Myners Principles

Paul Myners' report into institutional investment in the UK was published in 2001. The underlying concern was that key decision makers, such as pension scheme trustees, did not generally have the time, skill and expertise to carry out their responsibilities effectively.

Myners put forward a code of principles for trustees to follow covering aspects such as effective decision making, performance measurement and communication with members. Other proposals made by Myners included the legal requirement for trustees to have knowledge and understanding of various matters *(see above)* and the replacement of the Minimum Funding Requirement with a new funding regime *(see Section 20)*.

In October 2008, the Government announced changes to the Myners principles. There are now fewer, higher level principles covering:

- effective decision making
- clear objectives
- risk and liabilities
- performance assessment
- responsible ownership, *and*
- transparency and reporting.

The principles remain voluntary with a 'comply or explain' approach to reporting.

The Government also established the Investment Governance Group to oversee the principles and provide further guidance, when necessary. In particular, the Group is responsible for reviewing the principles as they relate to defined contribution arrangements.

THE ROLE OF THE EMPLOYER

The employer is a party to the trust and retains certain duties and powers which may be specified in the trust deed. The employer normally carries a substantial burden of the cost of the scheme benefits, or its administration, or both, and would therefore expect to retain certain powers, especially in areas where there is a cost element, for example the power to augment benefits or to amend the scheme. The employer generally has the ultimate power to cease contributions to the scheme, which will lead to the scheme either winding up or ceasing to provide any further benefit accrual, according to the provisions of the trust deed. In normal circumstances, the employer should act in a reasonable manner to ensure that the trustees can operate the scheme satisfactorily; this includes providing information on members, paying contributions when due, and meeting any obligations imposed on them by the trust deed or by legislation.

Although the Pensions Act 2004 extends the trustees' statutory powers in relation to scheme funding, the method and assumptions, statement of funding principles, any recovery plan, and the schedule of contributions are all, generally, subject to the agreement of the employer. *See Section 20 for further details*.

The employer is also required, under the Pensions Act 2004, to consult with scheme members about proposed changes to scheme rules, if these fall within prescribed categories. *See Section 7*.

THE ROLE OF THE ACTUARY

Responsibilities of the scheme actuary

The scheme actuary appointed by the trustees has a number of statutory responsibilities, many of which are connected with the funding of the scheme. Included in these are the following:

- advising the trustees on various aspects of scheme funding, as required by the Pensions Act 2004 *(see Section 20)*
- producing actuarial valuations for funding purposes *(see Section 20)*
- certifying the technical provisions and schedule of contributions as required by the scheme funding legislation *(see Section 20)*
- completing required certification for contracted-out salary-related schemes *(see Section 6)*
- along with other parties who are involved in running the scheme, reporting material breaches of statutory responsibilities by the employer or trustees to the Pensions Regulator *(see Section 11)*
- advising the trustees on various matters in relation to the calculation of individual transfer values *(see Section 16), and*
- certifying bulk transfers of members without their consent *(see Section 26)*.

Other actuarial advice

Most schemes require the trustees to take actuarial advice before taking decisions, on such matters as augmentations and bulk transfers, which will affect the finances of the scheme (and this is encouraged by the 'notifiable events' framework – *see Section 11*). Actuaries also provide expert advice in benefit design and implementation, and assist both employers and trustees in ensuring that the pension provision offered to employees is both appropriate and soundly based. They also assess the pension cost to be disclosed in the company's accounts *(see Section 27)*.

THE ROLE OF THE AUDITOR

Responsibilities of the scheme auditor

The statutory duties of the scheme auditor include the following:

- producing a report stating whether or not in his opinion the scheme accounts have been prepared in accordance with regulations
- producing an auditor's statement as to whether or not in his opinion the required contributions have been paid to the scheme
- if the auditor's statement is negative or qualified, giving a statement of the reasons, *and*
- along with other parties who are involved in running the scheme, reporting material breaches of statutory responsibilities by the employer or trustees to the Pensions Regulator *(see Section 11)*.

THE ROLE OF THE ADMINISTRATOR

The scheme administrator has many duties. Some of these are imposed by statute and regulations, some arise as a condition for being a registered pension scheme, and others are set out under a contract between the trustees and an administrator for providing services to the scheme. Requirements for occupational pension scheme administrators, from 6 April 2006, are set out in the Finance Act 2004 and associated regulations. HMRC requires every registered pension scheme to appoint a scheme administrator to be responsible for providing information including scheme returns and event reports, accounting for tax and monitoring benefits against the lifetime allowance. *Further details of the Finance Act 2004 tax regime can be found in Section 12.*

Day-to-day administrative responsibilities are very varied, ranging from organising the payment of benefits to individual beneficiaries in accordance with the scheme rules, to tasks such as organising the submission of information required by the Pensions Regulator. These may be carried out by someone other than the formal scheme administrator.

In January 2009 the Pensions Regulator published guidance on record keeping. This is aimed at trustees, providers and administrators. The Regulator's objective is to improve the standard of record keeping across the industry and the guidance should be viewed as good practice. The guidance includes a framework for testing and measuring data and specific events are noted which give rise to an urgent need to review record keeping: wind-up, entry to PPF assessment, change of administrator or buy-out. These reviews should provide Trustees with information on the quality of the member data held by their administrators. Where results indicate further investigation or data improvement is needed, action plans should be developed to address gaps and weaknesses according to the risks involved.

THE PENSIONS REGULATORY SYSTEM

Introduction

The regulation of pension funds has changed over recent years. This section covers the role of the current Pensions Regulator and other bodies involved in the regulation of pension schemes in the UK.

THE ROLE OF THE PENSIONS REGULATOR

The Pensions Regulator was created under the Pensions Act 2004 and replaced the Occupational Pensions Regulatory Authority (Opra) with effect from April 2005. The Regulator has wider powers than Opra. These fall into three broad categories: investigating schemes, acting against avoidance and putting things right.

The Regulator has statutory objectives to protect the benefits of members of work-based pension schemes, to reduce the risk of situations arising which might lead to calls on the Pension Protection Fund, and to promote and improve the understanding of the good administration of work-based pension schemes. A fourth statutory objective will be introduced with the Personal Accounts regime in 2012: maximising employer compliance with the new regime. *(See Section 9 for details.)*

In April 2009, the Regulator published its corporate plan setting out four key themes for the next three years (2009–12), to support these objectives:

- to improve the governance and administration of work-based pensions *(see Section 10)*
- to reduce risks to DB scheme members by continuing to regulate scheme funding effectively *(see Section 20)* and to ensure 'non-insured buy-out' products are properly managed *(see Section 25)*
- to reduce the risks to defined contribution scheme members *(see Section 8)*, and
- to prepare for 2012 *(see Section 9)*.

Scheme returns

The Regulator requires all schemes to complete a regular scheme return. This provides a wide range of information about schemes, including details of membership, sponsoring employers, trustees, advisers, administration, funding and investment. These returns include the information required by the Board of the Pension Protection Fund (PPF) to determine its annual levies *(see Section 22)*. A return is required only when the Pensions Regulator issues a 'scheme return notice'. The Regulator issues scheme return notices annually for all but the smallest schemes.

It is the trustees' legal duty to complete the scheme return online by the completion date notified on the form. The online system also allows trustees and administrators to regularly update scheme details during the year.

Codes of Practice and Guidance

The Regulator is required to publish codes of practice giving practical guidance on implementing certain parts of the legislation and indicating the conduct and practice expected. The codes are not 'law' but nevertheless would be taken into account by a court in deciding whether or not legislation had been complied with. The following codes are in force:

- Reporting breaches of the law
- Notifiable events
- Funding defined benefits *(see Section 20)*
- Early leavers – reasonable periods
- Reporting late payment of contributions to occupational money purchase schemes
- Reporting late payment of contributions to personal pensions
- Trustee knowledge and understanding *(see Section 10)*
- Member-nominated trustees and directors *(see Section 10)*
- Internal controls *(see Section 10)*
- Modification of subsisting rights
- Dispute resolution – reasonable periods, *and*
- Circumstances in relation to the material detriment test.

In addition to publishing codes of practice the Regulator has also issued regulatory guidance for trustees and employers on a number of subjects including clearance, abandonment of defined benefit pension schemes, transfer inducement offers, defined contribution schemes (various guides), setting mortality assumptions for valuations, cash equivalent transfer values, winding up and conflicts of interest.

Notifiable and reportable events

As noted above, the Regulator has issued codes of practice relating to notifiable events and reporting breaches of the law.

Trustees and/or employers are required to notify the Regulator in writing of certain 'notifiable events'. Notification is only required for schemes which are eligible for the PPF. The purpose of notification is to reduce the risk of the circumstances which might lead to compensation being payable from the PPF, by providing an early warning of possible insolvency or underfunding. The events to be notified include augmenting benefits without sufficient funding, granting large benefits and decisions which might result in a debt to the scheme not being paid in full.

Separately, and not restricted to schemes eligible for the PPF, there is a duty to report significant breaches which are 'likely to be of material significance to the Regulator'. The duty to 'blow the whistle' applies to a wide range of people, including trustees, employers, scheme administrators and professional advisers. Criteria for deciding whether or not a breach is likely to be of material significance are set out in the code of practice and guidance and cover the cause and effect of the breach, the reaction to it and any wider implications.

In both cases, notification should be made in writing and where possible the standard form available from the Regulator's website should be used.

Late payments by employers

The Regulator has issued two codes of practice relating to the reporting of late payments by employers to occupational money purchase pension schemes and personal pension schemes. These set out reasonable periods within which trustees/managers must report late payments of contributions to the Regulator (within 10 working days of identifying that a late payment is material) and to members/employees. Late payments must be reported if the trustees/managers have reasonable cause to believe that the late payment of contributions is material. The code includes a guide to which circumstances would be considered material, such as where a contribution remains unpaid 90 days after the due date. The code for personal pensions also includes guidance on what is a reasonable period for employers to provide payment information to the managers (within 30 days of the formal request), and for managers to report to the Regulator if this information is not received (within 60 days of the formal request).

Similar requirements apply to late payments to defined benefit occupational pension schemes. These are included in the code of practice covering scheme funding *(see Section 20)*.

Acting against avoidance

The Regulator has powers to act where it believes that an employer is attempting to avoid its pension obligations (deliberately or otherwise), leaving the PPF to pick up the pension liabilities. These are referred to in the pensions industry as 'moral hazard' provisions. These provisions were extended in 2009 to cover situations, in particular 'non-insured buy-out' business models *(see Section 25)*, where the previous powers were insufficient or difficult to implement. They allow the Regulator to issue any of the following:

(a) *Contribution notices.* If the Regulator determines that a company or individual has taken action with the main purpose of avoiding an obligation to meet a debt on the employer under section 75 of the Pensions Act 1995, he may direct that those involved pay a 'contribution' to the scheme. The aim of this is to recover the amount that would otherwise have come from the section 75 debt.

The Pensions Act 2008 introduced the ability for the Regulator to issue a contribution notice if the 'material detriment' test is met. This is met if, in the Regulator's opinion, 'the act, or failure to act, has been materially detrimental to the likelihood of accrued scheme benefits being received'. The Regulator has issued a code of practice and guidance relating to the test.

(b) *Financial support directions.* These are intended to apply in cases where corporate structures exist for legitimate business reasons but where the effect is that the 'employer' in relation to a scheme is 'insufficiently resourced' to deal with a potential section 75 obligation. Here the Regulator can require the company group to put in place 'financial support' arrangements. To date, the Regulator has only issued two financial support directions, both against Sea Containers Limited in February 2008, in respect of two schemes belonging to its UK subsidiary.

    (c) *Restoration orders.* If there has been a transaction at an undervalue involving the scheme's assets, these allow the Regulator to take action to have the assets (or their equivalent value) restored to the scheme.

Companies considering corporate transactions where there is an underfunded defined benefit pension scheme can apply to the Regulator for a clearance statement. This gives assurance that the Regulator will not use its anti-avoidance powers in relation to the transaction once it is completed. The decision is binding on the Regulator unless the circumstances differ materially from what was disclosed in the clearance application.

Intervention

When the Regulator decides action must be taken to protect the security of members' benefits, there is a range of options available. These include:

- issuing an improvement notice to one or more persons
- taking action to recover unpaid contributions from the employer
- disqualifying trustees, or issuing prohibition or suspension orders to trustees
- appointing trustees, including independent trustees in certain circumstances, *and*
- imposing fines (maximum: £5,000 for individuals or £50,000 in other cases).

THE ROLE OF THE DWP

The Department for Work & Pensions (DWP) provides the 'overarching regulatory and legal framework' governing the Regulator and the PPF. It has no responsibility for the day-to-day running of the Regulator and the PPF, but expects to be informed by them of potentially significant problems.

    A tripartite Memorandum of Understanding between the DWP, the Regulator and the PPF establishes the framework for cooperation between them, including discussion forums, and sets out the role and responsibilities of each body.

THE ROLE OF HMRC

Since pension benefits are often costly, employers will generally wish to take advantage of the tax reliefs that are available to schemes that meet certain criteria. This is monitored by Pension Schemes Services (PSS) within HM Revenue & Customs (HMRC). Schemes which wish to benefit from these tax reliefs must be registered *(see Section 12 for details)*.

    Following registration, PSS monitors schemes to ensure that they continue to meet their requirements. Scheme administrators are required to supply HMRC with the information necessary to enable its monitoring to be effective. This includes an Event Report which must be completed annually, giving details of specified events (such as large benefit payments or payment of benefit to members with enhanced or primary protection) that have occurred during the tax year to which the report relates. They also require quarterly income tax returns to be completed and a copy of the audited annual accounts to be submitted.

THE PENSIONS ADVISORY SERVICE (TPAS)

TPAS (The Pensions Advisory Service) is a non-profit, independent and voluntary organisation giving free help and advice to members of the public who have problems concerning State, occupational or personal pensions. The service is available to anyone who believes he or she has pension rights: this includes working members of pension schemes, pensioners, deferred pensioners and dependants. TPAS is grant-aided by the DWP.

TPAS has no statutory powers and any decisions it reaches are subject to the agreement of the parties involved. Where no agreement can be reached, cases may be referred to the Pensions Ombudsman (*see below*).

THE PENSIONS OMBUDSMAN

The Pensions Ombudsman's role is to investigate disputes and complaints concerning occupational and personal pension schemes. Complaints may be made by actual or potential beneficiaries against the trustees, employer or anyone involved in the administration of a scheme. The Ombudsman's jurisdiction also covers complaints made by the trustees against the employer, and vice versa, and disputes between trustees of either the same scheme or different schemes.

During an investigation, the trustees of the scheme involved, and anyone else against whom a complaint has been made, are given a chance to explain their position, and the Ombudsman can require any necessary information or documentation to be provided to him.

Unlike TPAS, the Pensions Ombudsman has statutory authority with regard to the complaints brought to him. In particular:

- he has the same powers as the court in respect of the examination and attendance of witnesses
- anyone obstructing an investigation, for example by refusing to give certain information, can be taken to court and, following representations by either or both sides, be dealt with as if he or she had been in contempt of that court, *and*
- the Ombudsman's decision, and any directions he gives, are final and binding, and are enforceable in a county court as if they were judgments of that court. An appeal can be made to the High Court on any points of law involved in the case.

The Pensions Act 2004 expanded the powers and jurisdiction of the Pensions Ombudsman. The Pensions Ombudsman is now able to appoint one or more Deputy Ombudsmen who will have the power to carry out any of the Ombudsman's duties. One-off acts of administration were brought within the Ombudsman's remit, by expanding the definition of a person concerned with the administration of a scheme.

Merging the Pensions Ombudsman and the Financial Ombudsman Service was considered but a full merger was ruled out in December 2008. However, the two services will work more closely together, after further consultation.

LEVIES

Occupational pension schemes are generally required to pay the following levies:

- the General Levy (which also applies to personal pension schemes)
- the Fraud Compensation Levy, *and*
- the Financial Reporting Council Levy.

Schemes which are eligible for future entry into the PPF are required to pay additional levies to the PPF *(see Section 22)*.

General Levy

The General Levy covers the cost of the Pensions Regulator, the Pensions Ombudsman and any grants to support TPAS.

The current levy rates, which were last reviewed for 2008/09, are set out below:

Band	Number of Members:	Occupational Schemes:		Personal Pension Schemes:	
		General Levy (per member):	Min. Payment (per scheme):	General Levy (per member):	Min. Payment (per scheme):
1	2–11	–	£33	–	£14
2	12–99	£3.35	–	£1.34	–
3	100–999	£2.42	£340	£0.94	£140
4	1,000–4,999	£1.88	£2,420	£0.81	£940
5	5,000–9,999	£1.43	£9,400	£0.54	£4,050
6	10,000+	£1.00	£14,300	£0.41	£5,400

Fraud Compensation Levy

The Board of the PPF are responsible for operating the Fraud Compensation Fund *(see Section 22)*.

This is funded by a 'Fraud Compensation Levy' on all schemes eligible for this compensation at a rate determined by the PPF Board. Regulations allow for this levy to be a maximum of £0.23 per member per year. This levy has not been charged since 2004/05.

Financial Reporting Council Levy

Since April 2006, the Board for Actuarial Standards, which is part of the Financial Reporting Council, has had responsibility for actuarial standards and regulation. The cost is met by an annual levy. For 2009/10 this is £2.6m and is collected:

- 10% from the Actuarial Profession
- 45% from life and general insurance companies, *and*
- 45% from pension schemes with 1,000 or more members (at the rate of £3.00 per 100 members).

PENSIONS TAXATION –
REGISTERED PENSION SCHEMES

The current pensions tax regime came into force on 6 April 2006 ('A Day') under the Finance Act 2004, and replaced the previous tax regimes for all types of pension scheme. Regulations, together with parts of subsequent Finance Acts, have added much detail and clarification.

This section sets out the main features of the current regime. These include changes in the treatment of certain *de minimis* and other payments, under regulations that came into force in 2009. Further changes, restricting tax relief for high earners to basic rate with effect from April 2011, were announced in the 2009 Budget *(see Section 30)*. 'Anti-forestalling' measures, brought into effect by the Finance Act 2009, *are described in Section 13.* At the end of this section is a brief summary of the previous regimes, parts of which are still relevant under transitional provisions.

FINANCE ACT 2004 TAX REGIME

Subject to two allowances, members can receive tax-advantaged benefits; this applies to all members of all 'arrangements' in 'registered' pension schemes:

- the *lifetime allowance* – an overall limit on an individual's tax-privileged retirement savings, *and*
- the *annual allowance* – an annual limit on an individual's 'total pension input'.

The government reviews the allowances quinquennially; the figures for the first five years are set out below. The allowances will be frozen at the 2010/11 levels for another five years, up to and including 2015/16.

Tax Year	Lifetime Allowance	Annual Allowance
2006/07	£1,500,000	£215,000
2007/08	£1,600,000	£225,000
2008/09	£1,650,000	£235,000
2009/10	£1,750,000	£245,000
2010/11	£1,800,000	£255,000

For the purpose of specifying the benefits that may be paid and testing against the above limits, the regime distinguishes between three main types of pension 'arrangement'. These are the two familiar ones, 'defined benefit' and 'money purchase', and a new one, 'cash balance', which is expressed as a sub-category of money purchase.

- Under a defined benefit arrangement, the 'pension input' for the purposes of the annual allowance is the value of any increase in the accrued pension over the year, using a factor of 10:1, plus the amount of any separate lump sum accrued
- under a money purchase arrangement (other than a cash balance arrangement), the pension input is equal to the amount of the contributions

paid by, or in respect of, the individual; if the scheme is contracted out, flat-rate 'minimum payments' and age-related payments are excluded, *and*

- under a cash balance arrangement, the pension input is the fund value at the end of the year, assuming the member retired, less the corresponding value at the start of the year increased by the greater of 5% and the RPI increase over the year. The amount is reduced by any flat-rate rebates received if the scheme is contracted out.

The value of benefits must be tested against the lifetime allowance (or the part of it that remains after any previous 'crystallisations') on each occasion that benefits come into payment, or 'crystallise'. A single factor (for all ages) of 20:1 is used for valuing *scheme pensions* (*see below*) on crystallisation. The valuation of annuities provided under money purchase arrangements is based on their cost. On crystallisation, up to 25% of the value of benefits crystallised (or their cost, under money purchase arrangements) within the lifetime allowance is available as a tax-free lump sum.

A number of transitional provisions are available to protect benefits accrued prior to A Day. These include:

- a facility *(primary protection)* to register the value of benefits already accrued if in excess of £1.5m at A Day, which will become a personal lifetime allowance, to be indexed in line with the statutory lifetime allowance, *and*

- a facility *(enhanced protection)* for individuals to have existing benefits (whether or not already in excess of £1.5m) ring-fenced by opting out of any future 'accrual' under the new regime.

'Employer-financed Retirement Benefit Schemes' ('EFRBS') replaced former unapproved arrangements ('FURBS' and 'UURBS') – *see Section 14*.

Registration

'Registration' of a pension scheme has replaced HMRC approval as the process by which schemes obtain tax-advantaged status. A new procedure was introduced, primarily intended for use by new schemes established after A Day.

Pension schemes that had HMRC approval prior to A Day, including occupational pension schemes, personal pensions, retirement annuity contracts and 'old code' schemes approved under s608 ICTA 1988, automatically became 'registered schemes' on 6 April 2006 unless they explicitly opted out.

Compliance requirements

Under the Act, registered schemes have to comply with a number of administration requirements. These include providing HMRC with quarterly returns for tax accounting purposes, reports on the occurrence of certain events and, if requested, a *Pension Scheme Return*.

BENEFITS THAT MAY BE PROVIDED BY REGISTERED PENSION SCHEMES

Pension payable to member

A defined benefit arrangement may pay a member pension only in the form of a *scheme pension*, as described below.

For a money purchase arrangement, there are essentially three options as to the type of member pension that may be provided:

- a *scheme pension* as for defined benefit arrangements, provided the member had been offered an open market option
- a *lifetime annuity*, which may be level, increasing or investment/index-linked, payable by an insurance company chosen by the member, *or*
- an *unsecured pension* consisting of income drawdown and/or a short-term annuity (while the member is under 75) *or* an *alternatively secured pension,* i.e income drawdown (age 75 onwards). The rate at which income is drawn down is subject to strict limits, particularly in the case of an alternatively secured pension, which is intended primarily for members with religious objections to pooling of mortality risk.

Scheme pensions must be payable at least annually and may not be reduced from one 12-month period to the next, except in specified circumstances including the cessation of an ill-health pension, a bridging pension ceasing between ages 60 and 65, as a consequence of a pension sharing order, or where reductions are applied to all scheme pensions.

All pensions payable from registered schemes are subject to income tax at the recipient's marginal rate and they must be paid under PAYE, where applicable.

Minimum age from which pension may be paid
Subject to transitional provisions, member pensions (including income drawdown) must not commence before *normal minimum pension age*, except on ill-health retirement. *Normal minimum pension age* is 50 before 6 April 2010 and 55 thereafter.

Period of payment
Secured pensions must generally be payable for life and may, additionally, carry a guarantee of up to 10 years payable (to any person) in the form of continued pension instalments.

Lump sums payable to member

Apart from additional authorised payments prescribed under regulations and additional transitional provisions (*see below*), the only lump sum benefits that may be paid to a member of a registered pension scheme are set out below; generally they can only be paid if the member is aged under 75.

Pension commencement lump sum
A tax-free pension commencement lump sum of up to 25% of the value of the benefits crystallised (*see above*) may normally be paid in connection with a member becoming entitled to a *scheme pension*, a *lifetime annuity* or an *unsecured pension*.

Serious ill-health lump sum

Where a member is expected to live for less than one year, a serious ill-health lump sum may be paid in respect of uncrystallised benefits. Up to the available lifetime allowance, this is tax free.

Short service refund lump sum

A refund of the member's contributions (without interest) may be paid from an occupational pension scheme on leaving service, if the member has no right to preservation. The scheme administrator is liable for tax on the first £10,800 of such refunds at 20% and on the remainder at 40%. Interest may be paid in addition to the short service refund lump sum as a 'scheme administration member payment' (*see below*) and is taxed at the member's marginal tax rate.

Trivial commutation lump sum

Trivial commutation is permitted only if *all* of a member's benefits under *all* pension arrangements are valued in aggregate at or below 1% of the standard lifetime allowance. The commutations must take place within a single 12-month window, chosen by the member, between ages 60 and 75. If the member has uncrystallised rights immediately before the lump sum is paid, 25% of the value of such rights is tax free, with the balance taxed at the member's marginal rate. Under regulations which came into force in 2009, the range of authorised lump sum payments was significantly extended to include *de minimis* payments; *see below*.

Winding-up lump sum

A winding-up lump sum not exceeding 1% of the standard lifetime allowance may be paid, subject to certain conditions, to extinguish the member's entitlement to benefits under the pension scheme. If the member has uncrystallised rights immediately before the lump sum is paid, 25% of the value of such rights is tax free, with the balance taxed at the member's marginal rate.

Lifetime allowance excess lump sum

Where none of a member's lifetime allowance is available, any remaining uncrystallised benefits may be taken as a lifetime allowance excess lump sum. This may not be paid until *normal minimum pension age* (unless the member is in ill health), and is taxed at 55%.

Refund of excess contributions lump sum

Where in any tax year a member's pension contributions exceed the maximum that qualify for tax relief (£3,600 or relevant UK earnings, if greater), a refund of the excess may be paid without giving rise to liability for income tax. Any excess contributions that had been paid net of basic rate income tax under a 'relief at source' arrangement cannot be included in the refund. A 'scheme administration member payment' *(see below)*, taxable at the member's marginal rate, may also be made in respect of interest or investment growth.

Scheme administration member payment

A scheme administration member payment is defined as 'a payment by a registered pension scheme to or in respect of a member of the pension scheme which is made for the purposes of the administration or management of the pension scheme'. The legislation expressly states that payments of wages, salaries or fees to persons administering the scheme and payments made for the purposes of scheme assets are scheme administration payments, whereas a loan is not. A scheme administration payment may not exceed the amount that might be expected to be paid on arm's length terms.

Pensions payable on death

A pension death benefit is a pension payable to a dependant on the death of a member, other than continuing payments of member pension for a limited period under a permitted member pension guarantee. The forms of the dependant's pension that may be provided under the different types of arrangement correspond to those for members' pensions. A dependant's *scheme pension* is restricted to 100% of the member's pension (plus an adjustment for any tax-free lump sum taken) if the member was over 75 years of age at the date of death. All dependants' pensions payable from registered schemes are subject to income tax at the recipient's marginal rate and must be taxed under PAYE, where applicable.

Recipient
Eligible 'dependants' are:

- a member's spouse or civil partner at date of death
- a person who was married to, or a civil partner of, the member when the member first became entitled to the pension
- a child of the member who either has not reached age 23 (extended in some circumstances under transitional provisions) or who, in the opinion of the scheme administrator, was dependent on the member at the date of the member's death because of physical or mental impairment, *and/or*
- any other person who, in the opinion of the scheme administrator, at the date of the member's death:
  - was financially dependent on the member
  - had a financial relationship of mutual dependence with the member, *or*
  - was dependent on the member because of physical or mental impairment.

Lump sums payable on death

Apart from additional authorised payments prescribed under regulations and transitional provisions (*see below*), the only lump sum death benefits that may be paid by a registered pension scheme are those described below. Except where otherwise indicated, the legislation imposes no restrictions on the recipient of the benefit. Most types of lump sum death benefit may only be paid in respect of members who die before age 75.

Defined benefits lump sum death benefit
A lump sum of unrestricted amount, tax free up to the amount of the member's remaining lifetime allowance.

Uncrystallised funds lump sum death benefit

On the death of a member of a money purchase arrangement, a lump sum not exceeding the amount of the uncrystallised funds, tax free up to the amount of the member's remaining lifetime allowance.

Pension/annuity protection lump sum death benefit

On the death of a member whilst in receipt of a scheme pension or lifetime annuity, a lump sum, taxable at 35%. This benefit may not exceed the amount by which the instalments paid up to date of death fall short of the amount originally crystallised.

Unsecured pension fund lump sum death benefit

On the death of a member of a money purchase arrangement, or of a dependant, who was entitled to income withdrawal at the time of death, a lump sum, taxable at 35%.

Charity lump sum death benefit

On the death, leaving no dependants, of a member of a money purchase arrangement (or of a dependant) who was in receipt of a post-age 75 alternatively secured pension, a charity lump sum death benefit may be paid to a charity nominated by the member or dependant as appropriate, or (if no such nomination has been made) by the scheme administrator.

Trivial commutation lump sum death benefit/winding-up lump sum death benefit

In specified circumstances, a lump sum not exceeding 1% of the standard lifetime allowance may be paid to a dependant, taxable at his or her marginal rate.

New authorised payments

Under regulations that came into force on 1 June 2009, the list of authorised payments was extended.

Commutation payments

With effect from 1 December 2009, the following became authorised member payments. Certain conditions apply including that, except for the last described, the payment does not exceed £2,000 and extinguishes the member's entitlement under the scheme. The payment is taxed in the same way as a trivial commutation lump sum, or as a trivial commutation lump sum death benefit if not paid to the member.

- A *de minimis* payment from a public service or occupational pension scheme to a member between ages 60 and 75; in this case, all benefits including those in related schemes must be within the £2,000 limit

- a payment by a larger public service or occupational pension scheme (with at least 50 members) where the payment is from a defined benefit arrangement, to a member between ages 60 and 75

- a payment under the Financial Services Compensation Scheme

- a payment after a 'relevant accretion', for example where a scheme passes on an unexpected additional allocation received after a member has transferred out or purchased an annuity

- a payment to or in respect of a member who has reached age 75 and was untraceable, *and*

- a payment to a member that would be a trivial commutation lump sum but for the continued payment of a lifetime annuity under the same scheme. The total value of the member's benefits under all schemes must not exceed 1% of the lifetime allowance.

Pension errors and arrears

With retrospective effect from 6 April 2006, the following are authorised payments, taxable as pension accruing in the tax year of payment:

- pension paid in error or up to six months after the pensioner's death (including payments after the error is discovered, provided that all reasonable steps had been taken to prevent payment), *and*

- payment of arrears of pension after death under a defined benefit arrangement, where the member died before age 75 and, if he or she had died on or after 6 April 2006, the scheme could not reasonably have been expected to make the payment before his or her death.

Lump sum errors

With retrospective effect from 6 April 2006, the following are authorised payments and not subject to tax:

- commencement lump sum based on an incorrect pension figure, or on an incorrect annuity or scheme pension purchase price, *and*

- commencement lump sum paid under a defined benefit arrangement, no more than a year after the scheme administrator first knew (or could reasonably have been expected to know) of the member's death, if entitlement was not established and payment could not reasonably have been expected before the member died.

TAXATION CHARGES IN CONNECTION WITH REGISTERED PENSION SCHEMES

The tax treatment of the main types of 'authorised' benefit that may be paid under registered pension schemes is as described above.

The treatment of member contributions and the other tax charges that may arise in particular circumstances are discussed below. The Finance Acts allow these charges to be varied by order. This gives the government scope to increase them to reflect the new 50% top rate of income tax from April 2010.

Member contributions

Member contributions that attract tax relief are limited to 100% of relevant UK earnings (or £3,600 if higher) in any one tax year. Further contributions may be paid, but attract no tax relief.

As well as taxable benefits in kind, 'relevant UK earnings' includes taxable income arising from share schemes and taxable redundancy payments.

Unauthorised payments charge

If a benefit paid from a registered scheme is not authorised *(see above)* the member (or other recipient in the case of a death benefit) is liable for an *unauthorised payments charge*, at a rate of 40%. A 15% surcharge (resulting in an overall charge of 55%) applies if the unauthorised payment exceeds 25% of the value of the member's benefits. A payment subject to an unauthorised payments charge is, however, exempt from any further income tax charge. Unauthorised payments (subject to exceptions permitted by the transitional arrangements) include death benefits paid in lump sum form after age 75 and children's pensions that continue to be paid when the beneficiary no longer falls within the statutory definition of 'dependant'.

Scheme sanction charge
The scheme administrator is potentially subject to a scheme sanction charge at a rate of up to 40% in respect of most unauthorised payments.

Lifetime allowance charge

A *lifetime allowance charge* is payable if the value of the benefits being crystallised exceeds the balance of any lifetime allowance available. The rate is 25% if the benefits being crystallised are taken in pension form or 55% (equivalent to the 25% charge plus income tax at 40%) if taken as a lump sum.

If the charge is met by the administrator (and the member's benefits under the scheme are not reduced to reflect this), the tax payment is itself treated as part of the excess benefit value on which tax is calculated.

Annual allowance charge

Where the 'total pension input' exceeds the annual allowance, the member is normally liable for a charge of 40% on the excess. However, there is an exemption from the annual allowance charge in any year in which an individual's benefits under an arrangement are taken in full.

Special annual allowance charge

The special annual allowance charge was introduced under the anti-forestalling measures in the Finance Act 2009 *and is covered in Section 13*.

TRANSITIONAL ARRANGEMENTS

Primary protection

This applies where total relevant pension rights in approved pension schemes as at 5 April 2006 were valued in excess of £1.5m and were registered by 5 April 2009.

The value of the accrued rights at 5 April 2006 is determined in a similar manner to values at crystallisation. However, pensions already in payment must be valued as 25 times the annual rate of pension in payment, to allow for the lump sum that is presumed to have been taken. If the member is taking drawdown, the maximum possible pension under the relevant drawdown provisions must be used.

There is an overriding limit on the benefits to be registered for protection corresponding to the maximum permitted on leaving service at 5 April 2006 under whichever of the previous tax regimes was applicable prior to A Day.

Under primary protection, the individual is granted a personal lifetime allowance (PLA), based on the total value calculated as above, in place of the standard lifetime allowance (SLA). The PLA is increased annually in line with the SLA and is subject to adjustment if a pension debit arises as a result of a pension sharing order implemented on or after A Day.

Enhanced protection

An alternative form of protection is known as 'enhanced protection'. Where this applies, there are no lifetime or annual allowance charges in respect of the individual. This means that, broadly speaking, accrued defined benefit rights at A Day can continue to be linked to salary (although any pre-A Day restriction due to the Earnings Cap will still apply), and money purchase funds accrued at A Day can be increased by the full investment return achieved subsequently.

To retain enhanced protection, no further 'relevant benefit accrual' (or money purchase contributions) are permitted under any registered scheme after 5 April 2006. Registration by 5 April 2009 was required.

However, in a defined benefit arrangement, continuation of contributions or of pensionable service does not in itself count as relevant benefit accrual. Instead, for enhanced protection not to be lost, the resulting benefits must not breach the member's 'appropriate limit' at the first or a subsequent crystallisation date (or where there is a permitted transfer out of the scheme). This, in effect, means that, if the pre-A Day service benefits turn out to be lower than expected (e.g. because a reduction applies for early retirement), post-A Day service benefits may be able to be provided without enhanced protection being lost.

As under primary protection, there is an overriding limit on the benefits to be registered corresponding to the maximum permitted immediately before A Day. Where enhanced protection applied, any benefits at A Day in excess of this maximum had to be surrendered. In the case of surplus AVCs, a refund was permitted, subject to tax under the previous provisions.

Individuals could apply for both primary and enhanced protection – this means that if the conditions for enhanced protection are breached (and therefore this protection is lost) the individual can rely on primary protection.

Protection of lump sum rights that exceed £375,000

Existing lump sum rights of more than £375,000 at A Day are protected if the individual registered for primary or enhanced protection. If the lump sum rights were over both £375,000 and 25% of the value of the benefits but the individual did not register, lump sum protection is available as set out below.

Protection of lump sum rights that exceed 25% of the value placed on total benefit rights under a scheme

Existing rights to a lump sum of more than 25% can be protected if the individual has not registered for either primary protection or enhanced protection, or his lump sum rights at 5 April 2006 are valued at less than £375,000. This is subject to the condition that all benefits under the scheme (that had not already been taken on or before 5 April 2006) are taken on the same date.

Overrides during a transitional period

HMRC regulations override the rules of approved schemes that have become registered schemes. These deal with issues arising where existing scheme benefits are not 'authorised' under the new regime, or are restricted by reference to the Earnings Cap, and where scheme provisions enable benefits to be increased up to the pre-A Day 'Revenue maximum'.

These 'Revenue overrides' apply until 5 April 2011 (or for longer if HMRC extend this transitional period). However, a scheme's rules may be amended so that they cease to apply.

Additional protections

Further protections under the Act, or introduced in subsequent legislation, extend the scope for paying benefits arising under pre-A Day scheme rules without incurring unauthorised payments or lifetime allowance charges. These include:

- it is permissible to take benefits as authorised payments before *normal minimum pension age* (55 from April 2010) in certain cases where such a right existed before A Day

- individuals granted a pension credit before A Day can register for 'pension credit protection' which provides an enhanced lifetime allowance in a similar way to primary protection above

- pensions may in some circumstances be paid to children who are over age 23 and are still in full-time education or vocational training, are suffering from serious physical or mental deterioration, or were financially dependent on the member

- benefits accrued in 'lump sum only' schemes at 5 April 2006 can be taken as tax-free lump sums on and after 6 April 2006 provided no 'relevant benefit accrual' (as for enhanced protection above) has occurred

- certain benefits may continue to be paid, as authorised payments, in respect of pensioners who retired before 6 April 2006 but die after age 75, including a funeral expense death benefit of up to £2,500 and a tax-free lump sum of the remaining pension payments within a 5-year guarantee period; the limit on the amount of a dependant's scheme pension is also disapplied, *and*

- lump sum death benefits that exceed the protected amounts under primary or enhanced protection may be protected.

OVERSEAS ASPECTS

Scheme membership

There is no restriction on non-UK-resident individuals becoming members of registered pension schemes.

The annual and lifetime allowance charges apply, whether or not the individual is resident, ordinarily resident or domiciled in the UK. However, the lifetime allowance may be enhanced in respect of overseas periods of membership falling after A Day during which contributions to the scheme are not eligible for UK tax relief.

Transfers may be accepted by registered schemes from any overseas pension schemes. Transfers from *recognised overseas pension schemes (see Appendix 2, Glossary of Terms)* do not normally count when testing against the lifetime allowance. Transfers may be made from registered schemes to *qualifying recognised overseas pension schemes* and count as benefit crystallisation events for lifetime allowance purposes.

Migrant member relief

Migrant member relief allows UK tax relief on contributions paid to overseas schemes where a *relevant migrant member* comes to the UK, and was a member of a qualifying tax-relieved overseas pension scheme at any time in the previous 10 years. The manager of that scheme must provide HMRC with details of any relevant benefit crystallisation events that occur. Contributions and benefits accruing after A Day would normally count towards the annual and lifetime allowances, although from 2008 this excludes benefits and contributions in respect of earnings that are not subject to UK taxation.

OTHER MATTERS

Investment

There is one set of tax rules covering investments for all registered pension schemes. These allow schemes to invest in any type of investment where this is held for the purpose of the scheme, and generally exempt them from income and capital gains tax. However, other non-tax regulations do limit or prohibit certain types of investment.

These rules allow 'authorised employer loans' subject to conditions. However, occupational schemes are still prevented from making such loans by the 'employer-related investment' provisions under the Pensions Act 1995 *(see Section 10)*. Investment in residential property is also allowed in certain circumstances, but not in cases where the members can direct the investment policy.

Surplus

A repayment of surplus funds to the employer is only authorised in limited circumstances and is taxed at 35%. For instance, a refund cannot reduce the assets of the scheme below the level required to buy out all members' benefits with an insurance company.

PREVIOUS TAX REGIMES

Previous tax regimes limited benefits and/or contributions by reference to parameters such as earnings, company service and age in order for schemes to have a tax-advantaged status. Benefits outside these limits had to be provided in a separate, less tax-advantaged scheme (FURBS or UURBS).

The features of the main tax-approved regimes that existed prior to A Day are summarised below.

Occupational pension schemes

'Revenue limits' set out maximum pensions and lump sums in three categories, according to the date the member joined the scheme ('pre-1987', '1987' and '1989'). The three categories are similar, and generally allow a member to be provided with a pension of 1/60 × final remuneration, and by commutation of this pension, a lump sum of 3/80 × final remuneration, for each year of service with the employer (up to a maximum of 40), regardless of retained benefits from previous employers' schemes or personal pensions. However, higher benefits could often be provided, with the maximum pension of $\frac{2}{3}$ × final remuneration (including retained benefits) payable after 10 or 20 years.

Ill-health and death benefits were based on a similar calculation but allowing for potential service up to the scheme's normal retirement age. Spouses' pensions were generally allowed to be up to $\frac{2}{3}$ of the member's pension, and an additional lump sum of 4 × final remuneration plus a refund of the member's own contributions could be provided on death in service. There was a limit on member contributions (including AVCs) of 15% of remuneration in any tax year.

The 1989 limits introduced the 'Earnings Cap' – a limit on the amount of final remuneration that could be used in calculating benefits under that regime. The 1987 limits included a monetary cap on lump sum retirement benefits but not on pension benefits.

Personal pensions and retirement annuity contracts

Personal pension schemes (and some money purchase occupational schemes) were subject to a different regime. Instead of restricting benefits, this set a maximum amount of contributions that could be paid in any tax year, which from 1989/90 onwards ranged from 17.5% of 'net relevant earnings' for those aged 35 and under to 40% for those aged 61 and over. There were no limits on the amount of pension that could be provided at retirement, although the maximum lump sum was generally limited to 25% of the member's fund.

Retirement annuity contracts were the forerunner to personal pensions, and had a similar regime, although there were lower limits on contributions.

Executive pensions

Small Self-administered Schemes ('SSASs') were set up to provide benefits for controlling directors and other senior employees. These generally allowed greater investment freedom, e.g. loanbacks to the employer, but were subject to stricter requirements from the Revenue in order to maintain their tax-advantaged status.

SPECIAL ANNUAL ALLOWANCE CHARGE

In the April 2009 Budget, the Government announced that tax relief on pension contributions will be reduced to basic rate tax for individuals whose annual income exceeds £180,000 from April 2011. Higher-rate relief will be phased out for those whose earnings are between £150,000 and £180,000. The changes will apply to both member- and employer-financed benefits. There are limited details of the new rules to apply from 2011, and the Government plans extensive consultation to ensure that the value of benefit accrual under defined benefit schemes is measured fairly relative to money purchase contributions.

Pending the abolition of higher-rate tax relief on high earners' pension contributions from April 2011, Finance Act 2009 has introduced anti-forestalling provisions for the 2009/10 and 2010/11 tax years in the form of a 'special annual allowance charge'. This section summarises the new provisions, which were brought into immediate effect from the date of the Budget.

FINANCE ACT 2009 REGIME

Finance Act 2009 imposes additional tax charges on individuals with income in excess of £150,000 p.a. who, on or after 22 April 2009:

- change their normal pattern of regular pension contributions or the normal way in which pension benefits accrue, *and*

- whose total pension contributions and/or benefit accrual after the change exceed the 'special annual allowance' of £20,000 in the year.

The new charge will apply to an individual where:

- 'relevant income' for the relevant tax year or in either of the two tax years preceding the relevant year exceeds £150,000, *and*

- their total pension input for the year exceeds the special annual allowance.

A higher special annual allowance of up to £30,000, based on the average level of 'infrequent' contributions made in the past, is available to those who had not contributed regularly before 22 April 2009.

Relevant income

'Relevant income' for this purpose is determined as:

- total income chargeable to income tax from employment and self-employment/partnership earnings, state, occupational and personal pensions and savings, rental and trust income, before personal allowances and other reliefs and deductions, *plus*

- pension contributions paid under the net pay arrangement (pension contributions paid under a relief-at-source arrangement will be included in the first bullet), *plus*

- any amount of employment income foregone by salary sacrifice in return for pension contributions or additional pension benefits if the agreement was put in place on or after 22 April 2009, *less*

- any normal deductions for reliefs (such as trading losses), *less*

- deductions for pension contributions but limited to a maximum of £20,000, *less*

- any Gift Aid deductions.

Amount of the special annual allowance

The special annual allowance is £20,000 for both 2009/10 and 2010/11 and the pension input periods are the tax years 2009/10 and 2010/11.

The special annual allowance is increased where:

- money purchase contributions have been paid on an infrequent basis (less than quarterly) in the tax years 2006/07 to 2008/09, *and*

- the annual average of these infrequent contributions, over these three tax years, exceeds £20,000.

The enhanced special annual allowance will then be the average of these infrequent contributions, but subject to a maximum of £30,000. This provision may be of assistance to individuals, such as self-employed high-earners, who do not make regular contributions but who have made significant irregular contributions in the past. However, where protected regular contributions or defined benefit accrual already exceeds £30,000 in value, the tax charge payable will be unchanged.

To calculate the amount subject to the special annual allowance charge, the special annual allowance is reduced by:

- pension input amounts that are 'pre-22 April 2009 pension input amounts', *and*

- pension input amounts that are 'protected pension input amounts'.

Amount of the special annual allowance charge

As for the existing annual allowance charge under Finance Act 2004, the pension input amount for the special annual allowance charge is the sum of defined benefit pension accrual multiplied by 10 and any money purchase contributions.

The special annual allowance charge is at a rate of 20% for 2009/10. It may increase to 30% for 2010/11 when the top-rate tax band of 50% is introduced. The charge is applied to any pension input in excess of the special annual allowance which is not protected.

It will be collected through individuals' self-assessment tax returns. If pension saving would be subject to both the normal annual allowance charge and the special annual allowance charge, there will be relief from double taxation.

PROTECTED AMOUNTS

Pre-22 April 2009 pension input amounts

Where an individual made irregular money purchase contributions between 6 April 2009 and 21 April 2009 inclusive (before the Budget announcement), or had additional irregular defined benefit accrual in respect of that period, these amounts are pre-22 April 2009 pension input amounts, and are protected.

Protected pension input amounts

Protected pension input amounts are the individual's normal regular ongoing defined benefit pension accrual and money purchase contributions. Money purchase contributions paid regularly, at least quarterly, and defined benefit accrual at rates unchanged from those applying at 21 April 2009 will be protected pension input amounts. Increases in money purchase contributions or defined benefit accrual arising from salary increases or promotions will also be protected pension input amounts.

Money purchase contributions for which there is no record of quarterly, or more frequent, payment such as annual contributions of varying amounts made by the self-employed and others, are not classed as protected pension input amounts. The alternative calculation of the enhanced special annual allowance may be of some assistance in such cases, *as discussed above*.

The following scenarios will also result in protected pension input amounts.

New pension arrangements

On a change of employment, any pension input amount to an occupational pension scheme or a group personal pension scheme will normally be protected if the pension contributions/accrual of benefits are at the same rate as other members of the scheme. However, payments into a new individual personal pension will not be protected. The specific conditions required for protection of a new pension arrangement set up on or after 22 April 2009 or an old scheme being reactivated are:

- the arrangement is under an occupational pension scheme, a public service pension scheme or a group personal pension scheme
- the arrangement relates to an employment of the individual, unless the scheme is a public service pension scheme
- twenty or more other members, who are employees of an employer who is an employer in relation to the arrangement (unless it is a public service scheme), are accruing benefits under the same arrangement on the same basis
- there is no material change to the way benefits are calculated from the date the arrangement is made and the end of the relevant tax year or such earlier date as the member ceases to accrue benefits under the arrangement, *and*

- the contributions are not additional voluntary contributions, nor for the purchase of 'added years'.

There is also an exception for individuals who applied in writing to join an individual money purchase arrangement before 22 April 2009 and where the application was received by the scheme administrator before 12 noon on 22 April 2009.

Changes to existing pension arrangements

Some material changes to arrangements are protected from the special annual allowance charge. The conditions depend on the type of arrangement, as set out in the following table.

Defined benefit and cash balance arrangements	Defined contribution arrangements
<ul><li>The scheme is:<ul><li>an occupational pension scheme, *or*</li><li>a public service pension scheme</li></ul></li><li>the individual was accruing benefits under the arrangement prior to 22 April 2009, *and*</li><li>there are at least 50 active members whose benefits are similarly affected.</li></ul>	<ul><li>The scheme is:<ul><li>an occupational pension scheme</li><li>a public service pension scheme, *or*</li><li>a group personal pension scheme</li></ul></li><li>the individual was an active member of the arrangement prior to 22 April 2009</li><li>contributions have been paid regularly on a quarterly or more frequent basis under terms in place before 22 April 2009, *and*</li><li>the increased rate of contribution was expressly agreed before 22 April 2009.</li></ul>

EXEMPTIONS

Drawing benefits

Unlike the normal annual allowance charge, there is no blanket exemption from the special annual allowance charge in the year in which individuals draw all their benefits or die. An individual will only be exempt from the special annual allowance when they draw all their benefits or die if:

- the benefit is under a defined benefit arrangement, and there are at least 20 active scheme members or pensioners at the date the benefit is taken, and the benefits are not being taken for the purpose of avoiding the charge, *or*

- the member meets the 'ill-heath condition' as defined in Finance Act 2004 and the arrangement is under an occupational pension scheme, a public service pension scheme or a group personal pension scheme.

REFUNDS OF CONTRIBUTIONS

If an individual has inadvertently made a payment that would be taxed under the special annual allowance charge, a refund of the individual's contribution may be paid, but it must be paid in the following tax year. Employer contributions will not be refundable other than under existing pre-22 April 2009 legislative provisions.

ANTI-AVOIDANCE

The new requirements include a number of provisions to restrict exemptions where a main purpose of an arrangement is to avoid the special annual allowance charge. For instance, if an increase in accrual is for a pension that starts artificially low and then subsequently increases in payment at above normal rates, this will be caught and an upward adjustment made to the pension input amount. There is also a new general anti-avoidance rule that specifically targets 'schemes' set up for the purpose of reducing the amount of special annual allowance charge payable.

ENHANCED PROTECTION

Individuals with enhanced protection will not be exempt from the special annual allowance charge, although they will remain exempt from the normal annual allowance charge. If enhanced protection is lost on the payment of a contribution that is subsequently refunded, enhanced protection is not restored.

OVERSEAS PENSION SCHEMES

The legislation for the special annual allowance charge includes provisions extending the special annual allowance charge to members of currently-relieved non-UK schemes, with certain modifications. As for the normal annual allowance as applied to overseas members *(see Section 12)*, contributions which would otherwise count towards the special annual allowance are excluded if they are in respect of earnings that are not subject to UK taxation.

EMPLOYER-FINANCED RETIREMENT BENEFIT SCHEMES

The tax advantages received by a registered pension scheme are limited by the Lifetime Allowance, the Annual Allowance and, from 22 April 2009, the Special Annual Allowance, *as discussed in Sections 12 and 13*. Although it is permissible to provide benefits in excess of these Allowances under a registered scheme, the tax penalties that apply may make it unattractive to do so, particularly since the introduction of the Special Annual Allowance Charge. Retirement and death benefits can instead be provided outside a registered pension scheme, in which case neither the tax advantages, nor the tax penalties referred to above, apply. Such arrangements are referred to as employer-financed retirement benefit schemes (EFRBS).

Under the Finance Act 2004, the previous types of unapproved pension arrangement, both funded (FURBS) and unfunded (UURBS), were replaced by EFRBS. The (limited) tax advantages previously given to unapproved arrangements ceased except where protected under transitional provisions.

Benefits accrued under an EFRBS will not be counted for the Annual Allowance or the Special Annual Allowance, nor will they be tested against the member's Lifetime Allowance when paid.

The most important tax consequences of providing benefits through an EFRBS from 6 April 2006 are as follows:

(a) the arrangement's investment income and capital gains are subject to tax

(b) lump sum and pension benefits are subject to income tax when received by the employee, *and*

(c) employers can deduct the costs of providing the benefits from taxable profits, but only when the benefits are paid from the scheme and chargeable to tax on the employee. (So corporation tax relief is not available until then.)

UNFUNDED EFRBS

An unfunded EFRBS may be distinguished from a funded EFRBS in that no contributions are paid in advance to meet the cost of the benefits.

Security

The main drawback of an unfunded arrangement is its inherent lack of security. A number of ways of overcoming this drawback are considered below:

Charges over assets
The establishment of a charge over assets to provide the security for an unfunded retirement benefit promise might be considered.

Insolvency insurance
It may be possible to arrange insurance cover to pay the benefits if an employer becomes insolvent and unable to do so. Premiums paid to insure against the

risk of default will be regarded as an employee benefit in kind and taxed accordingly.

Bank guarantees
Bank guarantees could be a source of external financial back-up for unfunded pensions, but are likely to be difficult to arrange and are available only for short-term cover.

ACCOUNTING

EFRBS, whether funded or unfunded, fall within the scope of FRS 17 and IAS 19 *(see Section 27)*.

DWP LEGISLATION

The Pension Schemes Act 1993, the Pensions Act 1995 and the Pensions Act 2004 are generally applicable to non-registered arrangements, although there are a large number of provisions from which such arrangements are exempt. For example, the protections against forfeiture of benefits do apply, but the scheme funding provisions do not and the disclosure requirements are limited.

Preservation and EFRBS

Preservation and transfer value rights for early leavers apply to funded EFRBS as to registered schemes. However, preservation does not apply to unfunded EFRBS unless it is explicitly written into the scheme documentation. If preservation does apply, then revaluation will also apply.

TAX TREATMENT OF EFRBS

A brief summary comparing the tax treatment of registered pension schemes and EFRBS is set out in the following table.

	Registered Pension Scheme	EFRBS[1]
Employer's contributions/allocations to reserves:		
– corporation tax relief for employer	yes	no[2]
– employer's NICs payable	no	no
– income tax charge on employee	no[3]	no
– employee's NICs payable	no	no
Member's contributions:		
– income tax relief for employee	yes[3]	no
Investment returns/growth in reserves:	no income tax or capital gains tax payable	income and capital gains taxable at rates applicable to trusts
Tax paid by beneficiary[4] on:		
– pension	income tax payable[5] (but no NICs)	income tax payable[5,8] (but no NICs[6])
– lump sum	tax-free (lump sum generally limited to 25%)	income tax payable[7,8] (but no NICs[6])

Notes:

1 The EFRBS is assumed to be established as an 'accumulation trust' with UK-resident trustees.

2 Corporation tax relief may however be claimed when benefits are paid and chargeable to tax on the employee. (However, if the EFRBS is set up so that the provision of the benefits results in a reduction in the benefits payable to or in respect of the employee under a registered pension scheme, or its payment is triggered by a reduction in the benefits payable under a registered pension scheme, then corporation tax relief for the employer will generally not be available, and may be witheld in respect of contributions to the registered scheme.)

3 However, the Special Annual Allowance Charge can be levied against certain employee and employer contributions, or in respect of the value of defined benefits accrued, in certain circumstances – see Section 13.

4 The Finance Act 2007 amended ITEPA 2003 to include a power to make retrospective regulations extending the definition of benefits from an EFRBS that are excluded from taxation.

5 All pensions, regardless of the type of arrangement, are taxed at source via the PAYE system.

6 Provided that the payments from the EFRBS meet specific conditions (including that the form of benefits would have been authorised if the scheme had been registered, and that employment has ceased and the member is not re-employed by the company), then no NICs are payable.

7 If the employee has paid contributions towards the provision of the lump sum, the amount of the lump sum that is taxable is reduced by the amount of those contributions. In addition, transitional rules provide for part of the lump sum to be tax-free if contributions, on which the employee was taxed, were paid to a FURBS before 6 April 2006; if no contributions have been made since then, the whole of the lump sum will be tax-free.

8 There is no exemption from inheritance tax for benefits payable from an EFRBS, except to the extent that they arose from contributions made to a FURBS before 6 April 2006.

The end to pensions information overload

Pensions Insight is the magazine that has taken the pensions industry by storm. First published in April 2009 it is relied upon by over 10,000 pensions professional every month.

Best described as "The Week" meets "The Economist" for the pensions industry, it will reduce the time spent researching and reading the information you need for your job. We scour hundreds of financial and business media to bring you the news and issues that really matter.

LEAVING SERVICE BENEFITS

PRESERVATION

The preservation legislation provides members of an occupational pension scheme with a legal right to short service benefit (SSB) if they leave pensionable service before normal pension age (NPA). The essential principle is that an early leaver's benefits should be calculated on a consistent basis with those of a member who remains in service up to NPA.

Entitlement to SSB is dependent upon the member either having at least two years' 'qualifying service' or having transferred benefits from a personal pension into the scheme. 'Qualifying service' is the sum of all actual pensionable service under the scheme plus pensionable service in any scheme from which a transfer payment has been received. Members who do not satisfy the preservation conditions may nevertheless be granted deferred benefits if scheme rules so provide. Alternatively, the scheme may provide for them to receive a refund of their own contributions, if any, less tax and their share of any premium required to reinstate contracted-out service back into the State scheme. However, no State scheme premium can be paid in respect of protected rights, which must be preserved within the scheme (this requirement will be removed when the restrictions that apply to protected rights are abolished, which is expected from 2012). In money purchase schemes, early leavers must normally be entitled to whatever benefit derives from contributions paid by or in respect of them.

Payment of short service benefits

Preserved benefits must normally be payable not later than the member's NPA. The preservation legislation defines NPA as the earliest age at which a member is entitled to receive benefits on retirement from the relevant employment, disregarding any special provisions for early retirement. Therefore, even if scheme rules define retirement age as 65, NPA could be earlier if members have an unqualified right to retire on an unreduced pension from an earlier age. However, until 5 April 2005, benefits need not have been paid before age 60, if scheme rules contain a specific provision to this effect. From 6 April 2005 this legislative provision was amended so that, if scheme rules so provide, benefits need not be paid before age 65.

The question of whether a scheme could have more than one NPA (for example when a member is entitled to part of his benefits from 60 and part from 65 following changes to scheme rules to comply with the *Barber* judgment) is a moot point following the 2007 Court of Appeal ruling in the case of *Cripps v TSL (see Section 32)*.

Leavers with 3 months' pensionable service

From 6 April 2006, the Pensions Act 2004 introduced a requirement for pension scheme leavers to be given the option of a transfer value (the 'cash transfer sum') in respect of accrued benefits, having completed between 3 and 24 months' pensionable service.

Trustees must notify members of this option, as an alternative to a refund of contributions, if applicable, within a 'reasonable period' of leaving pensionable service. If the member does not reply, a refund of contributions may be paid by default (within a further 'reasonable period'). Where it is paid, the cash transfer sum must be calculated in the same way as a cash equivalent transfer value under the scheme. The Pensions Regulator has issued a Code of Practice on what constitute 'reasonable periods' for this purpose.

REVALUATION

The position of early leavers from final salary occupational pension schemes improved significantly from 1986. Before then, with the exception of Guaranteed Minimum Pensions (GMPs), there was no legal requirement for preserved benefits to be increased during the period of deferment until the pension came into payment. Consequently, the purchasing power of the eventual pension could be seriously eroded by inflation.

The Social Security Act 1985 introduced the requirement to increase (or 'revalue') in deferment the part of a preserved pension in excess of GMP which relates to service completed on or after 1 January 1985, for a member who left pensionable service on or after 1 January 1986. The revaluation requirement was further extended to cover the whole of the member's pension in excess of GMP for members leaving pensionable service on or after 1 January 1991. The revaluation percentage was the *lesser* of the increase in the Retail Prices Index (RPI) and 5% per annum compound over the whole period of deferment.

The Pensions Act 2008 reduced the revaluation cap for pensionable service accrued after 5 April 2009 from 5% per annum to 2.5% per annum.

Deferred Pension Revaluation Percentages

Complete years since leaving	Calendar Year of Normal Pension Age		
	2009 (%)	2008 (%)	2007 (%)
1	5.0	3.9	3.6
2	9.1	7.6	6.4
3	13.0	10.5	9.7
4	16.1	14.0	12.8
5	19.7	17.2	14.7
6	23.0	19.2	16.6
7	25.1	21.2	20.5
8	27.2	25.2	21.8
9	31.4	26.6	25.7
10	32.9	30.6	30.2
11	37.1	35.3	33.0
12	42.1	38.2	38.2
13	45.1	43.5	41.2
14	50.7	46.7	43.7
15	54.0	49.3	48.9
16	56.8	54.7	55.0
17	62.4	61.1	71.9
18	69.1	78.6	85.0
19	87.5	92.2	95.5
20	101.8	103.1	103.7
21	113.3	111.7	110.0
22	122.3	118.2	
23	129.1		

GMPs

In addition to the revaluation requirements on the excess of the member's pension over any GMP, members of contracted-out schemes must also have their GMP revalued between leaving service and age 65 for men and age 60 for women, either:

(1)   in line with Average Earnings (Section 148 orders, *see page 49*); *or*

(2)   by fixed rate revaluation at the following rate per annum:

– leavers after 5 April 2007	4%
– leavers after 5 April 2002, but before 6 April 2007	4¹/₂%
– leavers after 5 April 1997, but before 6 April 2002	6¹/₄%
– leavers after 5 April 1993, but before 6 April 1997	7%
– leavers after 5 April 1988, but before 6 April 1993	7¹/₂%
– leavers before 6 April 1988	8¹/₂%

For leavers before 6 April 1997, schemes could choose to apply limited revaluation, which provided the lesser of Section 148 orders and 5% p.a. revaluation. A Limited Revaluation Premium was payable to the State. This option was withdrawn from 6 April 1997.

For members who left pensionable service after 31 December 1984, the revaluations on the GMP cannot be 'franked' against the excess pension over the GMP, or against revaluations on the excess.

GMP accrual ceased from April 1997, but GMPs earned prior to this date continue to be revalued as above on leaving service.

TRANSFER VALUES

Members of registered occupational pension schemes whose pensionable service has ended have the right to the cash equivalent of all or, in particular circumstances, part of their benefits to be paid as a transfer value to another registered scheme *(see Section 16 for further details on transfer values, including: transfers of contracted-out benefits; Finance Act 2004 restrictions; and overseas transfers)*.

TRANSFER VALUES

In 1986, pension scheme leavers acquired the statutory right to a cash equivalent as an alternative to deferred benefits under a scheme – *see Section 15*. For over 20 years, the actuary was responsible for approving the basis for the calculation of cash equivalent transfer values. However, under regulations which came into force on 1 October 2008, trustees are now responsible for setting assumptions. Trustees may also need to consider whether it is appropriate to offer members more than the minimum required by legislation – this may appeal to members and, if the transfer value is less than the prudent reserve required for scheme funding, the employer.

Right to a cash equivalent

Generally, members of occupational pension schemes whose pensionable service ended on or after 1 January 1986 have the right to the cash equivalent of all or, in particular circumstances, part of their benefits to be paid as a transfer value to another approved arrangement or, since 6 April 2006, registered scheme. From 6 April 1997, this right was extended to members whose pensionable service ended before 1 January 1986. This right is normally subject to there being a period of at least one year between the termination of the member's pensionable service and NPA, although, where NPA is earlier than 60, the right arises on termination of service at any time before NPA.

Members who opt out of pension schemes without leaving their jobs also have the right to transfer at least part of their benefits. This right only entitles the member to a 'partial' cash equivalent, related to service completed on or after 6 April 1988 (when members generally first had the right to opt out).

For transfer values from defined benefit schemes, there is a three-month window from the date of calculation in which the cash equivalent is guaranteed and may be taken without being subject to recalculation. There are other time limits and disclosure requirements *(see Section 17)* imposed on the process of making a transfer.

Calculation of transfer values

Prior to 1 October 2008, the approval of the basis for the calculation of transfer values was the responsibility of the actuary. The responsibility passed from the actuary to the trustees under regulations which came into force from this date.

However, the fundamental principle has not changed – the minimum cash equivalent transfer value remains broadly equal to the expected cost of providing the benefit within the scheme. Trustees are required to set financial and demographic assumptions on a 'best estimate' basis, having regard to the scheme's investment strategy and having obtained advice from the actuary. (This contrasts with the scheme funding requirement to use 'prudent' assumptions.) The Regulator has issued guidance that outlines the advice on assumptions that the trustees must seek from their actuary. Nevertheless, the trustees are responsible for determining, amongst other things, the interest rate used for discounting future benefit payments and the expected longevity of members.

Trustees also need to determine an appropriate allowance for member options and discretionary benefits. The Regulator's guidance makes it clear that only those options which increase the value of a member's benefits should be taken into account, although allowance can be made for the proportion of members likely to exercise such options. In deciding whether to make allowance for discretionary benefits, the guidance suggests that trustees should usually consult any person whose consent is needed, and consider past history and any allowance in scheme funding, amongst other things.

Paying more or less

For underfunded schemes, which would not have enough money to pay full transfer values for all members, the legislation permits the cash equivalent to be reduced in line with the extent of underfunding shown in an 'Insufficiency Report' commissioned from the actuary. The Regulator's guidance suggests that trustees should not normally make such a reduction where an employer's covenant is judged to be strong and any funding shortfall is being remedied over a reasonably short period.

The legislation also allows the trustees to pay transfer values at a level higher than best estimate. This may be appropriate if the scheme rules require it or where simpler calculations would make it cost-effective. Alternatively, the trustees may simply decide that it is appropriate to pay higher transfer values than the minimum required (perhaps following a request by, or in consultation with, the employer). Higher transfer values might encourage take-up, which, if transfer values remained below the prudent reserves required for funding the members' liabilities, could reduce a scheme's deficit (or increase its surplus).

Indeed, a transfer 'inducement' exercise may be proposed, in which members are actively offered enhancements to transfer values, direct cash payments or both as incentives to transfer. The Regulator has issued guidance on such exercises, which states that trustees should apply a high level of scrutiny, emphasises the importance of communication with and advice to members, and suggests that it may be appropriate for trustees to request an associated payment into the scheme from the employer.

Transfers of contracted-out benefit

Transfers of contracted-out benefits can be made freely between most arrangements contracted out on either the salary-related or the protected rights basis. In these cases, the nature of the contracted-out benefit may alter from GMP or 'post-97 Contracted-out Salary Related (COSR) rights' (that is, all non-AVC pension rights in the scheme accrued after 5 April 1997) to protected rights or vice versa, depending on the circumstances of the transfer.

A distinction is drawn between rights earned before 6 April 1997 and those earned on or after that date. Protected rights are also separately recorded as pre-97 and post-97 protected rights. The following system of transferability operates from April 1997:

- transfers where there are no pre-97 GMP or post-97 COSR rights, and no pre-97 or post-97 protected rights, can occur freely between salary-related or money purchase schemes, personal pensions and buy-out policies

- GMPs remain either as GMPs or become pre-97 protected rights (the basis of conversion being determined by the contracted-out status of the receiving scheme)

- pre-97 protected rights either remain as pre-97 protected rights or are replaced by GMPs based on the member's National Insurance contributions history (as determined by HMRC)

- post-97 COSR rights either remain as post-97 COSR rights or become wholly post-97 protected rights, *and*

- post-97 protected rights either remain as post-97 protected rights or become post-97 COSR rights.

Disclosure and payment

Disclosure requirements, including those in respect of transfer values, are described in *Section 17*.

A guaranteed cash equivalent may be accepted within the three-month 'guarantee period' without being subject to recalculation. Generally, the trustees are required to pay the transfer value within six months of the date of calculation where the cash equivalent is guaranteed and within six months of the original request where it is not (for example, where the benefits are money purchase in nature).

From 1 October 2008, trustees have also been required to inform members of salary-related schemes:

- that the Financial Services Authority, the Pensions Advisory Service and the Pensions Regulator provide information that may assist in their decision on whether to transfer

- of the existence of the PPF and that the scheme is eligible for it (eligible schemes only), *and*

- that it is recommended that they should take financial advice before making a decision.

Restrictions imposed by HMRC

Since 6 April 2006, the majority of restrictions on pension transfers and the benefits that could be provided in respect of them under previous tax regimes have been removed. In general, under the Finance Act 2004 tax regime, transfers of 'uncrystallised' pension rights can be made between registered pension schemes (or to deferred annuity contracts or buy-out policies) without restriction, provided that scheme rules permit. Transfers can also be made to 'qualifying recognised overseas pension schemes' *(see below)*.

The previous restrictions on partial transfers were removed by the Finance Act 2004. However, members only have a *statutory* right to a 'partial cash equivalent' in limited circumstances (e.g. on opting out *(see above)* or where contracting-out restrictions apply). Partial transfers will therefore generally be possible only where scheme rules permit.

Pensions already in payment can also be transferred, provided that scheme rules allow and certain conditions are met (e.g. the amount of the pension is not reduced except to the extent needed to meet the administrative cost of the transfer and any guarantee is no longer than that remaining before the transfer).

However, certain forms of transitional protection (see Section 12) may be lost on transfer, unless prescribed conditions are satisfied. In particular, enhanced protection (for high earners) will be lost unless the transfer is a 'permitted transfer' (requiring, inter alia, that the transfer is to a money purchase, but not cash balance, arrangement, or a bulk transfer that meets specified criteria).

Overseas transfers

Transfers to an overseas arrangement may only be made if that arrangement falls within the definition of a qualifying recognised overseas pension scheme (see Appendix 2, Glossary of Terms). If such a transfer takes place, the scheme administrator of the recognised pension scheme must ensure that an event report detailing the transfer is submitted to HMRC. Information must also be provided to HMRC by the manager of the overseas scheme.

DISCLOSURE OF
PENSION SCHEME INFORMATION

Pensions legislation including the Pension Schemes Act 1993 and the Pensions Act 1995 requires the trustees of occupational pension schemes to disclose actuarial and accounting information, as well as individual benefit details for each member. These rules override any provisions in schemes' trust documents if the two are in conflict.

Details to be disclosed differ depending on whether the benefits are of a defined benefit or defined contribution nature. One difference is that disclosures relating to defined contributions must, for members who have not yet retired, be provided automatically at least once a year, whereas disclosures relating to defined benefits need only be provided on request. Disclosure requirements also may differ for schemes with fewer than 100 members.

Information must also be disclosed to pension credit members and further disclosure requirements also arise at the time when pension sharing arrangements are being made. These are too extensive to describe in detail here, but an outline is included in *Section 19*.

The Government is considering restructuring and simplifying the existing disclosure legislation. A high-level overarching principle is proposed together with a new Code of Practice setting out reasonable periods which will replace specified time periods for providing information. The intention is to introduce new legislation from 6 April 2010.

The following summary sets out the main disclosure requirements for occupational schemes. Disclosure requirements for personal pension and stakeholder schemes are discussed in *Section 8*.

SUMMARY OF DISCLOSURE REQUIREMENTS

INFORMATION	TO BE DISCLOSED TO	IN WHAT CIRCUMSTANCES	TIME LIMITS/OTHER DETAILS
Trust Deed and Rules or other documents constituting the scheme, including names and addresses of participating employers.	**Members***, **Prospective Members,** their **Spouses** and **Civil Partners.** **Beneficiaries**. Recognised independent **Trade Unions**.	**For inspection on request**, free of charge. **A copy to keep on request**; any charge must be limited to the cost incurred in copying, posting and packaging.	Within two months of the request being made.

Note: * Throughout this summary 'members' includes pension credit members, as well as pensioners and deferred pensioners.

Information	To be Disclosed to	In What Circumstances	Time Limits/Other Details
Scheme Details including an address for enquiries.	Members*, Prospective Members, their Spouses and Civil Partners. Beneficiaries. Recognised independent Trade Unions.	On request, no more than once a year. In addition, new members must receive the information automatically within two months of joining the scheme.	Within two months of the request being made. Any material change in the scheme details, and any change in the address for enquiries, must be notified to all members and beneficiaries, within three months.
Estimate of Cash Equivalent	Active members of any scheme, and deferred members of schemes providing money purchase benefits.	On request, no more than once a year.	Within three months of the request.
Statement of Entitlement to Guaranteed Cash Equivalent	Deferred and pension credit members of schemes providing final salary benefits.	On request, no more than once a year.	To be calculated within three months of the request (although this is extended to six months in very limited circumstances) and passed to the member within ten working days of calculation (see Section 16).
Statement of Prospective Transfer Credits	Members and Prospective Members.	On request, no more than once a year.	Within two months of the request.
Benefit Statements	Members. Beneficiaries.	Automatically when benefit is due, or changes other than as described in a previous statement. To non-pensioner members of final salary schemes, on request, no more than once a year, within two months of request. To non-pensioner members of schemes with a money purchase element, automatically within 12 months of the end of each scheme year in respect of money purchase benefits including Statutory Money Purchase Illustrations (SMPIs) (see page 118).	Where benefits become due or are changed other than as described in a previous statement within one month, or two months in cases of early retirement. Leavers must be told their rights and options within two months of the trustees being notified that the member has left service. Options under money purchase benefits are to be notified to members at least six months before normal pension age (normal benefit age for pension credit members) or earlier agreed date of retirement. Beneficiaries over age 18 must be notified of rights and options within two months of trustees being notified of death.

DISCLOSURE OF INFORMATION

Information	To be Disclosed to	In What Circumstances	Time Limits/Other Details
Benefit Statements (continued)			Personal representatives of members who have died may request information, which must be provided within two months.
Summary Funding Statement	Members. Beneficiaries.	**Automatically**, annually, except where a member is entitled to only money purchase benefits. Must be issued within a **reasonable period** (generally three months) after the deadline for completion of actuarial valuation or actuarial report.	To include information on the funding and solvency positions of the scheme.
Trustees' Annual Report including: · audited accounts · latest certification or recertification of schedule of contributions · investment report.	Members, Prospective **Members,** their **Spouses** and **Civil Partners.** Beneficiaries. Recognised independent **Trade Unions.**	Reports covering the previous five years must be available: · **for inspection,** free of charge · a copy of the most recent report on request, **to keep,** free of charge · copies of earlier reports on request, **to keep,** for which any charge must be limited to the cost of copying, posting and packaging.	Within two months of the request being made. The report must be available within seven months of the end of the scheme year. The report should contain a statement that other information is available and from where it may be obtained.
Actuarial Valuation or **Report, Schedule of Contributions** or **Payment Schedule, Recovery Plan**†, **Statements of Funding Principles**† and of **Investment Principles,** and outline **Winding-Up Procedure** (if applicable)	Members, Prospective **Members,** their **Spouses** and **Civil Partners.** Beneficiaries. Recognised independent **Trade Unions.**	**For inspection,** free of charge. **A copy to keep, on request,** for which any charge must be limited to the cost of copying, posting and packaging.	Within two months of the request being made.

Note: † *See Section 20.*

SCHEME DETAILS

Scheme details must include:

- eligibility and conditions for membership
- the period of notice which a member must give to leave pensionable service
- whether re-entry to pensionable service is permitted and, if so, upon what conditions
- how employers' and members' normal contributions are calculated
- any arrangements made for members to pay Additional Voluntary Contributions (AVCs)
- taxation status
- contracted-out status, and whether the scheme is a contracted-out salary related scheme (COSRS), a contracted-out money purchase scheme (COMPS), or a contracted-out mixed benefit scheme (COMBS)
- for a COMBS, any potential changes in a member's accrual of benefits as a result of the scheme being a COMBS
- for a COMPS or COMBS that is not insured, a statement describing how the value of protected rights is increased, if this is not in line with actual investment returns, and the reason why this method is used
- normal pension age
- the benefits payable, and how they are calculated, including the definition of pensionable earnings and the accrual rate
- the conditions on which benefits, including survivors' benefits, and any pension increases in excess of statutory requirements, are payable
- whether the trustees accept transfers in to the scheme
- a summary of the method of calculating transfer values
- where cash equivalents do not take into account discretionary additional benefits, a statement to this effect
- the arrangements for providing refunds, preserved benefits, and estimated or guaranteed cash equivalents for early leavers
- a statement that the scheme annual report is available on request, except for public service pension schemes
- the procedure for internal resolution of disputes and the address and job title of the contact
- the functions and addresses of the Pensions Ombudsman, The Pensions Advisory Service and the Pensions Regulator, *and*
- a statement that further information is available and an address for enquiries.

BENEFIT STATEMENTS

Active and deferred members of salary-related schemes

On request, an active member must be given:

- a statement of accrued benefits, or benefits allowing for service up to normal pension age, based on current salary, *and*
- a statement of the benefits payable if the member were to die in service within one month of the date of receipt of the information.

The trustees need not comply with a request made within a year of providing the information, so if they provide benefit statements automatically once a year there is no need to respond to one-off requests.

Leaving service rights and options must be given automatically within two months of the trustees being notified that pensionable service has ceased.

On subsequent request, a deferred member must be given a statement of the date pensionable service ceased and the amount of his/her own benefits, and any survivors' benefits, payable from normal pension age or on death.

For both active and deferred members the information must include:

- the date on which pensionable service commenced and ceased
- the accrual rate or formula for calculating the member's own benefits and any survivors' benefits
- the amount of the member's pensionable earnings (at the date pensionable service ceased for a deferred member and at the current date for an active member), *and*
- details of how any deduction from benefits (e.g. offset for State pension or any pension debit) is calculated.

Pension credit members of salary-related schemes

On request, the member must be given a statement of the amount of his/her own benefits, and any survivors' benefits, payable from normal benefit age or on death. The information must include:

- the method or formula for calculating the member's own benefits and any survivors' benefits, *and*
- details of how any deduction from benefits is calculated.

All members of money purchase schemes (or schemes with a money purchase element)

Statements must be given automatically within 12 months of the end of each scheme year and must show, in relation to money purchase benefits:

- contributions credited to the member (before deductions) during the immediately preceding scheme year
- if the scheme was contracted out during the year, the contributions in respect of the member attributable to:

    (i)   minimum payments made by the employer

    (ii)   age-related payments made to the trustees by the DWP, *and*

    (iii) the date of birth used to determine any age-related payments and a contact name and address if this is incorrect.

- value of protected rights (if any) at a specified date
- value of other accrued rights (if any) at a specified date
- cash equivalents of protected rights and other accrued rights at the specified dates, if they differ from the values of these rights, *and*
- statutory money purchase illustrations (SMPIs) of projected benefits are required in addition to the above information (*see below*).

In addition, a member with money purchase benefits must be provided with an explanation of the different annuities available, his/her right to an open market option and a statement that the member should consider taking advice. This information must be provided no less than six months before the member's normal retirement date, or within seven days if a retirement date is agreed which is less than six months in the future.

TRUSTEES' ANNUAL REPORT

The report must include:

- audited accounts, including auditor's statement
- latest actuarial certificate certifying the adequacy of the schedule of contributions
- names of trustees or directors of the trust company, and the rules for changing trustees; names of the professional advisers, custodians and banks acting for the trustees, indicating any changes during the year
- a copy of the statement which any auditor or actuary of the scheme has made on resignation or removal as auditor or actuary during the year
- numbers of active, deferred and pensioner members and beneficiaries at a date during the year
- except for money purchase schemes, percentage increases made during the year to pensions and deferred pensions, in excess of those required by law – the extent to which increases were discretionary is to be stated
- except for money purchase schemes which are wholly insured, if transfer values paid during the year were not calculated in accordance with the law, an explanation as to why they have differed; if any were less than the full value of the member's preserved or pension credit benefits, an explanation as to why and when full values are likely to be available; and a statement as to whether discretionary benefits are included in the calculation and, if so, how they are assessed
- name of investment manager, and the extent to which the trustees have delegated their responsibility to him

- whether the trustees have produced a statement of investment principles and, if so, that a copy is available on request, and information on investments made other than in accordance with the statement

- except for wholly insured schemes, a statement of the trustees' policy on the custody of scheme assets

- investment report including review of performance, over the year and over a period of between three and five years, and of the scheme's assets

- details and percentage of any employer-related investment and steps taken or proposed to reduce excessive employer-related investment

- address for enquiries, *and*

- an explanation, where applicable, of why the auditor's statement about scheme contributions is negative or qualified and a statement as to how the situation has been, or is likely to be, resolved.

AUTOMATIC DISCLOSURE IN SPECIAL CIRCUMSTANCES

Trustees must disclose information automatically, rather than on request, in the following circumstances.

(a) **If any contributions are not paid by the due date,** and the trustees believe that this will be of material significance to the Pensions Regulator, members (and the Regulator) must be informed within a reasonable period (generally 30 days). The amounts and the due dates are those set out in the scheme's schedule of contributions or payment schedule.

(b) **Details of any proposed transfer without the member's consent** *(see page 165 of Section 26)*, including the value of the rights being transferred, must be provided at least one month before the proposed date of the transfer.

(c) **If a scheme is being wound up** *(see Section 24)*, all members and beneficiaries (except deferred pensioners and pension credit members who cannot be traced) must be given a notice within one month of the winding-up having commenced, and at least every 12 months thereafter. These notices must report on the action being taken to determine the scheme's assets and liabilities; give an indication of when final details are likely to be known; and indicate the extent to which the value of the member's accrued benefits is likely to be reduced (where the trustees have sufficient information to state this). In addition, the first notice must state that the scheme is winding up, together with the reasons; supply a name and address for further enquiries; provide a statement where relevant that an independent trustee is required; and provide a statement to active members as to whether death in service benefits will continue to be provided.

Once the assets have been applied in accordance with the legislative requirements, members and beneficiaries (except deferred pensioners and pension credit members who cannot be traced) must be told their benefit entitlements within three months, together with details as to who is responsible for paying the benefits, and the extent to which any benefits were reduced because the assets were insufficient. In addition the trustees must make periodic progress reports covering specified information to the Pensions Regulator. (A scheme for which a Recovery Plan is in place which commences to wind up must also prepare and provide to the Regulator a 'Winding Up Procedure'.) If requested, copies must be passed to members within two months.

(d) **If a COMPS ceases to be contracted out** *(see Section 6)* with respect to one or more employments, affected members must be told within one month and certain further information must be provided within four months.

(e) **Where a refund of surplus is proposed** *(see page 138 of Section 20)* to be made to the employer from a scheme that *is not winding up*, all members of the scheme must be sent a notice containing the following:

- a statement that the trustees have decided to make a payment to the employer

- the amount and date of the payment (which must be at least three months after the date of the notice)

- a statement that the trustees are satisfied that the payment is in 'the best interests of the members'

- a copy of the relevant valuation certificate, *and*

- a statement that the scheme is not subject to a freezing order.

For a scheme that *is winding up*, all members and beneficiaries must be given two written notices (the first running for at least two months and the second for at least three months) setting out the proposal and inviting representations.

(f) **Details of any independent trustee appointed on employer insolvency** *(see page 155 of Section 24)* must be provided to all members and recognised independent trade unions within a reasonable period of the appointment being made. Details of the scale of fees chargeable to the scheme and of the actual fees charged by the independent trustee in the previous 12 months must be provided on request to members, recognised independent trade unions and prospective members within a reasonable period of the request.

(g) In the selection of **member-nominated trustees or directors** *(see page 67 of Section 10)*, active and pensioner members (or organisations that adequately represent them) have to be invited to participate in the nomination and election process. Nominations and results of the election process should be communicated appropriately to members.

(h) **Consultation by employers** (*see page 53 of Section 7*) with members and prospective members of occupational pension and personal pension schemes is required before they can make certain 'listed changes' to the scheme. This is generally the employer's responsibility, but trustees are likely to have an interest in the process.

(i) **Modification of the accrued benefits provided by an occupational pension scheme** (*see page 53 of Section 7*) requires notification to members. The Pension Regulator's Code of Practice 'Modification of subsisting rights' provides guidance on the trustees' duties and responsibilities under the various stages of the requirements, including the process for communicating with and, where necessary, obtaining the consent of, members.

EXEMPTIONS FROM DISCLOSURE

- Schemes with fewer than two members.

- Schemes providing only death-in-service benefits.

- Schemes neither established in the UK nor with a trustee resident in the UK.

- Certain public service pension schemes are not required to obtain audited accounts or an actuarial valuation, or to publish an annual report.

- SSASs where all the members are trustees, in relation to information to be provided by the trustees to active, deferred or pensioner members (but not in relation to prospective members).

STATUTORY MONEY PURCHASE ILLUSTRATIONS

The legislation requires schemes under which any money purchase benefits are provided to supply members with annual illustrations of such benefits on a prescribed statutory basis, referred to as Statutory Money Purchase Illustrations (SMPIs). This legal requirement applies to any arrangement which is already required to issue annual benefit statements and covers occupational pension schemes (even those which are primarily on a defined benefit basis), free-standing and other AVCs, personal pensions, stakeholder schemes, and benefits bought out in the name of scheme trustees rather than members. Retirement annuities and non-registered arrangements are excluded, as are members within two years of retirement and with 'small' benefits (generally less than £5,000).

The overall aim is to provide illustrations of the amount of pension at retirement (in today's terms) on a broadly consistent basis for the different types of money purchase arrangement. The illustrations must be prepared in accordance with the Technical Memorandum (TM1).

The methodology and assumptions are specified in detail in TM1. In particular, it must be assumed that the pension will be index-linked in payment and will generally include a 50% contingent spouse's pension (although the provider need not include this if the member is single or, in other cases, agrees to its exclusion). Any regular contributions and the member's existing contracting-out status are assumed to continue. Version 1.3 of TM1, effective from 6 April 2009, allows for the forthcoming abolition of defined contribution contracting out, assumed to take place on 6 April 2012. Illustrations must assume that the member ceases to be contracted out no later than that date.

For the period before retirement, a long-term nominal return of up to 7% per annum together with inflation of 2.5% per annum must be assumed. Allowance for expenses must be in accordance with FSA rules where applicable, or otherwise based on actual experience. The assumed cost of purchasing annuities at retirement will generally be based on the yield on index-linked gilts on 15 February in the previous tax year, with a 4% allowance for expenses. No allowance is to be made for mortality before retirement. After retirement, it must be assumed to be in line with the PMA92 (males) and PFA92 (females) tables with medium cohort mortality improvement rates (published by the Actuarial Profession) applicable to the member's year of birth.

Specified information about the nature of the illustration and an overview of the assumptions must be included, together with other details listed in TM1. The value of the member's current fund may (but need not) also be included, as well as further illustrations on alternative bases, but it must be made clear which of the illustrations is on the statutory basis.

TM1 will be kept under review and it is likely that the assumptions will be changed from time to time.

EQUAL TREATMENT

Over recent years, the UK Government has incorporated into UK statute a number of provisions mostly designed to implement the various equal treatment requirements imposed by European law. Under EU law, there are a number of equal treatment principles that are of particular relevance to UK pensions.

The first, which stems from Article 141 (originally Article 119) of the Treaty of Rome as amended by the Treaty of Amsterdam, requires men and women performing work of equal value to receive equal pay. Case law at the European Court of Justice (ECJ) has shown that occupational pensions (though not social security schemes) fall within the definition of pay and that the principle of equal treatment must be applied in relation to both access to, *and* benefits provided by, occupational pension schemes.

Other equal treatment principles that followed are that part-time and fixed-term workers should be treated equally to comparable full-time workers and permanent employees respectively.

Regulations on discrimination on grounds of disability, religion or belief and sexual orientation have also been enacted. These prevent trustees from discriminating against or harassing members and prospective members, and trustees may only indirectly discriminate if they are able to justify their actions objectively. The catalyst for much of this new legislation was an EU Directive on Equal Treatment, adopted in November 2000.

Legislation tackling age discrimination came into effect from 1 October 2006, with the exception of the pensions provisions, which came into force on 1 December 2006.

In 2009, the Government published the Equality Bill which is intended to consolidate and extend existing discrimination legislation.

Further details of the principles of equal treatment, and how UK law seeks to implement them, are given below.

GENERAL PRINCIPLES OF EQUAL TREATMENT BY SEX

Equal benefits

Occupational pension schemes must provide equal benefits for men and women. In this respect, equality is only required for benefits in respect of service on or after 17 May 1990, except for claims initiated earlier.

Equal access

Men and women must have equal rights to join their employer's scheme. The exclusion of part-timers may thus constitute 'indirect' sex discrimination if the exclusion affects a much greater number of one sex than the other, *unless* the employer shows that it may be explained by objectively justified factors unrelated to sex. The right to join a scheme may be claimed in respect of service back to 8 April 1976, although time limits for bringing actions under national laws may apply *(see below)*.

Role of trustees, employers and the courts

Trustees must observe the principle of equal treatment in performing their duties. Both trustees and employers are bound to use all the means available under national laws in order to eliminate discrimination. National courts must apply the principle of Article 141 in the context of domestic laws, taking due account of the respective liabilities of employers and trustees. Article 141 may be relied on in claims against trustees as well as against employers.

APPLICATION OF PRINCIPLES OF EQUAL TREATMENT BY SEX TO OCCUPATIONAL AND STATE PENSIONS

Member contributions

The equal treatment principle of Article 141 applies to the whole benefit paid by an occupational pension scheme, and no distinction need be made between the parts derived from the employer's and from the employee's contractual contributions. However, benefits derived from members' additional voluntary contributions are not pay and so do not fall within the scope of Article 141.

Pension age and benefit accrual

Normal pension ages for men and women must not be discriminatory for benefits accrued since 17 May 1990. In respect of service from 17 May 1990 up to the date benefits are equalised (the equalisation date), the provisions applying to the less-favoured sex must be levelled up to those of the more-favoured sex, regardless of any difficulties this may cause the occupational scheme or the employer. For periods of service after the equalisation date, Article 141 does not preclude equal treatment being achieved by levelling benefits down, e.g. by raising the lower pension age. If members have a right to retire early, this right must not be discriminatory for benefits accrued since 17 May 1990.

Benefit accrual for service since 17 May 1990 must be equalised not only for scheme members but also for their dependants. For benefits not linked to length of service, e.g. lump sum benefits on death in service, equal benefits must be provided for men and women when the event triggering payment of the benefit occurs on or after 17 May 1990. In schemes where members have always been all of one sex, there is no need to equalise the respective benefits with those of a hypothetical member of the other sex. Where the funds held by the trustees are insufficient, any decision on how equalisation of benefits should be achieved must be resolved on the basis of national law.

Under the provisions of the Pensions Act 1995, all occupational pension schemes are deemed to have an 'equal treatment rule' covering both admission of members and benefits. The rule effectively levels up any unequal terms relating to service on or after 17 May 1990.

Bridging pensions and State pension offsets

Under the Pensions Act 1995 and associated regulations, unequal bridging pensions (and State pension offsets) that allow for the difference between men's and women's State pension ages are permitted. The extra pension payable to a man may not exceed the total Category A State retirement pension (i.e. basic plus additional component) payable to a woman with the earnings history of the individual in question in respect of their period of pensionable service under the scheme. Furthermore, it may be paid only between the corresponding female and male State pension ages.

On 19 April 2002, the High Court ruled in the *Shillcock* case that, for the purposes of calculating contributions and benefits, the operation of a Lower Earnings Limit (LEL) deduction from pensionable pay without pro-rating for part-timers did not constitute indirect sex discrimination and was, in any case, a reasonable method of implementing the legitimate objective of integration with state benefits and so was objectively justified.

Transfers

Schemes may, if they wish, calculate transfers out using actuarial factors which vary according to sex. The benefits to which the factors are applied are required to be equalised for service since 17 May 1990. Where a transfer value has in fact been based on unequal benefits for a period of service after 16 May 1990, the transfer value might be lower than it would have been if it had been based on equalised benefits. In such circumstances the *receiving* scheme must increase the benefits provided to those which could have been bought by the higher transfer value that should have been paid.

Actuarial factors

Actuarial factors that vary according to sex may be used for commutation, early and late retirement, and surrender of pension for a dependant. Emerging pension benefits from AVCs and money purchase schemes may also be calculated using sex-dependent factors.

Contracting-out problems

Contracted-out schemes have particular difficulties in equalising the benefits they provide because GMPs accrued at different rates and are required to come into payment at different ages for men and women. This issue was partly addressed by regulations under the Pensions Act 1995, which give contracted-out schemes some scope to provide unequal pension increases that reflect sex-related differences in the ways in which the increase in members' State pensions are calculated. While this exemption might appear to ease the position for schemes with unequal post-16 May 1990 GMPs *when pensions are in payment*, it does not address the problems associated with differences under the anti-franking legislation (primarily concerning increases in deferment). In January 2000, when the Pensions Ombudsman ruled that GMPs should be equalised for accruals since 17 May 1990, it looked as though schemes would soon be forced to address this issue. However, in February 2001, the High Court set aside the Ombudsman's ruling, principally because the judge considered the Ombudsman to have acted outside his jurisdiction. In practice, therefore, the majority of schemes are still waiting for clarification of what is required before implementing changes.

On 6 April 2009, regulations under the Pensions Act 2007 came into effect allowing trustees to convert GMPs into 'normal' scheme benefits. However, the lack of clarity on what must be done in order to comply with equal treatment requirements prior to conversion is likely to act as a deterrent to trustees considering using this facility.

The Pension Protection Fund (PPF) consulted, in 2008, on equalising compensation to allow for differences in GMPs, where schemes enter the PPF. However, at the time of writing, the PPF was still due to publish its proposal for GMP equalisation.

Time limits for bringing claims and backdating membership

Under equality provisions of the Pensions Act 1995, in force until August 2005, claims by members and prospective members of occupational pension schemes for unlawful unequal treatment had to be brought to industrial tribunals under the provisions of the Equal Pay Act 1970 within six months of leaving service, and backdated membership was generally limited to two years. However, the validity of these restrictions under European law (which overrides UK law) was challenged in the ECJ in the indirect sex discrimination part-timer case of *Preston v Wolverhampton*. After further legal proceedings, it was ruled that the UK's time limit of six months for bringing claims was consistent with EU law, but the two-year limit on backdating was not. Individuals may therefore claim in respect of service back to 8 April 1976.

UK regulations made in 1995 required the employer to pay the full cost for up to two years' backdated service between 31 May 1995 (or the deemed date of entry if later) and the actual date of entry. The requirement for the payment of the full cost was a more stringent requirement than that imposed by the European Court, which ruled that the employee could be required to pay full arrears of member contributions. The UK regulations were changed accordingly in August 2005.

Statutory occupational pension schemes

Schemes for government employees are subject to the equal treatment requirements of Article 141.

Maternity, adoption and paternity leave

The Employment Rights Act 1996 requires *all* benefits in kind, including pension accrual, to be maintained during *statutory* ordinary maternity leave (whether paid or unpaid). The Employment Act 2002 provisions, which generally took effect from April 2003, gave similar rights to adoptive parents with the introduction of statutory adoption leave, and also introduced new requirements for continued pension accrual during statutory paternity leave and statutory parental leave. Further requirements regarding pension rights are contained in the Social Security Act 1989 (SSA 89) which requires all *paid* maternity, adoption and paternity absence to be treated as a period of normal service as far as an employer-related benefit scheme is concerned. When assessing benefits it should be assumed that the normal pay for the job was received; for adoption and paternity leave, this only applies from 6 April 2005. However, the member is required to pay contributions based only on the remuneration actually received. For paid (but non-statutory) 'family leave' (other than maternity, adoption or paternity leave), SSA 89 only requires benefits to be based on actual (not on normal) remuneration.

The Work and Families Act 2006 introduced various amendments with effect from 1 April 2007. These include:

- extending statutory maternity pay, maternity allowance and adoption pay to nine months
- extending to carers the right to request flexible working
- introducing 'keeping in touch' days, so that where employees and employers agree, a woman on maternity leave can still go into work for a few days without losing her right to maternity leave or a week's statutory pay, *and*
- extending the period of notice for return from maternity leave to two months, enabling employees and employers to plan return to work more effectively.

Changes to the Sex Discrimination Act 1975, which apply to women who expected to give birth on or after 5 October 2008, have created some ambiguity over whether unpaid additional maternity leave must be pensionable. While the Employment Rights Act 1996 states that this is not required and HMRC have stated that this Act's provisions should be followed, there remains doubt arising from what some lawyers consider to be contradictory legal requirements.

State pension ages

From April 2020, State pension age will be equalised for men and women. The change is being phased in over a 10-year period from April 2010. From that date, State pension age for women increases by one month for every two months elapsed (*see table below*). Women born before 6 April 1950 are not affected by the change; women born after 5 April 1955 will have a State pension age of at least 65.

Female pension ages during phasing-in period

Date of Birth	Pension Date	Date of Birth	Pension Date
Before 6.4.50	60th birthday	. . .	. . .
6.4.50–5.5.50	6.5.2010	6.3.53–5.4.53	6.3.2016
6.5.50–5.6.50	6.7.2010	. . .	. . .
6.6.50–5.7.50	6.9.2010	6.3.54–5.4.54	6.3.2018
. . .	. . .	. . .	. . .
6.3.51–5.4.51	6.3.2012	6.3.55–5.4.55	6.3.2020
. . .	. . .	6.4.55 and after	65th birthday
6.3.52–5.4.52	6.3.2014		

The Pensions Act 2007 increases the State pension age from 65 to 68. The increase will not affect anyone born before 6 April 1959, and will be phased in between 2024 and 2046 as follows:

- from 65 to 66 over a two-year period from April 2024

- from 66 to 67 over a two-year period from April 2034, *and*
- from 67 to 68 over a two-year period from April 2044.

EQUAL TREATMENT FOR PART-TIMERS

In 1997, the EU adopted a part-time work directive requiring member states to outlaw all discrimination against part-time workers, and not just in cases of indirect sex discrimination covered under the general 'equal pay' provisions. UK regulations implementing the directive came into force on 1 July 2000, and applied with immediate (although not retrospective) effect. Under these regulations, it is no longer possible to treat a part-timer less favourably than a 'comparable' full-timer, unless the less favourable treatment is justified on objective grounds. The regulations provide that, in determining whether or not treatment is unfavourable, a 'pro-rata' principle applies, 'unless it is inappropriate'. The extent to which it is legal to provide inferior (or no) benefits to part-timers (on grounds such as non-comparability with full-timers, 'objective justification' or inappropriateness of a pro rata principle) is only likely to become clear as case law is built up. Complaints by individuals under this legislation must generally be taken to an employment tribunal within three months of the last day on which they consider they were unfavourably treated.

EQUAL TREATMENT FOR FIXED-TERM WORKERS

UK regulations implementing the EU fixed-term worker directive came into force on 1 October 2002. Under these regulations, direct discrimination against fixed-term workers in relation to terms and conditions including pensions is prohibited, unless it is justified on objective grounds. The regulations specifically provide that less favourable treatment in relation to some contractual terms is objectively justified where the fixed-term employee's overall employment package is no less favourable than that of a comparable permanent employee. Complaints by individuals under this legislation must generally be taken to an employment tribunal within three months of the last day on which they consider they were unfavourably treated.

EQUAL TREATMENT AND SEXUAL ORIENTATION

From 1 December 2003, pension schemes may not directly discriminate against members on grounds of their sexual orientation. Indirect discrimination is also unlawful, unless the practice is a 'proportionate means of achieving a legitimate aim'. However, preventing or restricting access to a benefit by reference to marital status remained lawful (*but see below*), as did discriminatory benefits in respect of service before 1 December 2003.

From this date, scheme rules are deemed to include an anti-discrimination clause which prevents trustees from illegally discriminating against, or harassing, members and prospective members. The legislation also gives trustees the power to make appropriate amendments to scheme provisions in respect of anti-discrimination clauses by resolution, where use of the scheme's existing powers would be impractical.

The Civil Partnership Act took effect from 5 December 2005. It introduced a facility for same-sex partners to register civil partnerships and thereby receive increased legal recognition. It extended the divorce pension sharing and earmarking regulations and social security legislation in line with the principle that civil partners should be treated in the same way as married people. Under the Act, contracted-out schemes have to provide the same contracted-out benefits to civil partners as to spouses for all service after 5 April 1988. In addition, the Government amended the 2003 sexual orientation regulations so that all schemes have to treat civil partners in the same way as spouses for service on or after 5 December 2005.

However, a recent ECJ judgment in a German case has cast doubt on whether equality of civil partners' benefits can legitimately be restricted to service from 5 December 2005. In the *Tadao Maruko* case, the ECJ held that a registered same-sex partner should be provided with the same dependant's pension as a surviving spouse and that the pension should not be limited to pension accrual from a specific date. The UK Government has yet to comment on the implications of this case for UK legislation.

The Gender Recognition Act came into force on 4 April 2005. It is designed to give formal recognition to transsexuals who successfully register in their acquired gender.

EQUAL TREATMENT AND RELIGION OR BELIEF

In respect of rights that accrue from 2 December 2003, pension schemes may not directly discriminate against members on grounds of their religion or belief, and may indirectly discriminate only where the offending practice is a 'proportionate means of achieving a legitimate aim'. The anti-discrimination requirements cover admission to schemes as well as treatment once admitted. Particularly in the realm of indirect discrimination, potential issues could possibly arise for pension schemes, for example where all investment funds offered under a DC arrangement are unacceptable to members of a particular religion. In the same way as for equal treatment and sexual orientation, from 2 December 2003 scheme rules are deemed to include an anti-discrimination clause.

EQUAL TREATMENT AND DISABILITY

The Disability Discrimination Act 1995 (Pensions) Regulations 2003 took effect from 1 October 2004. Under the regulations, in the same way as above, a non-discrimination rule is deemed to be included in the scheme rules. From this date, any direct discrimination in relation to occupational pension schemes is unlawful, and indirect discrimination (or 'disability-related discrimination', as it is referred to in the statutory Code of Practice issued under the legislation) is only allowed if it is 'justified' by a reason that is 'both material to the circumstances of the particular case and substantial'. From 1 October 2004, trustees also became subject to the general requirement under the Act to make 'reasonable adjustments'. Although the new legislation does not in general affect benefits earned before October 2004, it does extend to communications with members in relation to such rights.

The precise effect of the new regulations is unclear and legal advice should be sought in respect of specific circumstances. However, one potential effect is that it may not be possible to exclude disabled people from some death and ill-health benefits. The position may be complicated by the fact that there is a facility under the Act for insurers to discriminate against disabled people on sound actuarial grounds but this facility does not extend to trustees or employers.

EQUAL TREATMENT AND AGE

The Employment Equality (Age) Regulations 2006 took effect from 1 October 2006. The Regulations relating to pensions were delayed and took effect from 1 December 2006. They implement measures against age discrimination designed to satisfy the requirements of the EU Equal Treatment directive.

Both direct and indirect discrimination by employers and by trustees of pension schemes are prohibited, unless such a practice can be objectively justified as a 'proportionate means of achieving a legitimate aim'. There are a number of occupational pension scheme practices which are specifically exempted from being age-discriminatory under the Regulations. These include:

- the use of a minimum or maximum age for admission to a scheme
- the use of age-based actuarial factors in benefit calculations
- the use of a maximum period of service for benefit calculations
- limiting the payment of benefits to a minimum age
- the application of age restrictions which would be required to ensure the scheme is eligible for taxation concessions under the Finance Act 2004
- the provision of age-related employer contributions to money purchase schemes, where the aim is to provide benefits that do not vary by age of member (or to provide 'more nearly equal' benefits) in respect of each year of pensionable service, *and*
- the payment of equal contributions to money purchase schemes, irrespective of age, even though this will provide different levels of benefit to members of different ages.

Many common occupational pension scheme practices are, however, not exempt under the legislation. For example, benefit accrual may not generally cease at a fixed retirement age. In addition, there is a great deal of uncertainty concerning how much of the legislation will be interpreted, and clarification is expected to emerge only slowly as actual cases are considered by tribunals and courts.

Mandatory retirement ages have generally been outlawed, but the Regulations allow for a default retirement age of 65. An employee has the right to ask to work beyond this age, but the employer is not obliged to accept the request. Heyday, an organisation developed by Age Concern, challenged this in the ECJ. The case was referred back to the UK High Court, which, on 25 September 2009, ruled that the default retirement age of 65 is legal. The decision was based on the state of affairs in 2006 when the Regulation was adopted. In July 2009, the Government had announced that it intends to review the default retirement age in 2010, one year before it had been expected to do so. The judge stated that if the Regulation had been adopted in 2009, or there had been no indication of an imminent review, he would not have concluded that the choice of age 65 as a default retirement age was justified.

Complaints by individuals under this legislation must generally be taken to an employment tribunal within three months of the last day on which they consider they were unfavourably treated.

EQUALITY BILL

In April 2009, the Government published the Equality Bill, which it hopes will take effect from Autumn 2010. The Bill has two main purposes:

- to consolidate and harmonise existing equal treatment legislation, *and*
- to strengthen the law to support progress on equality.

Among the Bill's provisions, current non-discrimination rules deemed to be included in scheme rules will be replaced by a single rule in respect of discrimination on the grounds of gender reassignment, marriage and civil partnership, and sexual orientation. A new deemed sex equality rule will replicate and replace existing provisions, and a new maternity equality rule will be introduced. New regulations setting out the exceptions to the age discrimination requirements are also proposed.

PENSIONS AND DIVORCE

Courts are required to take benefits under pension schemes into account when considering financial provision on divorce. In many cases, this may be achieved by making a divorce settlement which distributes other marital assets in such a way as to keep pension rights intact. However, there are also two alternative approaches available for allowing both parties to the divorce to benefit directly from the benefit entitlements under a pension scheme of one of the two parties. The first alternative, earmarking, was introduced for petitions for divorce filed on or after 1 July 1996 (or 19 August 1996 in Scotland), and causes a specified amount of a scheme member's lump sum (all jurisdictions) and/or pension (England, Wales and Northern Ireland only) to be paid, instead, to his or her ex-spouse. The second alternative, pension sharing, is available where divorce proceedings began on or after 1 December 2000, and results in a 'clean break' between the divorcing parties.

Since December 2005, when the Civil Partnership Act 2004 took effect, the provisions for pension sharing and earmarking have been extended so that they also apply when civil partnerships are dissolved. In the remainder of this Section, 'divorce' should be read to include 'dissolution of civil partnership', 'ex-spouse' to include 'ex-civil partner' etc., as the context requires.

Some further changes were made under the Pensions Act 2008 and others are provided for but have not yet come into force.

Further details of the pension sharing regime are given below.

PENSION SHARING

Provision of information

If a benefit valuation is to be included, schemes have to supply basic information within three months of request; or within six weeks, where the member has notified them that proceedings for financial provision on divorce have commenced; or within such shorter period as may be specified in a court order. If no benefit valuation is to be included, the basic information must be provided within one month. Further information must be provided within 21 days of being notified that a pension sharing order may be made, unless the prescribed information has already been supplied. Additional information requirements arise subsequently if the divorcing parties proceed with a pension share.

What rights may be shared?

All rights under occupational and personal pensions and retirement annuity policies (including pensions in payment and annuities or insurance policies purchased to give effect to any such rights) may be shared. However, the regulations exclude survivors' pensions payable as a result of a previous marriage and Equivalent Pension Benefits (EPBs) where these are the only benefit under a scheme. SERPS/S2P rights are also included, but the State Graduated Scheme and the Basic State Pension are not. The Pensions Act 2008 contains provisions, not yet in force at the time of writing, which would allow for compensation payments under the PPF *(see Section 22)* to be shared on divorce in the same way as other pension rights.

What triggers pension sharing?

Any decision on sharing is triggered by a court order between the parties. The order is stayed until any appeals process has been completed. The order is expressed in terms of a transfer from one party to the other of a percentage of rights accrued prior to the date the order takes effect. In Scotland, these rights are restricted to those that accrued during the marriage and the transfer can alternatively be expressed as a fixed amount.

Rights to be provided to ex-spouse

The person receiving a share of his or her ex-spouse's rights usually has to be offered a transfer value in respect of those rights. Rights under unfunded schemes, including SERPS/S2P, are excluded from this requirement.

Schemes that are obliged to offer an external transfer may, but do not have to, offer the ex-spouse the option of a pension credit benefit within the scheme as an alternative to a transfer value. Ex-spouse members of pension schemes are, essentially, treated like deferred pensioners. If the ex-spouse is also an employee member of the scheme that provides the pension credit benefit, the scheme can insist that, on taking a subsequent cash equivalent, both sets of rights are transferred.

Basis of calculation for sharing

Calculations for pension sharing are based on the scheme's current established cash equivalent basis, extended to cover cases (like pensions in payment) where a transfer value would not normally arise. There is a facility for transfer values for ex-spouses (along with other transfer values) to be reduced if the scheme is under-funded. However, the legislation provides that such a reduction is to be applied only if the ex-spouse has been offered (but has declined) the alternative of a pension credit benefit within the scheme based on the unreduced transfer value.

Pension credit benefits

Pension credit benefits, if offered under the scheme, should be determined on the incoming transfer value basis, with appropriate adjustments where 'added-years' pensions are normally awarded and the ex-spouse is not himself or herself an active member of the scheme. Benefits are generally payable from 'normal benefit age' but can be paid early where the member has attained normal minimum pension age or qualifies for an ill-health pension. Pension credit benefits can also be partially commuted for a pension commencement lump sum, or fully commuted in certain circumstances, in accordance with the Finance Act 2004 requirements.

Except for pension credit benefits in money purchase form where the benefit had not come into payment before 6 April 2005, the regulations require LPI indexation of benefits derived from post-97 rights (other than those derived from AVCs). For this purpose, LPI is capped at 5% if the pension credit benefit was awarded before 6 April 2005, or 2.5% if awarded after 5 April 2005. Schemes are not prevented from indexing the whole of the pension credit benefit, in order to simplify administration.

Pension debits

In defined benefit schemes, the original member's benefit becomes subject to a debit, designed to be of equal value to the amount transferred to the ex-spouse. This is, essentially, a negative deferred pension. Each part of the member's vested benefit entitlement immediately prior to the date the pension sharing order takes effect is reduced in the same proportion (including, in particular, contracted-out benefits). Defined contribution scheme debits are the stipulated proportion of the fund value or, if applicable, of the benefit already in payment.

Contracted-out rights

Until 6 April 2009, restrictions applied to pension credit benefits derived from contracted-out rights. These were known as 'safeguarded rights'. The restrictions were removed, from that date, under the Pensions Act 2008, so safeguarded rights may now be treated in the same manner as other pension credit benefits. Previously, where contracted-out rights were 'shared', the ex-spouse would acquire safeguarded rights which essentially enjoyed the status, and carried the restrictions, of members' contracted-out rights.

Timing of implementation

Schemes generally have four months, after the date the relevant court order takes effect or (if later) receipt of all relevant divorce documentation and personal information about the divorcing parties, to implement the pension share in accordance with the option chosen by the ex-spouse or (if no valid instructions are given) in accordance with the scheme's chosen default procedure. The Pensions Regulator may (on application) extend the implementation period, in circumstances broadly similar to those which apply for the late payment of 'normal' cash equivalents.

Expense costs

Schemes are allowed to charge, to the divorcing parties, their reasonable costs incurred in providing information for and implementing the pension share, and are usually able to insist on receiving these before they have to provide the information or implement the share. However, most charges are allowable only to the extent previously disclosed in a Schedule of Charges at the outset, and no charge may be made for information that would be available free under the Disclosure requirements. The trustees can require that the costs are paid in cash, with deduction from the benefits being an alternative. Only costs specifically relating to an individual divorce case can be charged, and therefore initial costs involved in setting up administrative procedures to deal with pension sharing may not be passed on.

Tax treatment

Under the tax regime introduced from 6 April 2006 *(see Section 12)*, the benefits tested against an individual's lifetime allowance are the actual benefits payable after taking account of a pension debit or credit. In most circumstances, an individual whose benefits have become subject to a debit will have scope within his or her lifetime allowance to rebuild lost rights. A divorcing member with primary protection, however, will see his or her lifetime allowance reduced to take account of a post-5 April 2006 pension debit. For a member with enhanced protection, rights lost as a result of a post-5 April 2006 pension debit could – in general – be rebuilt, although not through a defined contribution arrangement.

An ex-spouse who became entitled before 6 April 2006 to a pension credit had until 5 April 2009 to register for an increased lifetime allowance, so that he or she would not lose scope to build up further tax-privileged pension rights. This did not apply to individuals with primary protection, who would however have been able to include the pension credit in the amount protected at A Day.

A pension credit received after 5 April 2006 gives rise to an increase in the personal lifetime allowance only if it arises from pension that had come into payment between 6 April 2006 and the date of the share, and the increase is registered within the required timescale. An ex-spouse with enhanced protection would lose this protection if a post-5 April 2006 pension credit were paid to his or her defined benefit or cash balance arrangement, causing the permitted limits to be breached. However, enhanced protection is not lost if the pension credit is paid to a money purchase arrangement which is not a cash balance arrangement, provided that this arrangement already existed at 5 April 2006.

PENSION SCHEME FUNDING

BACKGROUND

Pension scheme funding has come under close scrutiny in recent years. A new statutory funding regime was introduced under the Pensions Act 2004 in order to address the perceived shortcomings of its predecessor, the Minimum Funding Requirement (MFR), and to meet the requirements of the EU Pensions Directive. *The new regime is discussed in more detail later in this Section.*

ACTUARIAL VALUATIONS

Actuarial valuations are central to the process of funding defined benefit (DB) schemes. They are also used for other purposes, including accounting for pension costs *(see Section 27)*. Many different types of valuation may be called for in different circumstances. The basic principles of two of the main types, 'ongoing' and 'discontinuance' valuations, are described briefly below.

Ongoing valuation

When a defined benefit scheme is established, the actuary's calculations of the amount of contributions to be paid have to be based on assumptions about how the scheme will evolve. However, events will invariably unfold differently from the original assumptions, and it is necessary to examine the scheme periodically to value the assets and liabilities and to revise the contribution rate.

To value the liabilities, the actuary receives individual details of the scheme's current, retired and deferred members. Data relating to changes in membership since the previous valuation are also supplied to enable a reconciliation of the membership numbers to be carried out and to test actual experience against the assumptions of the last valuation.

Various assumptions need to be made; these are financial (e.g. the discount rate and rates of salary and pension increases) and demographic (e.g. rates of mortality, ill-health, early retirement and leaving service). Nowadays, the starting point for the financial assumptions is usually the yields on fixed-interest and index-linked securities available in the market at the valuation date.

Various different valuation methods are used according to the individual needs of the scheme and the employer, and to meet statutory requirements. Common valuation and funding methods include:

(a) *Projected Unit Method*: an 'accrued benefits' funding method which determines the cost of providing the benefits earned in the year (or other specified period) following the valuation date, allowing for salary increases to retirement, leaving service or death, as appropriate. Past service calculations are the same as for the attained age method *(see below)*. This is currently the most popular method.

(b) *Current Unit Method*: an 'accrued benefits' funding method similar to the projected unit method, under which salaries are only projected to the end of the year (or other specified period) following the valuation date. Increases in benefits after the end of the specified period are assumed to follow the scheme rules or overriding legislation applicable to members with deferred benefits.

(c) *Attained Age Method*: a 'prospective benefits' funding method based on the total prospective service of the existing membership, allowing for salary increases to retirement, leaving service or death, as appropriate. Past and future service components are considered separately. The future service contribution rate is adjusted to allow for any past service surplus or deficit.

The actuary also requires details of the assets held by the scheme. Assets are given at market value in the audited accounts, and this is the value that is now normally used in actuarial valuations in conjunction with market-based yields for valuing liabilities. Other methods of calculating asset values have been developed and used in the past, under which the value attributed to the assets in the valuation report may have differed significantly from their market value.

Discontinuance valuation

The discontinuance valuation assesses whether the scheme's assets would be sufficient to cover the liabilities if the scheme were to be discontinued at the valuation date and no further contributions were received from the employer. The liability for active members is usually based on service to and salary at the valuation date. Future expenses should be allowed for.

This assessment can be made on various bases. However, the latest scheme funding legislation and professional guidance require the actuary to disclose the extent to which the assets of the scheme would be sufficient, at the valuation date, to cover the liabilities assessed on an annuity buy-out basis, regardless of whether or not the scheme would be likely to secure benefits in this way if it were to discontinue. As an alternative to using the cost actually quoted by a suitable insurance company for buying out the benefits at the valuation date, the actuary may use an estimate of the buy-out cost based on the principles likely to be adopted by an insurance company. Liabilities must include a realistic allowance for expenses, and assets must be taken at no more than market value. Where the assets would not have been sufficient to secure the benefits in full, an estimate must be included of the percentage level of cover for each priority order class of benefits (*see Section 24*).

SCHEME FUNDING UNDER THE PENSIONS ACT 2004

The Pensions Act 2004 has brought about widespread changes to the regime governing the funding of DB pension schemes. The new scheme-specific funding requirements came into force on 30 December 2005 for valuations with effective dates on or after 22 September 2005. Previously, a Minimum Funding Requirement (MFR) regime required schemes to maintain sufficient assets to cover the value, calculated on prescribed assumptions, of scheme benefits, and to take remedial action if the level of cover fell.

Scheme-specific funding regime

Under the 'statutory funding objective', a DB scheme is required to 'have sufficient and appropriate assets to cover its technical provisions', i.e. 'the amount required, on an actuarial calculation, to make provision for the scheme's liabilities'. Regulations require the technical provisions to be determined on a (normally 'ongoing') scheme-specific basis. There is no legal requirement for schemes to fund at a prescribed level. Each valuation must, however, include an estimate by the actuary of the solvency of the scheme normally based on quoted 'annuity buy-out' costs or made using similar principles. The trustees have ultimate responsibility for the funding decisions, but are required to take advice from the scheme actuary and – normally – to obtain the employer's agreement. However, where the trustees have power under the scheme's rules to set contribution rates without the employer's agreement, that requirement is replaced by one for consultation (although agreement should be obtained if possible). If the rules provide for the actuary to determine the contribution rate, the rate must be certified as being no lower than the actuary would have set had he or she retained this responsibility.

Actuarial valuations are required with effective dates no more than three years apart, with additional written 'actuarial reports', covering developments since the last valuation, in each intervening year. There is a general exception from the scheme funding requirement for schemes in wind-up but, where this commenced on or after 30 December 2005, the exception is conditional upon the preparation of an annual solvency estimate by the scheme actuary (on a buy-out basis) and a winding-up procedure (see Section 24). Schemes that went into wind-up before 30 December 2005 are no longer required to obtain MFR valuations.

Cross-border schemes (see Section 7) are subject to more onerous requirements, including a specified deadline for meeting the statutory funding objective and full actuarial valuations every 12 months.

Statement of funding principles

The trustees must have a written statement of funding principles (SFP) setting out their policy for securing that the statutory funding objective is met and recording decisions as to the basis for calculating the technical provisions and the period within which any shortfall is to be remedied. The SFP must be reviewed at each valuation and, if amended, finalised (along with the valuation report and schedule of contributions) within fifteen months of the effective date of the valuation.

Calculation of technical provisions

The trustees must choose an 'accrued benefits' funding method, such as the projected unit or current unit method, for calculating the technical provisions.

It is also the trustees' responsibility (having received advice from the scheme actuary) to choose the assumptions to be adopted for the calculation of the scheme's technical provisions. The trustees should also agree the assumptions with the employer (unless there is only a requirement for consultation – see above).

The Pensions Regulator's code of practice on scheme funding states that trustees should set assumptions 'with a level of prudence consistent with the overall confidence they want to have that the resulting technical provisions will prove adequate to pay benefits as they fall due'. Other factors the trustees should consider include the sensitivity of the technical provisions to small changes in individual assumptions, economic and investment market conditions and factors particular to the employer or industry concerned.

Recovery plan

If an actuarial valuation shows that the statutory funding objective is not met, the trustees must prepare a 'recovery plan' setting out the steps to be taken (and over what period) to make up the shortfall. The trustees should aim for the shortfall to be eliminated as quickly as the employer can 'reasonably afford', taking into account his business plans and the likely impact of the additional contributions. The Regulator has stated that what is possible and reasonable will depend on the trustees' assessment of the employer's covenant. A copy of the recovery plan must be sent to the Regulator.

Schedule of contributions

As was the case under the previous MFR legislation, the trustees must have in place a schedule of contributions setting out the rates and due dates of contributions payable to the scheme, which will normally have been agreed with the employer, *as discussed above*. The schedule must be certified by the actuary as being sufficient to ensure that the funding objective will continue to be met for the next five years, or will be met by the end of the recovery plan period. In the latter case, a copy of the schedule must be sent to the Regulator. If contributions are not paid or are paid late, the trustees (and actuary or auditor, if they become aware of this) must inform the Regulator if they believe that the failure is likely to be 'of material significance'.

Intervention of the Regulator

In May 2006, the Regulator issued a statement detailing how it will regulate the funding of DB schemes. This sets out the circumstances and manner in which it may take action to intervene in a scheme where it forms the opinion that the scheme's funding plan is not compliant with the new requirements, and outlines steps it will have expected the trustees to have taken to ensure compliance.

The Regulator has set triggers to alert it to schemes where its intervention in the funding arrangements may be warranted, which are:

(a) that the technical provisions are set below a point, commensurate with the strength of the employer and the scheme's maturity, somewhere between the level of liabilities under the PPF's 'section 179' valuation *(see Section 22)* and those under the FRS 17 (or IAS 19) accounting basis *(see Section 27), and/or*

(b) that the recovery plan exceeds ten years, is significantly 'back-end loaded' or uses inappropriate assumptions.

The Regulator has stressed that the triggers do not set a new funding standard; the trigger points are not targets, and scheme-specific circumstances will also be used to determine whether or not the funding plan is compliant: in particular the employer's strength and ability to pay off the shortfall, and the maturity of the scheme.

If a scheme does 'trigger' (or comes to the Regulator's attention by some other means) the Regulator may ask for 'readily available' information, such as management accounts, scheme valuation reports and trustee minutes, before deciding whether to intervene. For valuations after 22 September 2008, the Regulator will also look specifically at the assumption for future improvements in life expectancy adopted by the scheme *(see Section 21)*.

The Regulator has issued a number of more recent statements confirming that its approach is sufficiently flexible to deal with adverse market conditions, particularly general falls in asset values and pressure on employer covenants. It expects trustees to consider reviewing recovery plans where there is a significant change in such circumstances. For example, recovery plans lasting more than ten years or back-end loaded recovery plans may be appropriate in order not to jeopardise the financial position of the employer. However, the Regulator says that recovery plans should not suffer to enable the employer to continue to pay dividends, and that the trustees should consider themselves as unsecured creditors and therefore take priority over shareholders.

The Regulator also has powers to intervene in cases where agreement cannot be reached between the trustees and employer or where the actuary is unable to provide the necessary confirmation. In addition, the Regulator now has powers to intervene if it views the technical provisions as insufficiently prudent, even if the trustees and employer are in agreement. Possible courses of action include imposing a funding basis, modifying future accrual and freezing or winding up the scheme. However, the Regulator has stated that it aims to use its formal powers sparingly, preferring to achieve its desired outcome by more informal means.

Disclosure to members

Schemes are required to send members an annual 'summary funding statement' including information about the funding and discontinuance positions of the scheme and an explanation of any changes since the previous statement. Where a valuation under the new regime has not yet been carried out, the statement should include information from the most recent ('ongoing') valuation carried out under the previous regime.

Employer covenant

The Regulator has stated that it is essential for the trustees to form an objective assessment of 'the employer's financial position and prospects as well as his willingness to continue to fund the scheme's benefits'. This assessment should be used to inform the trustees' decisions on both the technical provisions and any recovery plan needed. In order to carry out this assessment, the trustees will need to obtain information about the employer, either directly from the employer or by using commercially available services such as credit specialist advisers.

Trustees should continue to monitor the employer's covenant between valuations, and should consider reviewing their funding policy in the light of any material improvement or decline in the employer's covenant.

Contingent assets

Although they may not be taken directly into account in determining whether the statutory funding objective is met, or when estimating solvency, the Regulator has issued guidance about the way in which 'contingent assets', such as group company guarantees or bank letters of credit, might be used to support technical provisions or a recovery plan.

Refunds of surplus

From 6 April 2006 a power to repay surplus from the scheme can only be exercised by the trustees (subject to the agreement of the employer, if it was originally conferred on him) and only if it is in the members' interest and they have been notified. Furthermore, a payment of surplus from the scheme to the employer will only be permitted to the extent that the scheme's assets exceed the full buy-out cost of the accrued liabilities, as indicated by a valuation carried out under the Pensions Act 2004 funding regime or a special valuation carried out for this purpose.

The DWP has issued an informal discussion paper setting out ways in which the refund of surplus rules could be relaxed. The options considered include lowering the funding threshold from the full buy-out level, taking account of contingent assets, and sharing surplus between the employer and members. However there has been no indication as to whether these proposals will be taken any further.

MORTALITY

Dramatic recent increases in life expectancy – particularly for men – have received much publicity, and the extra cost of paying pensions for longer has perhaps added to talk of a 'pension crisis'. Trustees of defined benefit schemes in particular need to understand the risks involved and how they can manage them.

LONGEVITY RISK

Different types of mortality-related risk can be identified. One such risk, commonly referred to as 'mortality risk', is the risk of dying sooner than expected. 'Longevity risk' refers to the risk of living longer than expected. This is arguably more of an issue for pension schemes, given the recent increases in life expectancy and the uncertainty over how these will persist. We will concentrate on 'longevity risk' in the rest of this section.

Longevity risk has different elements. Past data may tell us fairly accurately the mortality rates for the general population. But for any given pension scheme there must be uncertainty over:

- how mortality rates for its members differ from those for the general population (because of factors like location, social class, diet and smoking)
- how mortality rates will change in the future – will past improvements continue? *and*
- whether there might be a 'jump' change in mortality rates in the future (e.g. caused by an epidemic or, in the other direction, a medical breakthrough).

Longevity risk can fall on different parties depending on what type of pension scheme we are considering. At one extreme, the risk under a traditional final salary scheme falls entirely on the trustees and the sponsoring employer (although members' future benefit accrual could be reduced if increases in life expectancy cause the scheme to become too expensive). At the other extreme, the risk under a pure defined contribution scheme buying annuities for its pensioners falls partly on the scheme members (since they do not know how much pension their money will buy when they retire) and partly on the insurance company (since the annuity rates it sets may turn out to be wrong).

ASSUMPTIONS

To place a value on the liabilities of a defined benefit pension scheme, its trustees need to make assumptions about how long its pensioners will live. An insurance company selling annuities needs to do the same thing in order to set its annuity rates.

Mortality rates

Life expectancies are usually calculated based on mortality rates. 'Mortality rate' in this context means the assumed probability that an individual of a given age will die in the next year. The lower the mortality rates are, the longer the life expectancy is. The assumptions needed are in two parts: the rates assumed to apply for the next 12 months (the 'base tables') and how these rates are expected to change in future years. Different rates are calculated for men and women.

Base tables

Larger schemes will often have enough data to carry out an investigation of their own mortality experience, looking at their own recent data and using this to set the assumed mortality rates for the next year. But, in most cases, published standard tables are used as a starting point. These are usually tables prepared by the Continuous Mortality Investigation (CMI), a research body under the aegis of the UK Actuarial Profession, based on data collated from life insurance companies or from self-administered pension schemes.

The three most recent CMI tables are the '92' series and the '00' series (based respectively on life office experience from 1991 to 1994 and 1999 to 2002) and the 'S1' series (based on self-administered pension scheme experience from 2000 to 2006). The trustees and actuary may adjust the mortality rates from the standard tables to make them more appropriate for their own scheme's members (to reflect, for example, their locations and former occupations). Such adjustments may be based on an analysis of the scheme's own experience or, if this is not available or not large enough, on broad principles.

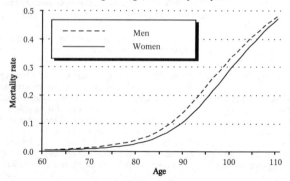

Mortality rate (probability that an individual of a given age will die in the next year)

Source: From the S1 series (pensioners, amounts), adjusted for use in 2010, allowing for long cohort projection factors but with a projected long-term minimum improvement in life expectancy of 1.25% p.a.

Future improvements

Longevity has improved dramatically in recent years, and it is now normal to make an explicit allowance for further improvements in the future. These are of course unknown, and one way of dealing with the resulting uncertainty is to carry out calculations on two or more different sets of assumptions. By 2002, it had become clear that longevity was improving at a faster rate than had previously been assumed, with the improvements being particularly marked for the generation (or 'cohort') of pensioners born between the two World Wars. In response to this, the CMI published three sets of improvement factors for use with the '92' series of tables: the 'short', 'medium' and 'long' cohort improvement factors, allowing for the increased rates of improvement to continue until 2010, 2020 and 2040 respectively. In autumn 2009 the CMI published a spreadsheet program, known as 'CMP v1.0', that it is expected will supersede the use of the cohort improvement factors.

Another possibility, although one that is rarely used at present, is to adopt a stochastic approach. This involves assigning an assumed probability distribution for future mortality rates and then carrying out a large number of simulations to assess the range of outcomes. (A similar approach is often used at present to illustrate the effect on schemes' funding levels of different rates of future investment return.)

LOOKING AHEAD

Predicting future improvements in longevity is extremely difficult, not least because of the huge uncertainties surrounding the impact that future events may have. Medical advances, changes in social behaviours (e.g. the impact of the smoking ban in enclosed public spaces in England from 1 July 2007) and increases in obesity will all have an impact.

Some experts caution against making forecasts based purely on past experience, believing instead that life expectancy will level off in the future and ultimately start to fall. Others disagree, arguing that as one disease is conquered scientists will move on to the next, and that improvements in life expectancy due to medical advances will continue at a similar rate. With research indicating that a 35-year-old non-smoker has over double the chance of living to age 80 that a 35-year-old smoker has, the impact of further reductions in the incidence of smoking could be significant.

Such wide-ranging views make it difficult for trustees and actuaries to decide what allowance to make for future improvements in longevity. However, the Pensions Regulator's guidance on mortality assumptions for scheme-specific funding (see Section 20) states that, in its view, these should be chosen prudently, specifically requiring an allowance for prudence in the base table rather than necessarily in the allowance for future improvements.

MANAGING THE RISK

The requirement for 'prudence' means that trustees need to consider carefully whether they remain comfortable with the assumptions made at previous funding valuations. For many schemes, significant changes have already been made to the mortality assumptions, leading to a significant increase in the calculated value of their liabilities.

One way of reducing the longevity risk a scheme faces is by changing benefit design. This might involve moving away from the traditional defined benefit structure, for future service, to:

- defined contribution

- cash balance, where a lump sum based on service and salary is used to purchase pension based on conversion terms that can change over time, *or*

- defined benefit, but where the accrual rate depends on population life expectancy, so that the longevity risk is shared with members.

Purchasing annuities with an insurance company removes the longevity risk entirely, but this can be expected to be more expensive in the long term than paying pensions from the scheme itself (because the insurer will look to charge a price for taking on the risk). Some financial institutions are now offering longevity swaps whereby the issuer pays the scheme an amount of money each year based on the difference (for a reference population or for the scheme itself) between the actual survivorship and what this was predicted to be. Trustees therefore receive money when fewer pensioners than expected die, and pay money to the issuer when more pensioners than expected die *(see Section 25)*.

In the future, it may also be possible for schemes to reduce their longevity risk by investing in 'longevity bonds'. These would run for a specified term, paying out an amount of money that reduced each year in line with the survivorship of a specified reference population.

THE PENSION PROTECTION FUND AND LEVY

The Pension Protection Fund (PPF) was formally established under the Pensions Act 2004 and commenced on 6 April 2005, with the aim, in the words of the Government, of 'guaranteeing members a specified minimum level of pension when the sponsoring employer becomes insolvent'. It is run by the Board of the Pension Protection Fund, which includes a Chairman, Chief Executive, and (at the time of writing) eleven other members.

The PPF covers eligible schemes where an insolvency event occurs to the employer on or after 6 April 2005. Schemes already in wind-up on that date are not covered by the PPF. The PPF is not underwritten by the Government, but is funded by levies on eligible schemes *(see below)*. A separate Financial Assistance Scheme (FAS) provides assistance to members of schemes that went into wind-up between 1 January 1997 and 5 April 2005 *(see below)*. The Fraud Compensation Fund became the responsibility of the Board of the PPF from 1 September 2005 *and is also discussed below*; previously it had been the responsibility of a separate Pensions Compensation Board.

ADMISSION

The principle of the PPF is that the Board will 'assume responsibility' for 'eligible schemes' if their assets immediately before the insolvency event are insufficient to cover the 'protected liabilities' *(see below)*. 'Eligible schemes' excludes, in particular, pure money purchase schemes. 'Assuming responsibility' entails the Board taking over the assets of the scheme and paying members the benefits provided under the 'pension compensation provisions'. The trustees are discharged from their obligations to pay benefits and administer the scheme.

The assessment period

During the 'assessment period', the Board will determine whether or not the scheme is eligible. This period begins with the employer's insolvency (or, in certain circumstances, with either the trustees' application for the Board to assume responsibility or a notification from the Pensions Regulator to the same effect). The legislation contains a lot of detail on the process for notifying insolvency events and confirming whether or not a 'scheme rescue' is possible (if, for example, the employer can continue as an ongoing concern).

An actuarial valuation on a prescribed basis has to be carried out to determine whether or not the scheme has sufficient assets to cover the 'protected liabilities' (i.e. the cost of securing the benefits provided for under the pension compensation provisions, together with any non-benefit-related liabilities and the estimated costs of wind-up). Once the Board has approved the valuation, normally either it will proceed to assume responsibility and issue a formal 'transfer notice' to the trustees, or (if there are sufficient assets to meet the protected liabilities) the trustees must proceed with winding up. In the latter case, the trustees can make an application to the Board for reconsideration. Where winding up takes place, this may be subject to directions made by the Board and/or the Regulator.

During an assessment period, lots of restrictions apply. Further benefits may not accrue and further contributions may not be made. Normally, transfers out are not permitted and a wind-up cannot be started. Benefit payments must be restricted to those payable under the pension compensation provisions. The Board can also give directions to the trustees regarding, for example, scheme investment.

The assessment period ends when the 'transfer notice' is served, or when the Board ceases to be involved with the scheme, or if the scheme winds up. Reasons for the Board ceasing to be involved include a scheme rescue and a refusal to assume responsibility for the scheme because it has been set up to exploit the PPF. A transfer notice cannot be given until the assessment period has run for at least a year.

Closed schemes

Schemes that are too well funded to be taken on by the PPF but are too big to be able to find an insurer to buy out the liabilities must apply to the Board to continue as 'closed schemes'. These closed schemes would then be subject to the same restrictions on contributions and accrual of benefits, and to directions from the Board, that apply during an assessment period. Closed schemes are required to undertake regular valuations and, if at some point the assets have fallen below the value of the PPF liabilities, the PPF will then assume responsibility.

COMPENSATION

The admissible rules

The starting point for determining the benefits payable to members under the pension compensation provisions is the scheme's 'admissible rules'. Essentially, this means the rules as at the assessment date (i.e. the start of the assessment period), but disregarding rule changes within the previous three years that would increase the level of PPF compensation. Discretionary pension increases within the same period are also excluded, unless they do not exceed the increase in the RPI since the pension was last increased. Discretionary early retirement pensions that came into payment under a rule that is to be disregarded may have to cease, and the Board can review – and, if necessary, adjust – ill-health pensions granted in the last three years.

Members' and dependants' benefits

Members over NPA at the assessment date and ill-health pensioners are entitled to 100% of the benefits under their scheme's admissible rules. Payments made by the scheme during the assessment period are offset from the PPF compensation. Members under NPA, including those already receiving pension, are entitled to 90% of accrued benefits under the admissible rules.

A future widow or widower is entitled to 50% of the pension payable to the member (unless the admissible rules had no provision for a survivor's pension). A 'relevant partner' (of either sex, living with the member as 'man and wife') has the same entitlement. Benefits for children are payable until age 18 (or 25 in some circumstances); their amount depends on the number of children and on whether or not there is a widow, widower or relevant partner.

The Pensions Act 2008 provides for PPF compensation to be shared on divorce, in a similar way to occupational pension scheme benefits, but, at the time of writing, these provisions are not yet in force.

The compensation cap

For members whose compensation is subject to the 90% restriction, the initial rate of compensation is limited to a stipulated 'maximum permitted rate' at the date benefits come into payment. For 2009/10, a maximum pension of £28,743 p.a. at age 65 will apply. The level of this 'cap' increases in line with earnings each year. The Board has set adjustment factors to derive amounts applicable where benefits come into payment at ages above and below 65.

Revaluation and indexation

Benefits not in payment and accrued before 6 April 2009 are revalued between the assessment date and NPA (or earlier retirement) in line with RPI increases or, if lower, by 5% p.a. The 5% p.a. limit is reduced to 2.5% p.a. in respect of benefits accrued from 6 April 2009. This reflects the change in the statutory requirement for scheme revaluation *(see Section 15)*.

A new provision to deal with 'non-revaluing benefits' was introduced from 1 April 2009. Under this, PPF compensation benefits are not revalued, but only where the scheme provides no revaluation to any member in any circumstances.

For deferred pensioners, revaluation between date of leaving and assessment date is based on the scheme rules.

Benefits in payment are increased in line with RPI increases or, if lower, 2.5%. Increases apply only to benefits attributable to service from 6 April 1997.

Options

Lump sum commutation, of up to 25% of benefits, is permitted using factors specified by the Board. Early payment of benefits after age 50 (to be increased to 55 by no later than April 2010) is permitted subject to actuarial reduction using factors specified by the Board. Trivial commutation and terminal ill-health lump sums are also available in certain circumstances.

Adjustments by the Board

Where the scheme rules are such that the appropriate compensation benefits cannot be determined in accordance with the legislation, the Board can decide the level of compensation that will apply to members.

The Board has the ability (after consultation) to adjust the rates of revaluation and increases in payment if necessary. If both of these have been reduced to zero they can recommend that the Secretary of State reduce the 90% and/or 100% levels of compensation. Such reductions would only apply in 'extreme circumstances'.

VALUATIONS

The introduction of the PPF has given rise to two new types of actuarial valuation.

Levy valuation

A 'section 179 valuation', carried out by the scheme actuary, is required to determine the PPF levy payable by a scheme. The deadline for submitting the first such valuation was 31 March 2008. Subsequent valuations are needed at intervals of no more than three years.

For the purposes of the valuation, assets are generally taken at the value shown in the scheme's audited accounts.

Liabilities are valued, using assumptions set out in guidance issued by the Board, to reflect the estimated cost of 'buying out' the benefits with an insurance company. The benefits valued are broadly those provided under the scheme's rules, but allowing for members under NPA receiving 90% (not 100%) of benefits, the compensation cap, and the PPF levels of revaluation, indexation and spouse's pension.

Entry valuation

A 'section 143 valuation' is required by the Board of the PPF to determine whether or not it should assume responsibility for a scheme. The Board will obtain it from the trustees, who will usually ask the scheme actuary to carry it out. It has to be obtained as soon as reasonably practicable after the insolvency event. Assets are generally taken at the value shown in the audited accounts. Liabilities are valued using assumptions set out in guidance issued by the Board (which are similar to those for levy valuations), but the actual PPF compensation benefits are taken into account, rather than the broad approximations used in the section 179 valuation.

LEVIES

Schemes that are eligible for future entry to the PPF may be required to pay three PPF levies. These are charged in respect of each levy year, which begins on 1 April.

Pension Protection Levy

The Pension Protection Levy consists of two parts: the *risk-based levy* (which must represent at least 80% of the total collected from all schemes) and the *scheme-based levy*. There are limits each year on the total estimated levy and the amount by which it can increase. These limits can only be changed by the Secretary of State following consultation and with the approval of the Treasury.

For 2009/10, the PPF intends to collect £700 million. This is line with the PPF's 2007 commitment that for 2008/09 and the following two years the total levy amount would remain stable, subject only to increases in line with average earnings.

The risk-based levy is based on:

(a) The *assumed probability of insolvency of the employer* (or a weighted average probability for multi-employer schemes), derived by assigning the employer to 1 of 100 risk bands corresponding to failure scores calculated by Dun & Bradstreet.

(b) *Underfunding risk*. This is calculated as a specified percentage of the scheme's estimated PPF liabilities, the percentage depending on the funding level revealed by the levy valuation *(see above)*. Where the funding level is 120% or lower, the underfunding risk is the difference between 121% and the funding level. A sliding scale applies for funding levels between 120% and 140%, and the underfunding risk (and hence the risk-based levy) is zero for funding levels of 140% or above.

A scaling factor (2.22 for 2009/10) equates the proposed levy estimate with the estimated risk exposure across all schemes. The risk-based levy is capped (at 1% of estimated PPF liabilities for 2009/10) in order to protect the weakest levy payers. The Board also reduces the risk-based levy if a scheme voluntarily submits details of:

- *deficit reduction contributions*, over and above the cost of accruing scheme benefits, made since the valuation date as certified by the scheme actuary – this reduces the underfunding risk, *and*
- *contingent assets* (if in a standard form and legally binding) that produce cash for the scheme when an insolvency event occurs in relation to the employer – this reduces the underfunding risk or the assumed insolvency probability, depending on the type of contingent asset.

The scheme-based levy is based on a percentage of the scheme's estimated PPF liabilities – the scheme-based levy multiplier (0.0162% for 2009/10).

At the time of writing, the PPF had given a firm indication that, for 2010/11, the levy estimate would be £720 million, and the scaling factor and scheme-based multiplier 1.64 and 0.0145% respectively.

In November 2008, the PPF published a consultation document on the future development of the levy. It proposed a new formula which would take account of short-term underfunding and insolvency probability, and the contribution to losses in adverse scenarios over a longer term. It also included a simple allowance for investment risk. In its July 2009 response to the consultation, the PPF recognised that there were concerns about key elements of the proposals. It announced that a steering group of industry representatives would formulate new proposals, to be consulted on in early 2010 and implemented no earlier than 2012/13.

PPF Administration Levy

This is charged to meet the costs of establishing and running the PPF (other than the cost of paying compensation). It is based on the number of members on the last day of the scheme year which ended before the beginning of the previous levy year.

PPF Ombudsman Levy

The legislation provides for regulations to be made for a levy to be charged to meet the operating costs of the PPF Ombudsman. There has been very little PPF

Ombudsman activity to date, and the regulations have not been made, therefore no levy has yet been charged.

FRAUD COMPENSATION FUND

An occupational pension scheme that has lost assets as a result of an offence (such as theft or fraud) committed after 6 April 1997 may be eligible for compensation if the employer is insolvent. The amount of any compensation payment is determined by the Board, and is limited to the amount of any loss that cannot reasonably be recovered. Applications for compensation may be made by the trustees, administrators or scheme members.

The Fund is financed by a Fraud Compensation Levy, potentially payable by all schemes eligible for this compensation (a wider group than for the PPF). Regulations cap the levy, at present, at 23 pence per member. The levy is only charged as and when needed, however, and no charge has been made since 2004/05.

FINANCIAL ASSISTANCE SCHEME

The Financial Assistance Scheme (FAS) was established on 1 September 2005, following the Government's announcement that £400 million of public money would be made available, released over 20 years, to support workers who lost pensions through company insolvency but who were not covered by the PPF. Though originally intended as an 'assistance' (rather than compensation) scheme, after successive changes, the levels of benefit are now similar to those under the PPF. The FAS has also been extended to cover some schemes with solvent employers.

CEASING ACCRUAL

This section sets out the issues that employers and trustees need to consider before stopping any further benefits building up in a final salary arrangement.

In recent years, many final salary arrangements have been closed to new members, with new employees instead being offered membership of a defined contribution (DC) arrangement or a defined benefit (DB) arrangement with lower costs and/or risks to the employer (e.g. CARE or cash balance: *see Section 7*). Current employees have generally continued to build up final salary benefits with these new benefit arrangements typically applying to new joiners only.

However, it is becoming more common for employers to go further and stop final salary benefits for all their employees. This is referred to as 'ceasing accrual'.

Ceasing accrual is not a simple exercise. There are a number of actions that have to be carried out by law, and others that employers may want to go through in order to maintain good employee relations. The process will require a significant amount of planning and involve a number of functions within the employer as well as other parties. Careful due diligence and good project management is important in order to identify potential issues and to set a realistic timeframe.

CONSIDERATIONS FOR EMPLOYERS

Business case

The main reason for ceasing accrual is usually to reduce the significant cost of pension benefits. However, employers may need to be able to justify the need for these cost savings to affected employees and other parties such as trade unions and the pension scheme trustees. These parties will often want to ensure that the employer has considered a range of possible options and be satisfied that ceasing accrual is a reasonable solution in the relevant circumstances. Many employers propose moving members to a DC scheme to achieve these cost savings. But it may be possible to arrive at similar cost savings by retaining a DB structure, and making a combination of changes to the benefits that are offered (e.g. moving from final salary to CARE, reducing the accrual rate, increasing member contributions etc).

Immediate financial savings may not be the only consideration. Employers may want to reduce the risk that the costs turn out to be higher than expected over the longer term. This would involve passing some or all of the risks inherent in a pension arrangement on to members.

Employers may also want to ensure that all employees are treated equally, irrespective of their length of service. If a final salary arrangement closed to new members a few years ago, the overall cost of a DC arrangement set up for new employees may have been designed to be similar to the cost of the final salary arrangement at that time. Now, because of increases in longevity and falling gilt yields, the expected cost of new benefits in the final salary arrangement is likely to be significantly higher than the cost of such a DC scheme. This means that the overall employment cost of two employees in identical jobs and on otherwise identical terms can be significantly different depending on when they joined the employer. This can lead to claims of a 'two-tier workforce'.

In proposing changes, employers should always bear in mind that they have a legal obligation to act in 'good faith' in dealings with employees.

Design of future benefits

Employers will need to consider what pension benefits they will offer to members to replace their final salary benefits. If an employer has already set up a new arrangement for employees who joined after a certain date, then it may want to move all employees to this arrangement. However, the employer will want to ensure that this arrangement continues to be appropriate.

In many cases, employees are moved into a DC arrangement. However, this can be seen as moving from one extreme to the other (with the member, rather than the employer, bearing all the risks). Some employers may consider that sharing risks to some extent is a more desirable outcome.

The accounting impact of both ceasing accrual in the DB arrangement, and the new benefit structure, will need to be considered *(see Section 27)*. The savings in cash terms are unlikely to be the same as the savings in accounting terms, and in some cases there could actually be an adverse effect on the employer's profit and loss account.

There are a number of other issues in changing benefit structures, particularly if moving from final salary to DC:

- whether the new arrangement should be under the same trust as the final salary arrangement: there can be complex issues including implications for funding cross-subsidies, contracting out and winding up

- benefits payable on death or ill health cannot be funded in a DC arrangement in the same way that they can in a DB arrangement: advice on appropriate insurance arrangements will be needed and the costs should be considered

- final salary arrangements have more flexibility to provide extra benefits in cases of redundancy and other workforce management exercises: DC arrangements are less flexible, and employers will need to consider how to provide such benefits, particularly if these are contractual entitlements

- there are additional considerations for executive benefits:
  ○ employers will need to consider whether the new arrangement will provide appropriate remuneration for senior employees or whether additional benefits need to be provided through a separate arrangement
  ○ new arrangements for executives might be subject to the Special Annual Allowance Charge *(see Section 13)*, particularly if higher contribution levels apply, *and*

- in order to avoid having to review pension arrangements again in a few years' time, employers should consider whether the proposed new arrangement will meet the minimum requirements to avoid also having to enrol employees in the Personal Accounts scheme from 2012 *(see Section 9)*.

Design of accrued benefits

There may also be various ways in which active members' benefits in respect of past service can be calculated. For example, depending on scheme rules, the employer may have the following options for increasing pension between date of implementation and retirement:

- statutory minimum increases in line with leaving service benefits
- increases in line with price inflation, *or*
- maintaining full salary linking.

This is an area in which legal advice is particularly important – *see below*.

If the scheme is contracted-out immediately before benefit accrual ceases, contracting-out legislation requires that a 'Protection Rule' is added to the scheme rules to ensure that any contracted-out benefits retained within the scheme (GMPs and post-1997 contracted-out rights) are protected at normal pension age and on death from being franked against benefits accrued during periods of non-contracted-out pensionable service. Separate anti-franking legislation requires GMPs to be protected at and after the age at which GMP becomes payable (65 for men and 60 for women).

Consultation and communication with employees

Ceasing accrual is a 'listed change' under the Pensions Act 2004 consultation requirements *(see Section 7)*. Employers will therefore have to carry out a 60-day consultation with affected members or their representatives and consider any representations made during the consultation before they can implement any changes. This process could take significantly longer than 60 days, particularly if member representative groups need to be set up.

Many employers will want to do more than the legal minimum, and put in place a detailed communication strategy to ensure members understand the reasons for change, the effect on their final salary benefits built up to date, and the likely benefits they will receive from the new arrangement. For many members, the headline is likely to be a significant reduction in their projected benefits at retirement. However the detailed implications will affect individual members in different ways.

In the case of a new DC arrangement, employers may wish to encourage former DB members to take more responsibility than they have in the past for ensuring their benefits will meet their needs at retirement. This is likely to involve taking decisions relating to the level of contributions paid and their investment options. Employers may want to provide a range of information to employees about this, reflecting the level of financial literacy of the workforce.

Legal issues

There are a number of areas where employers will need to take legal advice.

Members' employment contracts will need to be reviewed. This is to check how membership of the pension scheme is described. For example, some contracts give the right to membership of a final salary pension scheme. Some contracts may also contain individual pension promises.

The scheme's trust deed and rules should be consulted and may need amendment. They should be checked to ensure that the scheme does not restrict the types of amendment that can be made. If trustee consent is required for any amendment, the trustees may see this as an opportunity for negotiation *(see below)*.

One specific issue may arise if the employer wishes to break the link to final salary for accrued benefits. Case law has suggested that the wording of some trust deeds and rules may require members' benefits to be calculated by reference to their salary when they leave or retire from the employer. In such cases it would not be possible to calculate benefits using the member's salary at the date accrual ceases in the scheme. This may reduce the cost savings the employer would otherwise make.

In some cases, amending the scheme rules or members leaving the scheme as a result of ceasing accrual may trigger a wind-up *(see Section 24)* or a debt on the employer *(see Section 26)*. This could have significant financial implications, and the employer will usually want to ensure that the changes are carried out in such a way as to avoid this.

Other issues

If the current arrangement is contracted out of S2P but the new arrangement is not, the scheme employer will need to carry out the necessary actions in order to cease to contract out *(see Section 6)*. In particular, this requires the employer to give members, trustees and trade unions at least one month's notice of the intention to cease contracting out (or three months if there are trade unions involved who do not agree to a shorter period). Such a notice must include certain prescribed items of information.

There are additional considerations if the scheme has any ex-public sector workers, or if the employer might consider bidding for public sector outsourcing contracts in the future. Employers may be required to offer a certain level of DB pensions to ex-public sector workers. It is not always easy to identify ex-public sector workers, particularly if they have joined the scheme as a result of subsequent transactions between private sector companies.

CONSIDERATIONS FOR TRUSTEES

Trustees' duty

The conventionally accepted view is that trustees' primary duty is to safeguard accrued rights, and that it is the employer's role to decide the basis of pension benefits it wishes to provide to its employees for future service.

However, as well as protecting members' existing benefits, trustees will want to satisfy themselves that the employer's business case for any proposal to cease accrual is properly reasoned, the proposals are workable in practice, and that they do not breach any legal obligations. Trustees should also bear in mind that they need to consider the interests of all members of the scheme, not just the active members who will be directly affected by the ceasing of future accrual.

As noted above, if trustee consent is required in order to amend the scheme to allow the ceasing of future accrual, the trustees may use this as an opportunity for negotiation with the employer over funding, security of benefits, and even benefits themselves. The trustees may need to take legal advice, particularly where their trust deed and rules provides them with a power to veto changes to future benefits.

Safeguarding accrued rights

The issue of ceasing accrual may be raised during the valuation process *(see Section 20)*. The scheme funding regulations allow trustees to modify future accrual if it appears to them that it is not otherwise possible to obtain the employer's agreement. Alternatively, the issue may be raised by the employer during funding negotiations.

The trustees will need to consider whether a proposal to cease accrual, and the background to such a proposal, reflects a weakening in the employer's covenant – its ability and willingness to continue to fund the scheme *(see Section 20)*. This could have implications for the level of technical provisions the trustees consider necessary to safeguard accrued rights.

Even if the proposal is not made as part of the valuation process, the trustees will need to consider the effect of ceasing accrual on the funding position of the scheme *(see Section 20)*. This will include considering whether the current funding plan remains appropriate.

Ceasing accrual brings forward the possibility of winding up the scheme and buying out the liabilities with an insurance company. This may still be many years in the future, but once accrual has ceased there will come a time when it is more effective for the trustees to discharge their liabilities in this way, rather than continuing to invest funds and paying benefits themselves. Trustees might start to consider a 'flight plan' – a time scale with actions they need to take to achieve that ultimate objective. The main issues to consider will be investment and funding strategies. The employer may want to have input into these discussions.

Trustees are also likely to consider moving to a less risky investment strategy over time, as the proportion of the scheme's liabilities that relates to pensions in payment rises. This will have implications for funding assumptions. Trustees may also have to pay closer attention to cashflow requirements, and the disinvestment of assets. Buying out portions of the liabilities over time *(see Section 25)* or purchasing longevity swaps to reduce risk *(see Section 21)* may also be considered.

Any changes to the adopted funding principles are likely to require a review of actuarial factors, such as commutation and early retirement terms, as well as transfer value assumptions. The employer's consent may be required to change some factors.

Benefit changes

As part of any negotiation with the employer, trustees may decide it is appropriate to suggest alternative future benefits. As the employer's proposals are likely to be aimed at cutting costs, the scope for alternative approaches may be limited. Trade unions and representations from members may also suggest approaches which partially offset the removal of members' final salary benefits.

Administration and communication

If the new pension arrangement is being set up under the same trust, the trustees will need to consider how the administration of two separate benefit structures for the same members will work, and ensure that administration systems can cope with the new benefits. Trustees will need training to understand their responsibilities and the features of the new benefits with which they are not familiar.

Trustees may want to be involved in the employer's communication process, to ensure that the employer is explaining the issues clearly and properly. Once any changes have been implemented, trustees may want to review how they communicate with members more generally.

SCHEME CLOSURE AND WIND-UP

The winding up of occupational pension schemes can raise complex legal and practical issues. The process can take several years, although legislation was introduced from April 2002 with the intention of speeding it up. The trustees of a scheme that is being wound up need to understand their continuing responsibilities under the relevant provisions of the trust deed and rules, and should take legal and actuarial advice where appropriate.

Commencement of wind-up

The events that can trigger wind-up are normally set out in the scheme trust deed and rules. These can include the employer ceasing to contribute (or not being prepared to contribute at a rate the trustees consider adequate for funding the scheme), or becoming insolvent. However, the scheme rules may allow the alternative of postponing wind-up, and instead continuing to operate on a 'closed' fund basis. The trustees have an overriding power under the Pensions Act 1995 to choose to follow this route if the employer has gone into liquidation and they consider it appropriate. Continuing as a closed fund would be subject to neither the Pensions Regulator nor, if the employer is insolvent and a PPF assessment period (*see Section 22*) has been completed, the PPF Board requiring the scheme to be wound up.

It is important for the date on which wind-up is treated as having commenced to be clearly identified and recorded. This can vary depending on the circumstances, but for most purposes can be taken as the earliest date when there are no members in pensionable service and either (i) the scheme rules provide that wind-up should commence or (ii) the power to wind up is exercised by the trustees (or by any other person or body, such as the Pensions Regulator or a court, having the authority to do so).

Winding-up procedure

Regulations effective from 24 July 2006 imposed additional requirements on trustees of underfunded occupational schemes entering wind-up. In particular, the trustees of a scheme that enters wind-up during a recovery period (*see Section 20*) must as soon as practicable prepare a 'winding-up procedure'. This procedure includes details of the action that will be taken to establish the liabilities and the method that will be used to discharge them, an indication of any accrued rights or benefits that are likely to be affected by a reduction in actuarial value, and an estimate of the amount of time that will be taken to complete these steps. The procedure must be submitted to the Pensions Regulator.

Schemes in wind-up are generally exempt from the scheme funding requirements (*see Section 20*).

Appointment of an independent trustee and role of the Pensions Regulator

If the employer has become insolvent, the insolvency practitioner (or, if applicable, official receiver) must notify the Pensions Regulator. The Regulator then has the power to appoint an independent trustee although he does not have to do this (e.g. if one has already been appointed).

Subject to various safeguards relating to members' rights, the Regulator may modify a scheme with a view to ensuring that it is properly wound up following an application from the trustees (which must include specified information and documents). He may also order a scheme to be wound up, or give legally binding directions to trustees, administrators and others if he considers that these are necessary to speed up the process. In June 2008, the Regulator, the PPF and the DWP (on behalf of the Financial Assistance Scheme) published a joint statement saying that they expect the important parts of a wind-up should generally be completed within a two-year period. The Regulator has also published guidance that sets out examples of good practice in order to help schemes through the winding-up process.

Debt on the employer

Where a defined benefit scheme has insufficient assets to cover the scheme liabilities, the employer may have a legal obligation to make up the shortfall. For wind-ups starting on or after 15 February 2005, the liabilities for this purpose must be based on an estimate of the actual cost of buying out benefits and meeting the expenses of wind-up. For wind-ups that commenced before this date, the liabilities in respect of some or all of the benefits may instead be determined on the MFR (Minimum Funding Requirement) basis *(see Section 20)*, depending on when the wind-up commenced and on whether or not the employer was insolvent.

If the wind-up was 'triggered' by an 'insolvency event' of the sponsoring employer, any 'debt on the employer' must be treated by the trustees as having arisen immediately before this occurred. Otherwise, the debt can be treated by the trustees as having arisen at *any* time after the commencement of wind-up and before the employer goes into liquidation.

Discharging scheme liabilities

In order to wind up a scheme, its assets must be applied to discharge its liabilities. This can be done by transfer to another occupational scheme or to personal pensions, by purchasing insurance company annuities *(see Section 25)*, by assigning existing annuity contracts to members or, in certain cases where the entitlement is small, by the payment of a 'winding-up lump sum' *(see Section 12)*.

Priority order

Because of the possibility that the assets will be insufficient to fully discharge all liabilities in this way, scheme rules normally contain a 'priority order' setting out the order in which the different liability classes (e.g. pensions already in payment, accrued pensions of active members) are to be dealt with. However, with effect from 6 April 1997, such 'scheme-specific' priority orders have, in the case of defined benefit schemes, been overridden by the statutory priority order set out in the Pensions Act 1995 and modified by subsequent legislation. For the purpose of assigning them to appropriate priority classes, scheme liabilities are normally treated as having 'crystallised' according to their status at the date when wind-up commenced.

For wind-ups commencing on or after 6 April 2005, the statutory priority order is as follows:

(1) benefits under certain contracts of insurance

(2) benefits corresponding to those that would be provided if the scheme entered the Pension Protection Fund *(see Section 22)*

(3) benefits from AVCs, to the extent that these are not included in the categories above

(4) all other liabilities.

Any money purchase assets and liabilities are generally excluded from the above calculations. Such benefits would normally be expected to have priority over non-money purchase benefits, but this is dependent on the scheme rules. The classification of certain benefits as money purchase or non-money purchase is also the subject of much legal debate.

The liabilities set out in the statutory priority order must be valued by the scheme actuary using a specified basis. If the wind-up commenced on or after 15 February 2005, the basis used is the actual cost of securing the benefits, for example by means of an annuity buy-out. For earlier wind-ups, the basis used – depending on when the wind-up commenced and whether or not the employer was insolvent – may be either the MFR *(see Section 20)* or the actual cost of securing the benefits, in a similar but not identical way to the debt on the employer calculation *(see above)*.

Where wind-up commenced before 15 February 2005, any assets remaining, once all of the statutory liabilities have been dealt with, can be applied according to the priority order in the scheme rules to discharge (so far as possible) any remaining scheme liabilities. In practice, this includes any extra money needed to meet the full cost of buying out a benefit, where that benefit has been valued on the (lower) MFR basis for the purposes of the statutory priority order.

Deficiency

Where the full 'buy-out' debt basis *(see above)* does not apply, or such a debt cannot be collected, the assets of the scheme may be insufficient to discharge all of the scheme's liabilities. In this event, the benefits provided for the lowest priority class(es) will have to be cut back accordingly. Legislation was amended in 2009 to allow schemes in wind-up to reduce pensions already in payment, due to underfunding, without giving rise to unauthorised payments charges *(see Section 12)*.

The Pension Protection Fund (PPF) *(see Section 22)* was established with effect from 6 April 2005. It provides some protection for eligible schemes with employers that become insolvent on or after that date. The Financial Assistance Scheme *(see Section 22)* was established to provide some support for workers who have lost pensions through underfunding in schemes that went into wind-up between 1 January 1997 and 5 April 2005, and are not covered by the PPF.

Surplus

If a surplus of assets remains after all of the scheme liabilities have been discharged, this must also be dealt with in accordance with the scheme rules and relevant legal requirements. As well as providing for the augmentation of benefits, either at the sole discretion of the trustees, or in consultation with (or with the consent of) the employer, there may be provision for payment of a refund to the employer. Before this can be done, a number of requirements under the Pensions Act 1995 (as amended by the 2004 Act) must be satisfied. These requirements include sending written notices to members inviting them to make representations in respect of the proposal.

Previously, there was a requirement that Limited Price Indexation (LPI) increases be provided on *all* current and future scheme pensions (other than GMPs and money purchase benefits) before a refund could be paid to the employer. This requirement was removed with effect from 6 April 2006.

Disclosure and reporting requirements

A notice must be given to members within one month of the commencement of wind-up, followed by annual progress reports. For defined benefit schemes, members must also be provided with details of the trustees' proposals for discharging liabilities before they are implemented. In all cases, once the assets have been applied to provide benefits, members must be given full details within three months.

Periodic progress reports must also be given to the Pensions Regulator. Where wind-up commences on or after 1 April 2003, the first such report must be filed within three months of the third anniversary of commencement of wind-up. Where wind-up commences on or after 1 October 2007, the report must be filed within three months of the second anniversary of the commencement of wind-up. *(See also Section 17.)*

Operating as a closed scheme

The process of winding up can take several years. In the meantime the scheme will continue to operate as a closed scheme. During this period, trustees may pay provisional benefits to members on retirement, with final benefits to be confirmed when winding up is complete. From 6 April 2005, however, DWP legislation specifically provides for benefits paid during the winding-up period to be reduced in line with what the priority order will ultimately require *(see above)*. Trustees should also review the terms for member options and the scheme's investment strategy to ensure they remain appropriate, particularly if the employer has become insolvent. It is possible to apply to the Pensions Regulator for permission to delay paying cash equivalent transfer values.

It is important for the trustees to receive legal and actuarial advice throughout this period.

Schemes also sometimes operate as 'closed schemes' (with no further accrual of benefits) *without* having started a winding-up process. Also, the phrase 'closed scheme' is sometimes used to describe a scheme which no longer permits new entrants to join, but which allows existing members to continue accruing future service benefits.

BUY-OUT

In *Section 24*, scheme closure and wind-up is described. It is in this context that one typically associated the concept of pensions buy-out – as a means of discharging a scheme's liabilities prior to wind-up. However, in the last few years, the market for what are now described as 'buy-outs' encompasses many new products and the market has expanded rapidly.

In fact, the term 'buy-out' is now sometimes used to describe non-insurance options – pension regulatory environment (PRE) insurers offer models that involve a new company becoming the sponsoring employer of a scheme. As such, the pension promises remain under schemes subject to pensions legislation (particularly funding legislation – *see Section 20*), rather than being contracts with insurers, subject to the authority of the FSA (and in particular the more stringent reserving requirements that apply to insurance companies). These models have attracted the attention of the Government, which has increased the powers of the Regulator to counteract any undesirable consequences of such innovations.

Increased competitiveness in the insured buy-out market led to more attractive pricing and the development of options such as partial buy-outs and 'buy-ins'. Though pricing has subsequently hardened, these options may remain attractive for some schemes.

Other non-insurance products continue to be developed. In 2009, the first longevity hedge agreement was announced. These agreements can be used by trustees as part of a 'synthetic' or 'DIY' buy-out.

These developments have arisen as a result of employers becoming increasingly sensitive to the risks associated with defined benefit schemes and the potential impact on their financial statements *(see Section 27)*. There is increasing focus on managing these risks, including interest rate, inflation and longevity risks – recent increases in life expectancy have increased the cost of providing pensions *(see Section 21)*. Though the recent economic downturn has seen a decline in buy-out market activity since September 2008, the market appears likely to be sustained by the demand from trustees and companies for de-risking solutions.

BUY-OUT OPTIONS

The following describes the main buy-out alternatives available for pension schemes. Within each subheading below there are a number of options that continue to be developed to give schemes more flexibility.

Full buy-out

In the past, full buy-out was associated with the wind-up of a pension scheme. Annuities would be purchased from an insurance company for current pensioners and deferred annuities for other members. It would represent part of what was often (and still can be) a protracted wind-up process.

The buy-out exercise itself can take a significant time, as historic issues, such as incomplete data, may take years to resolve.

As required in a wind-up, liabilities are discharged from the scheme – the annuities purchased are in members' names. This means of discharging liabilities has been associated with schemes of insolvent employers. However, solvent employers have used this means to achieve a 'clean break' with their pension schemes. In some cases, this has been done via an intermediate stage by using a PRE Insurer – *see below*.

Partial buy-out

A partial buy-out allows for the discharge of some of the liabilities of a pension scheme. As with a full buy-out, annuity policies are purchased from an insurance company in the names of scheme members. They become policyholders of the insurer, ceasing to be members of the scheme. Typically, such transactions are 'pensioner buy-outs'; annuities for current pensioners are usually relatively less costly than deferred annuities, and these buy-outs can represent good value to sponsoring employers.

As with full buy-out, this may prove to be a lengthy exercise during which issues such as incomplete data have to be resolved. However, in exchange for an additional premium, insurers have been willing to take on liabilities where the data quality is less than ideal and accept the risk that data issues will subsequently increase liabilities.

Buy-in

As an alternative to pensioner buy-outs, many pension schemes have used 'pensioner buy-ins' to insure their pensioner liabilities. The trustees purchase an insurance policy which is intended to match the liabilities closely, but not necessarily exactly. Hence, for example, where there are issues with data quality or where discretionary pension increases may be given, any further liability is not covered by the insurer.

Such transactions are typically quicker to implement. The membership of the scheme is not affected – the individuals remain scheme members and the liability to pay their benefits remains with the scheme's trustees. The insurance policy can be regarded as an investment, which matches the corresponding liability more closely than alternative assets.

Pension Regulatory Environment (PRE) Insurers

Where full buy-out is the objective, but there is a desire to avoid the potentially lengthy process of wind-up, some insurance companies have structured offers to allow an immediate clean break by offering an intermediate non-insurance solution. For example, a subsidiary of the insurer may first replace the scheme's employer, or the assets and liabilities of the scheme are transferred to a new pension scheme sponsored by the insurer. Annuity policies are purchased with the insurance company itself at a later date, hence achieving full buy-out. In some cases, the insurer may take steps to reduce the eventual buy-out liabilities, for example by offering members the option to transfer their benefits out of the scheme.

The providers of these intermediate arrangements can be considered PRE insurers – the pension promises remain subject to pensions legislation, benefiting from the protection offered by the Pension Protection Fund (see Section 22), rather than being individual contracts with insurers, which are protected under the Financial Services Compensation Scheme (see Section 28).

An alternative model involves a company (perhaps the parent company of an insurer) taking on a company's pension liabilities, by, for example, purchasing the company, retaining the pension scheme and selling on the majority of the company. However, the benefits are not expected to be bought out with an insurer and, as such, this does not represent an insurance solution.

The most high-profile example of this to date involved the Telent pension scheme. In November 2007, Pensions Corporation bought Telent, the sponsor of the scheme. The trustees of the scheme asked the Pensions Regulator to intervene, as it felt a clear conflict of interest had arisen which had not been managed appropriately – see Section 10.

Subsequently, at least partly in reaction to such developments, the Pensions Act 2008 increased the Regulator's power to appoint trustees (see Section 11). The Act also extended the Regulator's powers to issue Contribution Notices and Financial Support Directions where there is a materially detrimental effect on the security of members' benefits. The Government stated that the new powers were particularly aimed at 'non-insured buy-outs' to ensure that members are protected in a changing environment without inhibiting innovation.

Synthetic buy-out

'Synthetic' or 'DIY' buy-outs, although lacking a number of the features of a traditional buy-out, have emerged as an important element of the buy-out market.

For many years, financial institutions – primarily investment banks and insurance companies – have provided protection against interest rate and inflation risks through the issue of 'swaps'. These require the purchaser to pay a series of cashflows (often fixed) over a period of time in return for a series of different cashflows that more closely reflect their own liabilities over that period (e.g. cashflows that increase in line with inflation). For pension schemes, the use of these swaps is similar to investment in bonds, but they can be structured much more flexibly to meet the estimated cashflows of a scheme.

Interest rate and inflation risks can be reduced significantly using swaps, leaving increasing longevity as the main risk remaining for a typical defined benefit pension scheme. 'Longevity swaps' can be used to reduce this risk. These allow the scheme to pay cashflows over a fixed period of time based on the expected longevity of a group of individuals, and receive cashflows over a period of time related to the actual longevity of that group. There are two main types of longevity swap for pension schemes:

(a) A bespoke longevity swap is based on the life expectancy of the actual members of a scheme. The provider agrees to meet the actual payments to members and the trustees pay a fixed schedule of payments to the provider. This removes the risk that members will live longer than expected. However, bespoke hedges are only available to relatively large schemes, and typically only those with a high proportion of pensioner members.

(b) An index-based longevity swap provides protection based on the general population rather than the scheme's membership. Therefore, the trustees retain a risk that members' longevity is not in line with that of the index population.

Schemes can therefore use a combination of swaps to replicate the effect of a buy-out or a buy-in – in return for a series of known payments (rather than a 'one-off' insurance premium) schemes can receive a series of payments to meet their (approximate) liabilities as they arise. This has become known as a 'synthetic' or 'DIY' buy-out.

THE BUY-OUT MARKET

At the end of 2005, there were two main players in the UK pensions buy-out market, typically insuring the liabilities of schemes in wind-up or of very small schemes. This equated to around £1 billion of business written each year.

In the following three years, dramatic expansion in the market saw more than 30 companies offering a range of options designed to transfer pension risk. There has been some consolidation, but although activity has reduced the market has remained competitive. In 2007, £3 billion of business was written, and in 2008, around £8 billion, but volumes of business in 2009, at the time of writing, have fallen significantly.

There have been a number of transactions of over £1 billion, including the buy-in of the pensioner liabilities of the Cable & Wireless pension scheme in September 2008 and the buy-out of the Thorn pension scheme in December 2008. In May 2009, Babcock International announced an agreement to a longevity swap for two of its pension schemes and around £800 million liabilities, the first UK schemes to enter such a deal.

SALES, PURCHASES & CORPORATE ACTIVITY

Background

The pensions aspects of corporate sales and acquisitions require careful consideration, particularly where defined benefit schemes are involved. All parties will need to take expert legal and actuarial advice. There may be considerable potential for conflicts of interest which will need to be identified and dealt with appropriately. This is particularly relevant in cases where scheme trustees have normally obtained advice from the same sources as the sponsoring employer.

TUPE

Employees' accrued rights are protected by the Preservation requirements under pensions legislation. The TUPE requirements protect the terms and conditions relating to future benefits for employees who are transferred as a consequence of a business transaction. Transferring employees entitled to occupational scheme benefits have to be provided with pension benefits by the new employer. Where the new employer offers defined contribution benefits (including a stakeholder scheme) he must pay contributions that match the employee's contributions, up to a maximum of 6% of basic pay. If the new employer offers a defined benefit scheme, it must *either*:

- satisfy the Reference Scheme Test (whether or not it is contracted-out), *or*
- provide for members to be entitled to benefits of a value equal to, or more than, the sum of 6% of pensionable pay for each year of employment and the total amount of contributions paid by the member.

Transferring employees with rights to pension schemes established under contract (such as group personal pension or stakeholder arrangements) may also have their current pension rights preserved by TUPE, depending on the terms of their contracts.

In some circumstances, early retirement terms and benefits may be preserved by TUPE requirements. Actuarial and legal advice should be taken on the issue and, in general, purchasers should seek appropriate indemnities against hidden liability.

PRICING PENSIONS IN THE DEAL

The cost of pension provision will have an impact on the pricing of most deals. Where manpower represents a material business cost and the deal is priced on the basis of future income, the purchaser should give full consideration to the future cost of providing appropriate pension benefits to acquired employees. It will also be necessary to consider the financial and employee-relations implications of mirroring or changing the previous level of benefits.

The purchaser may also take on defined benefit pension liabilities, for example by acquiring an entire pension scheme or accepting a 'bulk transfer' of accrued rights from part of a scheme *(see below)*. Actuarial advice would be required on the cost of taking on those liabilities compared to the assets on offer. The difference could be included in pricing the business.

The cost of and the responsibility for meeting any debt on the employer may also have to be allowed for *(see below)*.

ACQUISITION OF WHOLE SCHEME

If the company being acquired has its own pension scheme that will be taken over along with the business, this will need to be carefully examined. Although the matters to be considered are generally similar to those that arise from a routine review of pension arrangements, these will be thrown into sharp relief when a transaction is in prospect. The funding position as presented in the actuarial valuation or accounting costs may not be a suitable basis for pricing pensions in a deal.

In addition to investigating the adequacy of the existing fund to cover the benefits already accrued, the ongoing costs of benefits and administration will need to be assessed. These may have a substantial impact on the future profitability, and even perhaps viability, of the business. It will be necessary to consider the financial and employee-relations implications of retaining or changing existing benefits.

BULK TRANSFER ARRANGEMENTS

Issues arise if the employees of the company or business being acquired are members of a scheme that also covers other employees. Although there is no requirement, under pensions legislation, for the employees concerned to be treated other than as ordinary leavers, it is often desirable, in the interest of good employee relations, for a 'bulk transfer' to be arranged. The bulk transfer terms may be a matter of commercial negotiation between the purchaser and vendor and will normally be set out in the 'pensions clause' of (or 'schedule' to) the legal agreement governing the transaction (perhaps accompanied by a side letter between the actuaries advising these parties, in which the actuarial basis is set out in detail). The amount transferred need not be equal to the value placed on the liabilities for pricing purposes. As well as specifying the basis for calculating the amount of the bulk transfer payment, the pensions clause will usually also specify the benefits to which the transferring employees will be entitled in their new employer's scheme as a result of the transfer. It will also normally cover other aspects such as:

(a) Any transitional period during which the employees continue to participate in the vendor's scheme. This may be necessary, for example, to give time for the purchaser to establish a new scheme. The purchaser would need to be aware of a risk of triggering a debt on the employer *(see below)*.

(b) The procedure for calculating and agreeing the amount of the transfer payment and making the payment. This may include a timetable and perhaps provide for an interim payment to be made on account.

(c) The way in which any difference ('shortfall' or 'excess') between the amount calculated on the agreed basis and that actually paid is to be dealt with *(see below)*.

Trustee considerations

As the trustees of the vendor's scheme will not normally be party to the sale and purchase agreement, the agreed bulk transfer terms will not be binding upon them. Instead, it will be their responsibility to ensure that the members concerned are dealt with properly, in accordance with the scheme rules. They will need to consider, having regard to the interests of *all* scheme members and beneficiaries and taking expert advice where required, whether it is appropriate to pay a bulk transfer and, if so, the basis on which it should be calculated. This might lead them to conclude that a transfer on the agreed basis is appropriate. On the other hand, they might decide that the payment should be calculated on a different basis, or that a bulk transfer should not be paid at all, in which case the shortfall/excess clause (*see above*) would have effect. Similarly, the trustees of the purchaser's scheme would not be obliged to accept the bulk transfer payment or provide the agreed level of benefits in respect of it. Any issues that arose on this account would also need to be resolved.

Member consent or actuarial certificate

For a bulk transfer to be able to be paid, *either* the transfer must be restricted to include only the members who give their consent, *or* the actuary advising the trustees of the scheme from which the bulk transfer is to be made must provide a GN16 certificate confirming that the past service benefits of each transferring member will be 'broadly no less favourable' after the transfer. Where individual consents are sought, the trustees will need to ensure that members are provided with the information necessary to understand all of the options open to them and make an informed choice. Where a GN16 certificate is to be provided there are legislative requirements for the members to be provided with information beforehand. GN16 also requires the actuary to have given certain information to the trustees before or at the same time as the certificate was provided. However, GN16 is expected to be withdrawn in 2010 and it is not currently clear how or if it will be replaced.

EMPLOYER COVENANT

The trustees of a pension scheme will wish to consider carefully the impact of any corporate transaction on the covenant of the sponsoring employer(s). Where the ability of a sponsoring employer to meet future shortfalls in a scheme is to be reduced, trustees might consider requesting additional funding and/or reviewing the investment strategy.

POTENTIAL 'DEBT ON EMPLOYER'

If the corporate transaction results in a participating employer ceasing to be an employer in relation to the vendor's scheme, either at the time of the sale/purchase or at the end of a participation period, then a debt could become due from that employer, determined on a similar (but not identical) approach to that which applies on a wind-up *(see Section 24)*.

The debt on the employer can be a significant amount. It arises in respect of the benefits accrued whilst in service with that employer and covers all members, not just the current employees. In addition, the debt may include a proportion relating to any 'orphan' members. Orphan members are pensioners or deferred members with no currently participating employer. Depending on the previous corporate activity of the company, these orphan members can represent a high percentage of the total membership and therefore can substantially increase the debt for which a participating employer is liable.

The debt, which falls to the participating employer, should be taken into account in pricing the business or company for sale. The debt can sometimes fall on the vendor (if a business, rather than a company, is sold and as a result a company owned by the vendor ceases to have members in the scheme); but it is usually more likely to fall on the purchaser. Where the debt would fall on him, the purchaser might reduce the price on offer for the business, or obtain an indemnity from the vendor to cover the debt. Also, a debt may still be payable to the original scheme even where liabilities and assets are transferred to another scheme.

The 'default' basis for determining the debt is the departing employer's share of the deficit on a buy-out basis, but there are a number of ways in which it can be agreed that a lower debt will be paid:

- a Scheme Apportionment Arrangement is an agreement between the employers and trustees that some or all of the debt for the ceasing employer can be reapportioned to other participating employers

- a Withdrawal Arrangement is an agreement with the trustees that the ceasing employer will pay a lower amount, at least equal to its share of any deficit relative to technical provisions *(see Section 20)*, and that a contingent guarantor will stand behind the remaining debt, *or*

- an Approved Withdrawal Arrangement is similar to a Withdrawal Arrangement but Regulator approval is required and the amount immediately payable must be less than the employer's share of the technical provisions deficit.

For any of these to be agreed, the 'Funding Test' must be met. This requires the trustees to be reasonably satisfied that:

- when the arrangement takes effect, the remaining employers will be reasonably likely to be able to fund the scheme so that it has sufficient and appropriate assets to cover its technical provisions, *and*

- in the case of a Scheme Apportionment Arrangement, the security of members' benefits will not be adversely affected.

Purchasers should also be alert to the possibility that companies they are buying may have previously ceased to participate in a scheme or been involved in a scheme which has started to wind up and be liable for historical debts, as yet unpaid or even unidentified.

At the time of writing, the Government is consulting on changes to the debt-on-employer legislation. The most significant proposal would allow certain corporate restructurings to take place without triggering a debt.

THE PENSIONS REGULATOR

The role of the Pensions Regulator is described in *Section 11*. The 'notifiable events' framework requires the trustees of an underfunded scheme to notify the Regulator if a bulk or individual transfer payment exceeding £1.5 million (or, if lower, 5% of scheme assets) is made. Separately, clearance from the Regulator may be sought for certain transactions – which might include a bulk transfer – impacting on a defined benefit pension scheme *(see below)*.

MORAL HAZARD AND CLEARANCE

The 'moral hazard' provisions of the Pensions Act 2004 are designed to prevent situations where employers deliberately avoid their obligations. The Pensions Regulator has sweeping powers to act in these circumstances, including the power to issue Contribution Notices, Financial Support Directions and Restoration Orders *(see also Section 11)*.

Contribution Notices may be issued in relation to a variety of events, including (but not limited to) sale or acquisition of a business, group restructuring and capital restructuring. The Regulator's powers are not limited to the current employer of the scheme.

The Regulator's 'moral hazard' powers were extended in 2009. It is now able to issue a Contribution Notice where, regardless of the employer's intent, the effect of an act is materially detrimental to the security of members' benefits. A statutory defence prevents the Regulator acting in this way where the employer reasonably concluded that there was no material detriment and certain other conditions are met.

A company or individual can avoid the risk of the Regulator later taking action by applying for clearance. Once given, clearance is binding on the Regulator unless the actual circumstances were different from those disclosed at the time.

The Regulator has issued guidance on clearance applications and this can be found at *www.thepensionsregulator.gov.uk*. The guidance includes:

- a pension scheme in deficit should be treated like any other material creditor
- the Regulator wishes to know about all events having a materially detrimental effect on a pension scheme's ability to meet liabilities, *and*
- trustees and employers should work together in relation to potentially detrimental events, communicating and sharing appropriate information.

PENSION COSTS IN COMPANY ACCOUNTS

Pension cost accounting in UK company accounts has been undergoing significant change over the last few years. FRS 17 became mandatory for accounting periods beginning on or after 1 January 2005. For listed companies' consolidated group accounts for periods beginning on or after this date, however, international accounting standard IAS 19 must be used rather than FRS 17. The use of IAS 19, instead of FRS 17, has at the same time become an option for individual company accounts and for the consolidated group accounts of unlisted companies. This section describes the requirements of both standards.

In January 2008, the Accounting Standards Board (ASB) issued a discussion paper proposing fundamental changes to accounting for occupational pensions. The suggestions put forward include financial reports reflecting the actual, rather than the expected, return on assets and the use of a risk-free rate to discount liabilities. The ASB received a large volume of responses and intends to discuss the matters raised with interested parties.

The IASB (the board responsible for international standards) and the FASB (the body responsible for US accounting standards) are also undertaking linked projects to update and align their standards. In September 2006 the FASB issued FAS 158 (amending FAS 87, FAS 88, FAS 106 and FAS 132) which came into effect for years ending after 15 December 2006, addressing the first phase of its review project. The most significant changes are the requirement to reflect the accounting surplus or deficit of a scheme on the balance sheet and (for years ending after 15 December 2008) the requirement to use measurements made at the fiscal year-end date.

In March 2008, the IASB issued a discussion paper on possible amendments to IAS 19. Its proposals included the immediate recognition of all gains and losses in accounts (and consideration of which gains and losses should be recognised in the Profit and Loss account rather than in Other Comprehensive Income), which will be included in an exposure draft the IASB expects to publish in late 2009, with a view to it having effect in 2013. Other proposals, including measuring 'contribution-based' plans (which would include defined benefit plans that are not based on final salary) at 'fair value', may form part of a comprehensive review of pensions accounting, the timing of which is not yet known.

ACCOUNTING FOR PENSION COSTS UNDER FRS 17

Coverage

FRS 17 covers companies registered in the UK or in the Republic of Ireland, and their subsidiaries. It covers all retirement benefits (including medical care during retirement) which the employer is committed to providing, wherever they arise world-wide. Reporting entities applying the Financial Reporting Standard for Smaller Entities (FRSSE) are exempt from FRS 17, although FRSSE itself imposes requirements that are essentially a simplified version of FRS 17.

Transition

As a minimum, companies have had to phase in use of FRS 17 from 22 June 2001 (with earlier full adoption also being permitted). Full implementation is required for accounting periods beginning on or after 1 January 2005, including recognition of the relevant amounts in the primary statements, but five-year history disclosures may be built up over the following years (i.e. they need not be constructed retrospectively).

Application to Multi-employer Schemes

Where a number of companies participate in a multi-employer DB scheme, individual companies may not be able to identify 'their' assets and liabilities, or may be obliged only to contribute for benefits currently being earned. In such cases, the individual companies should account for the scheme on a cash basis (cost equals contributions paid), as in DC schemes, but must make appropriate disclosures. However, for the purposes of group accounts, multi-employer schemes are accounted for on a DB basis.

A: DEFINED CONTRIBUTION SCHEMES

Summary

For DC schemes, the charge against profits must be the amount of contributions due in respect of the accounting period.

A DC scheme is defined as one 'into which an employer pays regular contributions fixed as an amount or as a percentage of pay' without a 'legal or constructive obligation to pay further contributions if the scheme does not have sufficient assets to pay all employee benefits relating to employee service in the current and prior periods'. A scheme may be taken to be a DC scheme for the purposes of this definition, even where salary-related death-in-service benefits are provided.

Disclosure

The following disclosures should be made:

- the nature of the scheme (i.e. defined contribution; funded or unfunded)
- the pension cost charge for the period, *and*
- any outstanding or prepaid contributions at the balance sheet date.

B: DEFINED BENEFIT SCHEMES

Overview

A DB scheme is defined as a 'pension or other retirement benefit scheme other than a defined contribution scheme'. Financial statements should reflect pension assets and liabilities, measured at fair values. Retirement benefit-related operating costs, financing costs and any other changes in value of assets and scheme liabilities should be recognised in the period in which the benefit is earned or in which they arise, with no smoothing or spreading.

Benefits to Value

Benefits promised under the formal terms of the scheme must be valued. Benefits should be attributed to periods of service according to the scheme's benefit formula, except that uniform accrual should be assumed where the benefit formula is rear-end loaded.

Discretionary benefits are to be included only where the employer has a constructive obligation to provide them. Favourable early retirement terms should be reflected where there is an established practice of allowing retirement at the employee's request on these terms. No allowance should be made for future retirements at the employer's initiative.

Actuarial Assumptions and Methodology

Full actuarial valuations by a professionally qualified actuary are needed at least every three years; they should be updated to each intervening balance sheet date.

Pension scheme assets must be measured at fair value (bid price for quoted securities for accounting periods beginning on or after 6 April 2007; previously fair value was defined as mid-market value).

Scheme liabilities are measured using the projected unit method, which reflects the benefits the employer is committed to provide for service up to the valuation date and, where applicable, allows for projected increases to those benefits in line with pensionable earnings after the valuation date.

The expected costs of death-in-service or incapacity benefits should be charged on an insurance cost basis, to the extent they are insured. Any such benefits that are uninsured are to be charged on a projected unit method that reflects the proportion of the full benefits ultimately payable attributable to the accounting period.

The actuarial assumptions for projecting future outgoings in respect of the scheme liabilities are ultimately the responsibility of the directors (or equivalent), but should be set upon advice given by an actuary and must reflect market expectations at the valuation date, for consistency with the asset value. They should be mutually compatible and should lead to the best estimate of the future cashflows that will arise under the scheme liabilities. The projected outgoings must then be discounted. The discount rate to be used is the redemption yield at the valuation date on AA (or equivalent) rated corporate bonds of equivalent term and currency to the scheme liabilities.

Balance Sheet

Any surplus at the balance sheet date of assets over scheme liabilities calculated as above should be recognised in the balance sheet but is limited to the amount that the employer can recover through reduced employer's contributions in future and refunds which have already been agreed by the trustees at the balance sheet date.

A deficit (on the FRS basis) should be recognised as a liability to the extent of the employer's legal or constructive obligation to fund it. If the scheme rules require members' contributions to be increased to help fund a deficit, the liability should be reduced appropriately.

The net pension asset/liability shown in the balance sheet may differ from the above, due to deferred tax.

Pension Cost

The full cost of benefits, including actuarial gains and losses, is recognised in the performance statements in the accounting period in which the cost arises. The Profit and Loss account is protected from excessive volatility by the recognition of actuarial gains and losses in the Statement of Total Recognised Gains and Losses (STRGL) and the facility to vary the expected return on assets.

The different components making up the pension cost are shown in the table *on page 173*, along with definitions, details of where they should be recognised in the performance statements, and brief comments.

Disclosure

On 7 December 2006, the ASB published an amendment to FRS 17. It replaced the existing disclosure requirements with those of IAS 19. The following disclosures are mandatory for accounting periods beginning on or after 6 April 2007:

- a general description of the type of scheme (for example, flat-rate or final salary pension scheme, or retirement healthcare plan)
- a reconciliation of the scheme assets and liabilities to the net asset or liability recognised in the balance sheet, showing at least:
  o the present value of scheme liabilities that are wholly unfunded
  o the present value (before deducting the fair value of the scheme assets) of scheme liabilities that are wholly or partly funded
  o the fair value of any scheme assets
  o the past service cost not yet recognised in the balance sheet
  o any amounts which would, apart from the limits laid down by FRS 17, be recognised as an asset, *and*
  o the other amounts recognised in the balance sheet
- any self-investment included in the fair value of scheme assets
- reconciliations showing the movements over the period of the scheme assets and liabilities
- the total expense recognised in the profit and loss account for each of the following:
  o current service cost
  o interest cost
  o expected return on scheme assets
  o past service cost
  o any curtailment or settlement costs, *and*
  o the effect of any limit on the balance sheet asset (where recognised through the profit and loss account)
- the actual return on scheme assets
- the principal actuarial assumptions

- the amount recognised in the Statement of Total Recognised Gains and Losses, separately showing actuarial gains and losses and the effect of any limit on the balance sheet asset (where recognised outside the profit and loss account)
- cumulative gains and losses recognised outside the profit and loss account
- assets, showing the amount or percentage in each major asset category
- explanation of how expected return is derived, referring to the impact of each major asset category, but no requirement to disclose expected returns separately for each category
- five-year history of asset value, liabilities, surplus/deficit and experience gains and losses (there is no requirement to construct these retrospectively)
- expected contributions over the coming year, *and*
- explanation of any constructive obligations (e.g. to provide regular pension increases).

Where several defined benefit schemes are involved, disclosure can be combined in the way felt to be most useful.

In January 2007, the ASB released a Reporting Statement which recommends additional best practice disclosures. These are not mandatory and are intended to give a clear view of the risks and rewards arising from schemes. The Reporting Statement applies to UK companies using either FRS 17 or IAS 19, and the disclosures are complementary to those required under those standards.

The recommended disclosures include:

- information on the relationship between the company and the scheme trustees/managers, including how the investment strategy and funding principles are determined, and any significant and unusual trustee powers
- information on and sensitivity analysis for each of the principal assumptions, including mortality
- the buy-out cost of the liabilities, if available
- information on contributions agreed with the trustees, *and*
- other information that will enable the user to evaluate risks and rewards, including on the expected rate of return of each of the major asset classes.

FRS 17: SUMMARY OF CALCULATION OF PENSION COST

Component	Where recognised	Description and Notes
Current service cost	Staff cost section of operating cost in P&L[1]	The increase in the scheme liabilities expected to arise from employees' service in the accounting period, calculated using financial assumptions based on conditions at the beginning of the period. Includes insurance cost, for the accounting period, of insured death-in-service and incapacity benefits, and a charge calculated using a 'projected unit' method for their uninsured counterparts. Expected employees' contributions are offset from the gross cost.
+ Interest cost	Financing section of P&L	Expected increase during the period in the present value of the scheme liabilities because the benefits are one period closer to settlement.
− Expected return on assets	Combined with interest cost (above) to give a net entry in financing section of P&L	Based on actual assets held by the scheme at the beginning of the accounting period and the expected rate of return on those assets as follows: – for bonds, current redemption yields at start of period – for equities and other assets, the rate of total return expected over the long term at start of period in either case averaged over the remaining term of the related liabilities and net of scheme expenses. Appropriate allowance should be made for expected cashflows into and out of the fund during the year. May be restricted if there is an irrecoverable surplus.
+ Actuarial loss (gain)	STRGL[2]	Changes in actuarial surpluses or deficits that arise because events have not coincided with the actuarial assumptions made for the last valuation or because the actuarial assumptions have changed. An adjustment may be required where there is an irrecoverable surplus.
+ Past service cost, offset by surplus otherwise treated as irrecoverable	Staff cost section of operating cost in P&L	A past service cost (PSC) is any increase in the scheme liabilities related to employees' service in prior periods, arising in the current period as a result of the introduction of, or improvement to, retirement benefits. PSCs are required to be recognised on a straight-line basis over the period in which the additional benefits vest. Where these vest immediately, the PSC should be recognised immediately.
+ Loss (gain) on settlement/ curtailment, offset by surplus otherwise treated as irrecoverable	Staff cost section of operating cost in P&L, unless it attaches to an exceptional item immediately after operating profit in the P&L	Settlement occurs where the responsibility for, and risk attaching to, a pension obligation is irrevocably transferred to another party, e.g. by buying matching annuities or by paying a bulk transfer value. Curtailment is where defined benefit liabilities cease to accrue or current members' future service benefits are reduced, e.g. on termination of a final salary scheme and replacing it with a money purchase scheme, or due to a redundancy exercise. Losses or gains arising as a result of settlements and curtailments instigated by the employer and falling outside the scope of the actuarial assumptions are included in this component of pension cost.

Notes: 1 Profit and loss account.   2 Statement of Total Recognised Gains and Losses.
Where the surplus recognised in the balance sheet has to be restricted (as described under the heading 'Balance Sheet'), FRS 17 sets out details of the adjustments required to the performance statements.

ACCOUNTING FOR PENSION COSTS UNDER IAS 19

Requirement to Use International Standards

In May 2000, the International Organisation of Securities Commissions (IOSCO) issued a recommendation that stock exchanges which belong to IOSCO (which include all the major global stock exchanges) should permit non-domestic companies seeking a listing to use IASB standards rather than requiring them to use local standards.

In June 2002, the EU Council of Ministers adopted a Regulation that generally *requires* companies governed by the law of an EU Member State, whose securities are admitted to trading on a regulated market in any EU Member State, to prepare their consolidated accounts in compliance with International Accounting Standards for accounting periods starting on or after 1 January 2005. UK AIM (Alternative Investment Market) companies must also prepare their consolidated accounts in compliance with IASB standards for accounting periods starting on or after 1 January 2007.

In December 2007, the US Securities and Exchange Commission (SEC) ruled that non-US companies reporting under International Financial Reporting Standards (IFRS) would no longer have to reconcile to US accounting standards in order to obtain a listing in the USA. In November 2008, the SEC issued a proposal that, if adopted, would *allow* certain US-listed companies to prepare financial statements using IFRS from 2009, as an alternative to US standards, and would *require* US companies to report under IFRS from 2014.

Coverage

IAS 19 covers four categories of employee benefits, with separate requirements for each:

- short-term employee benefits, such as salaries and social security contributions
- post-employment benefits, such as pensions and post-employment medical care
- other long-term employee benefits, including long-service leave *and*
- termination benefits.

Equity compensation benefits, including share options, which were previously covered by IAS 19, are now covered by IFRS 2.

Application to Multi-employer Schemes

In December 2004, the International Accounting Standards Board (IASB) issued an amendment to IAS 19 which provides a simpler approach to accounting for group schemes than was the case under the original IAS 19.

Under IAS 19, only plans which are operated by companies which *are not under common control* are 'multi-employer' plans. If participants in a defined benefit multi-employer plan are unable to identify separately the assets and liabilities, they can account for the plan on a cash contribution basis.

Since December 2004, where a defined benefit plan is operated by a group of companies which *are under common control*, the principal

174

sponsoring employer has been required to account for the plan on a defined benefit basis and other participating employers have been allowed to use a cash contribution basis, unless there is a contractual agreement on the sharing of future pension costs, in which case each company should recognise its share of the defined benefit cost.

A. DEFINED CONTRIBUTION SCHEMES

Overview

The treatment of DC schemes under IAS 19 is essentially the same as under FRS 17. The only disclosure required by IAS 19 is the amount of expense recognised for the period.

B. DEFINED BENEFIT SCHEMES

Overview

The most significant difference from FRS 17 is in the choice of methods that IAS 19 allows companies to use to recognise actuarial gains and losses *(see Pension Cost, below)*. There are other small differences in approach and in the information which has to be disclosed.

Benefits to Value

The benefits to be valued under IAS 19 are basically the same as those required to be valued under FRS 17, although IAS 19 is not specific about what allowance should be made for future early retirements.

Actuarial Assumptions and Methodology

IAS 19 requires assets and liabilities to be valued regularly enough that the amounts recognised in the accounts are not materially different from the amounts that would be determined from an up-to-date valuation. The involvement of a qualified actuary is encouraged but not required.

Assets must be measured at fair value. Auditors may require fair value to be taken as bid value rather than mid-market. Liabilities are measured using the projected unit method.

IAS 19 is silent on the treatment of risk benefits. We understand that most auditors expect the 'attribution method' to be used. For benefits that are not service-related, this method allocates benefits in proportion to the ratio of completed years of service to either the vesting period or, if the benefit is unvested, total projected years of service.

The actuarial assumptions are the responsibility of the directors and must be unbiased and mutually compatible, being best estimates of the variables determining the ultimate cost of the benefits. The discount rate to be used should be determined by reference to market yields at the valuation date on high quality corporate bonds of consistent term and currency. The market yields on government bonds should be used if there is no deep market in corporate bonds, although IAS 19 is expected to be revised in late 2009 to require an estimate of the corporate bond yield to be used.

Balance Sheet

The amount recognised in the balance sheet should be calculated as:

The present value of the defined benefit obligation

+ Actuarial gains (or minus any losses) not yet recognised in pension cost

– Any outstanding past service costs not yet recognised in pension cost

– The fair value of scheme assets.

If the result is an asset, then it should be limited to the present value of:

The available future refunds of surplus

+ The available reduction in future contributions

+ Any outstanding actuarial losses or past service costs not yet recognised in pension cost.

In July 2007, IFRIC (the Interpretation Committee of the IASB) published an Interpretation which addresses the impact of minimum funding requirements, the limit on an asset for a defined benefit scheme and the interaction of these. IFRIC 14 explains that a refund or a reduction in future contributions may be considered available even if it cannot be realised at the balance sheet date. The company must have a right to any refund, without recourse to the trustees. The available reduction in future contributions must be restricted to allow for any contributions payable under any 'minimum funding requirement' that may apply. The balance sheet asset or liability must also be adjusted to reflect any irrecoverable surplus (on the accounting basis) that will be created in future by the payment of minimum contributions in respect of a past service deficit on the minimum funding basis. IFRIC 14 is mandatory for accounting periods beginning on or after 1 January 2008.

Pension Cost

With the exception of actuarial gains and losses, the components of pension cost are calculated in essentially the same way as under FRS 17.

The original IAS 19 required that unrecognised actuarial gains and losses only have to be included as components of pension cost if, at the beginning of the year, they fall outside a 'corridor' equal to 10% of the greater of the present value of the defined benefit obligation and the fair value of scheme assets. The excess outside this corridor can then be amortised over the employees' average remaining service period (or in a more stringent way if applied consistently and systematically from year to year). However, where a curtailment or settlement occurs, any associated unrecognised gains or losses will need to be recognised immediately.

On initial implementation, companies will normally recognise any opening surplus or deficit immediately, and thereafter recognise gains and losses using the 10% corridor and amortisation. Alternatively, a company can avoid the immediate recognition of the opening surplus or deficit by reconstructing IAS 19-style figures as if IAS 19 had existed since the beginning of the scheme.

The amendments to IAS 19 in December 2004 introduced an optional alternative approach. Under the alternative approach, gains and losses are recognised in full immediately, but through a secondary performance statement called the Statement of Recognised Income and Expense (SORIE) and not through the profit and loss account. This approach is analogous to the recognition of gains and losses through the Statement of Recognised Gains and Losses (STRGL) under FRS 17. The IASB have included this option as an interim measure.

Disclosure

The disclosure requirements are the same as those introduced by the December 2006 amendments to FRS 17 *(see page 171)* except that to cater for the alternative approaches to recognition of gains and losses under IAS 19, the company must also disclose:

- the accounting policy for recognising gains and losses, *and*
- the amount of gains or losses in the breakdown of the expense recognised in the income statement (where relevant, i.e. where gains and losses are amortised through the income statement).

RELATED PARTY DISCLOSURES (IAS 24)

Companies complying with IAS 19 also have to provide disclosure figures under IAS 24 – *Related Party Disclosures*. This Standard requires information to be disclosed for key management personnel (in aggregate) for each of the following categories:

- short-term employee benefits
- post-employment benefits
- other long-term benefits
- termination benefits *and*
- share-based payment.

IAS 24 defines key management personnel as persons having authority and responsibility for planning, directing and controlling the activities of the entity, directly or indirectly. This includes (but is not limited to) directors.

For each category, only a single figure is required. For some benefits this one figure is easy to access (for example, actual contributions paid to a defined contribution plan). Our understanding is that, in the case of defined benefit plans and other long-term benefit plans, the IAS 19 service cost for each relevant individual should be used rather than a proportion of the whole profit and loss charge.

DISCLOSURE OF DIRECTORS' PENSIONS

Previously, listed company accounts were subject to disclosure requirements in relation to directors' pensions imposed by the FSA's Listing Rules in addition to those generally applicable under the Companies Act 1985. For company accounts relating to financial years ending on or after 31 December 2002, the intention was that disclosures would be streamlined, with requirements broadly mirroring those of the FSA being incorporated into the Companies Act 1985, enabling the corresponding FSA requirements to be deleted. However, there was a flaw in the regulations amending the Companies Act, which was not corrected despite determined lobbying, and the FSA have confirmed that their requirements must also continue to be met. With effect from 6 April 2008, the Companies Act 1985 requirements were replaced by regulations made under the Companies Act 2006, but these did not change the legislative requirements for disclosure of directors' pensions. The legislative and FSA requirements apply in addition to the requirements of IAS 24 – *Related Party Disclosures* where applicable. A summary of the legislative disclosure requirements relating to directors' pensions is given below, together with a note of the additional FSA requirements (where these differ significantly).

Unquoted company disclosures

Unquoted companies are required to make the following disclosures in the notes to their accounts:

- the aggregate value of company contributions paid or treated as paid to a pension scheme to provide money purchase benefits in respect of directors' service
- the number of directors accruing retirement benefits under money purchase schemes and the number accruing benefits under defined benefit schemes
- except where, broadly, aggregate directors' pay and other specified emoluments fall below a specified threshold, the following must be disclosed in respect of the highest-paid director: company contributions in respect of money purchase benefits, and accrued defined benefit pension and lump sum (both excluding benefits from AVCs) at year-end, *and*
- the aggregate amount by which directors' retirement benefits in payment exceeded the amount they were entitled to at 31 March 1997, or the date the benefits became payable, if later. This does not apply if the benefits were sufficiently funded without recourse to additional contributions and benefits were paid to all pensioner members of the scheme on the same basis.

Quoted company disclosures

For each financial year, the directors of a quoted company must produce a directors' remuneration report which must include the following pension disclosures in relation to each person who has served as a director of the company at any time during that financial year:

Money purchase schemes only
Details of company contributions paid or payable for the relevant financial year or paid in that year for another financial year.

Defined benefit schemes only
(a) Changes during the relevant financial year in accrued benefits under the scheme.
(b) Accrued benefits under the scheme as at the year-end.
(c) Transfer value of accrued rights at year-end.
(d) Transfer value of accrued rights at previous year-end.
(e) Increase in transfer value over the year [i.e. (c) – (d)] less contributions made by the director during the year.

The Companies Act 2006 regulations require transfer values to be calculated in accordance with transfer value regulations (*see Section 16*).

However, the FSA's Listing Rules require calculation in accordance with actuarial guidance note GN11, even though the note is no longer effective.

To meet the FSA's requirements, the following details must also be included:

   (f) The amount of the increase in accrued benefit during the year (excluding inflation), and either:

     (i) the transfer value (less director's contributions) of the increase in accrued benefit net of inflation; *or*

     (ii) so much of the following information as is necessary to make a reasonable assessment of the transfer value in respect of each director:

- current age
- normal retirement age
- the amount of any contributions paid or payable by the director during the period
- details of spouse's and dependants' benefits
- early retirement rights and options, expectations of pension increases after retirement (whether guaranteed or discretionary), *and*
- discretionary benefits for which allowance is made in transfer values, and any other relevant information which will significantly affect the value of the benefits.

Money purchase and defined benefit schemes

In respect of each former or current director of the company as at the year-end, the amount by which retirement benefits paid exceeded those to which the person was entitled on the later of the date the benefits first became payable and 31 March 1997. This does not apply if the benefits are sufficiently funded without recourse to additional contributions and benefits were paid to all pensioner members of the scheme on the same basis.

In addition to the disclosures required in the directors' remuneration report, the Regulations also require quoted companies to include in the notes to their accounts the disclosures *in the first two bullet points of the* 'Unquoted company disclosures' *section above*, unless the information is capable of being readily ascertained from other information shown.

FINANCIAL SERVICES LEGISLATION AND PENSION SCHEMES

Introduction

The Financial Services and Markets Act 2000 (FSMA) is the principal legislation for the regulation of the financial services market. It specifies that regulated activities, such as dealing in investments, managing investments, arranging deals in investments, offering investment advice, taking custody of investments and establishing collective investment schemes and certain pension schemes, may only be carried out as a business in the UK by persons who are either authorised or exempt. Authorisation is granted by the Financial Services Authority (FSA), which is the sole regulator of the UK financial services market, although the Pensions Regulator also has a regulatory role in respect of workplace contract-based pension arrangements.

Professional firms may be licensed by 'Designated Professional Bodies', such as the Institute of Actuaries, to carry out a limited range of 'exempt' regulated activities that are incidental to their main business without FSA authorisation. Authorised firms that are managed and controlled by suitably qualified professionals and fall within the FSA's definition of 'Authorised Professional Firms' may also be able to avail themselves of corresponding exemptions when carrying out similar non-mainstream regulated activities.

Implications for pension schemes

Pension scheme trustees and administrators are clearly concerned with investments in various ways. They may be:

- responsible for the management of the scheme's assets (whether in insurance policies or directly invested)

- involved in giving advice to scheme members and prospective members *and/or*

- involved in arranging investments for individual members, such as additional voluntary contributions and insurance company buy-outs.

Each of the above can be a 'regulated activity' requiring authorisation by the FSA, for which stringent requirements must be met, unless covered by an exemption. Establishing whether authorisation is required for a particular action can be complicated, particularly when considering relationships between trustees and individual members. In May 2006, the FSA issued some formal 'perimeter guidance' setting out the circumstances in which authorisation is or is not required.

Definition of investments

Under the FSMA, the definition of investments includes cash deposits (and also mortgages and general insurance contracts), shares, debentures, Government and public securities, options and futures, units in unit trust schemes and long-term insurance contracts. However, the provisions relating to managing, dealing in and advising on investments do not apply to cash deposits. Property continues to be excluded.

Generally, a scheme member's interests under the trusts of an occupational pension scheme are not classed as investments. However, rights under a stakeholder scheme are specifically included (even if the stakeholder scheme is an occupational scheme) and, from April 2007, rights under a personal pension scheme similarly became explicitly included, bringing the establishment and operation of all such schemes, including in particular Self-Invested Personal Pensions, within the ambit of the FSMA.

Management of investments

The FSMA specifically provides that those engaged in the activity of managing the assets of occupational pension schemes must be authorised or exempt, even if (as is the case with many trustees) they would not normally be regarded as doing so as a business. However, the Act goes on to provide that authorisation will not be required if all day-to-day decisions about the management of investments are taken on their behalf by a person who is himself authorised or exempt. Trustees are also permitted to make 'day-to-day' decisions on pooled investment products and insurance contracts, provided that they have first obtained and considered advice from an appropriate authorised person.

The Pensions Act 1995 also imposes a requirement on pension schemes for trustees to appoint a competent and experienced fund manager who has the necessary authorisation or exemption. It identifies certain matters on which trustees are required to obtain investment advice and also sets out a requirement for a written statement of investment principles to govern the investment of the scheme's assets.

In response to Paul Myners' *Review of Institutional Investment*, a specific requirement for trustees to have 'knowledge and understanding' of the principles relating to pension fund investment was introduced from April 2006 under the Pensions Act 2004. This has been supplemented by a detailed Code of Practice from the Pensions Regulator. In October 2008, the Government updated the original Myners principles to ensure they remain relevant *(see Section 10 for further details)*.

Communications with members

To reflect the requirements of the EU Distance Marketing Directive, rules were introduced in 2004 which prevent an employee from being included in a scheme regulated by the FSA without a 'prior request'. This means that any information given to employees, offering membership of a stakeholder or group personal pension arrangement, will need to include a reply slip, unless consent is obtained and recorded by some other means.

However, with the introduction of the Personal Accounts regime *(see Section 9)*, from 2012 employers will be able to auto-enrol employees into workplace pension arrangements, including group personal pension and stakeholder schemes. Although these are regulated, contract-based schemes, the Government received confirmation from the European Commission that this was allowed under EU law.

The FSMA also places restrictions on financial promotion, prohibiting the communication of any 'invitation or inducement to engage in investment activity', unless it is issued or approved by an authorised person. There are certain exemptions set out in secondary legislation, covering some (but not all) communications involving trustees, beneficiaries and trust settlors (generally, employers in a pension scheme context), but these are generally relevant only to occupational schemes. However, from 1 July 2005, employers offering stakeholder or group personal pension arrangements to their employees have been able to avoid the restrictions, provided certain conditions are met. These include requirements that the employer must contribute and must not receive any direct financial benefit. There are further proposals to extend this exemption to cover also promotions by third-party administrators.

Other responsibilities of the Financial Services Authority

The FSA is the single statutory regulator under the FSMA. As part of its overall responsibility to regulate and authorise all financial businesses, unit trusts and open-ended investment companies (OEICs), and to recognise and supervise investment exchanges and clearing houses, the FSA regulates the marketing and promotion of all personal pension and stakeholder pension schemes, the authorisation of such schemes' managers, and the activities of pension scheme investment managers.

Role of the Pensions Regulator

The regulation of workplace contract-based pension schemes (such as stakeholder arrangements) is shared between the Pensions Regulator and the FSA. The two parties have produced joint guidance explaining their respective roles.

The Pensions Regulator's role includes dealing with late payment of contributions and other breaches of legislation, promoting good administration, and providing information and education. As part of this, the Pensions Regulator has published guidance on voluntary employer engagement in workplace contract-based pension schemes, to support employers. The guidance does not propose any new requirements and notes that there is no 'one-size-fits-all' governance solution. *(See Section 11 for more information on the Pensions Regulator.)*

The Financial Services Compensation Scheme (FSCS)

The FSCS is a safety net for customers of financial services firms, dealing with all financial-services-related claims. It was created under the FSMA and became operational on 1 December 2001.

The FSCS was set up to pay compensation where an FSA-authorised firm is unable, or unlikely to be able, to pay claims against it. This is generally when a firm is insolvent or has gone out of business. It covers deposit-related claims, insurance- and investment-related claims and claims related to mortgage advice and arranging.

From 29 March 2009, the FSCS can also be called upon by the Government to contribute to the costs associated with the exercise of a 'stabilisation power'; for example, where it intervenes to ensure the continued existence of a bank or building society.

5 Nov 08	The Institute of Actuaries published 20 new mortality tables (the 'S1' series), based on the mortality of pensioners of self-administered pension schemes.
24 Nov 08	The Chancellor of the Exchequer presented the 2008 Pre-Budget Report to Parliament, which included an announcement that the Lifetime and Annual Allowances would be frozen for five years from 2011 and that National Insurance rates for employees, employers and the self-employed would increase by 0.5% from April 2011.
26 Nov 08	The Pensions Act 2008 received Royal Assent. The Act contains various provisions relating to Personal Accounts including the automatic enrolment requirement. The Act also included changes to the operation of the PPF and the Pensions Regulator and measures to further reform State Pensions.
1 Apr 09	The requirement for the PPF to revalue benefits prior to retirement, when the original scheme did not provide revaluation in respect of the member, was removed.
6 Apr 09	Version 1.3 of the Board for Actuarial Standards' TM1 came into effect, allowing for the future abolition of contracting out for DC schemes in SMPIs. It must be followed for SMPIs issued after 31 August 2009.
6 Apr 09	The requirements to notify the Pensions Regulator when there are two or more changes in the holders of any key scheme post within the previous 12 months, two or more changes in the holders of any key employer posts within the previous 12 months or any change in the employer's credit rating were removed.
6 Apr 09	Regulations extended the look-back period for Financial Support Directions from 12 to 24 months. But during a transitional period from 6 April 2009 to 6 April 2010, the new 24-month period is reduced by the number of complete months remaining until 6 April 2010.
6 Apr 09	The restrictions on when and how pension credit benefits may be taken were removed.
6 Apr 09	Regulations allowing trustees to convert GMPs to normal scheme benefits, with a continuing requirement to provide survivor benefits, came into force.
6 Apr 09	The cap on statutory revaluation in deferment was reduced from 5% to 2.5%, for benefits accrued in relation to service from 6 April 2009.
6 Apr 09	The Upper Accrual Point replaced the Upper Earnings Limit for S2P and contracting-out purposes.

6 Apr 09   Safeguarded rights were abolished.

22 Apr 09   The Chancellor of the Exchequer delivered his second Budget, which included plans to restrict tax relief on pension contributions to the basic rate of tax from April 2011 for high earners, and the introduction of a special annual allowance for tax years 2009/10 and 2010/11. Income tax rates on investments held by EFRBS are to be increased to 50% from April 2010.

29 Apr 09   The Government published the Equality Bill, which it hoped would take effect from Autumn 2010. The Bill contains provisions that would extend and consolidate the current discrimination rules that apply to occupational pension schemes.

1 Jun 09   Regulations came into force, allowing certain payments made in error since 6 April 2006 to be treated as authorised payments.

29 Jun 09   The Pensions Regulator published the final Code of Practice on material detriment tests and announced new guidance on how it intends to use the 'material detriment test' powers. At the same time, it made minor amendments to its guidance on clearance and abandonment, updating them for changes introduced by the Pensions Act 2008.

1 Jul 09   Regulations came into force which, in certain circumstances, permit pensions in payment to be reduced on scheme wind-up without attracting unauthorised payments charges. The regulations are backdated to 6 April 2006.

21 Jul 09   The Finance Act 2009 received Royal Assent. The Act included provisions to introduce the 'special annual allowance charge', which imposes additional tax charges on high earners who, on or after 22 April 2009, make changes to either their normal pattern of regular pension contributions or the normal way in which their pension benefits accrue.

25 Sep 09   The High Court ruled in the *Heyday* case that the default retirement age of 65 could be justified. However, the judgment stated that the outcome might have been different if the Government had not previously announced in July 2009 that it intended to bring forward to 2010 its review of the default retirement age.

1 Dec 09   Regulations came into effect which allow some trivial payments to members (of up to £2,000) to be treated as authorised payments.

EMERGING DEVELOPMENTS

AGE DISCRIMINATION

On 6 December 2006, the High Court ruled that the issue of whether a default retirement age is unlawful should be referred to the European Court of Justice.

The 'Heyday' case was brought by Age UK (formerly Age Concern). They challenged the Employment Equality (Age) Regulations 2006 and argued that, in providing for a default retirement age, the Government has failed to properly implement the EU's equal treatment directive by denying people over 65 the right to choose to continue working.

In March 2009, the ECJ ruled that member states can provide for a default retirement age if it is justified by legitimate social policy objectives, such as those related to employment policy, the labour market or vocational training. In September 2009, the High Court ruled that the default retirement age of 65 does meet these conditions. However the judge made it clear that he was influenced by the Government's July 2009 announcement that it intends to review the default retirement age in 2010, one year earlier than previously expected.

Separately, in 2007, the Government consulted on the interaction between the Employment Equality (Age) Regulations and flexible retirement, including retirement after Normal Pension Age and the drawing of benefits while continuing to work. Following its initial consultation, the Government ran a second consultation, in March 2009, whilst explicitly stating that more discussion with interested parties would be required before any practical solutions could be agreed. At the time of writing, the Government's response to the second consultation was awaited.

STATE BENEFITS AND CONTRACTING OUT

The Pensions Act 2007 made some fundamental changes to state pensions and contracting out, including the abolition of contracting out under defined contribution schemes (probably from 2012) – *see Sections 5 and 6*. The Pensions Act 2008 made the following further changes:

- the calculation of state additional pension (SERPS and S2P) for individuals who have been contracted out and attain State Pension Age from 2020 onwards will be amended, *and*

- the abolition of all elements of protected rights at the same time as money purchase contracting out is abolished. Schemes will no longer be required to make special provision in relation to the protected rights of members.

SOLVENCY II AND ITS APPLICATION TO PENSION SCHEMES

Solvency II, a draft EU Directive, will dramatically change the way insurers reserve for their liabilities.

There has been much speculation about its possible extension to occupational pension schemes, including the possibility that it would introduce reserving requirements considerably in excess of technical provisions under the Pensions Act 2004 scheme funding regime *(see Section 20)*.

In September 2008, the European Commission issued a consultation, which discussed the issues for two types of occupational scheme: 'regulatory own funds' and cross-border schemes. Some commentators have taken the view that, in the absence of comment, there is no intention to apply a solvency requirement to other occupational schemes, the vast majority of schemes in the UK. This may be the case, but there could yet be further developments.

RISK SHARING

As part of the 2007 Deregulatory Review, the Government sought views on adding a third layer of legislation to cater for 'risk sharing' schemes. In June 2008, the DWP launched a detailed consultation, considering various options for risk sharing between employers and employees. The Government's response to the consultation confirmed that it would not remove mandatory indexation for defined benefit schemes or introduce conditional indexation, but would look in more detail at:

- introducing collective defined contribution schemes
- sharing longevity risk between members and employers, *and*
- reviewing the complexities of contracting out.

At the time of writing, it was not clear how or when these proposals would be taken forward.

PERSONAL ACCOUNTS

The Pensions Act 2008 puts in place the framework for the 'Personal Accounts' scheme, setting out the main rules for enrolment and contributions. The scheme is expected to commence in 2012. *See Section 9 for further information.*

PENSION PROTECTION FUND LEVY

The Pension Protection Fund is considering further changes to the formula for calculating schemes' levies, which are intended to take account of 'long-term risk'. These would not have effect before 2012/13. *See Section 22 for further information.*

EQUALITY BILL

In April 2009, the Government published the Equality Bill, which it hopes will take effect from Autumn 2010. *See Section 18 for further information.*

DISCLOSURE OF INFORMATION TO MEMBERS

The Government is considering restructuring and simplifying the existing disclosure legislation. New legislation is proposed, which would set out the high-level overarching principle that members should be given sufficient information to understand their benefits and make decisions in their own best interests. There would also be a Code of Practice on 'reasonable periods' for providing the information, which would replace the time periods specified in existing regulations. A new provision will also be introduced to allow information to be provided electronically.

The intention is to introduce new legislation from 6 April 2010.

TAX RELIEF FOR HIGH EARNERS

Plans to restrict pensions tax relief for high earners from April 2011 were announced in the 2009 Budget. Those with income above £180,000 p.a. would have tax relief limited to basic rate tax, with a taper applying for those with income between £150,000 and £180,000 p.a. The restriction will apply to both defined benefit accruals and member and employer money purchase contributions, but there are currently no details of how this will work. There will be extensive consultation on the precise details as there are likely to be significant practical issues in implementing this.

SIGNIFICANT PENSION DATES

AVCs

26.10.87	FSAVCs available.
06.04.88	Schemes must offer AVC facilities giving reasonable value for money.
March 1991	Refunds of surplus AVCs permitted (subject to tax charge).
06.04.06	(i) Requirement for occupational schemes to offer an AVC facility removed.
	(ii) Previous arrangements for taxation of AVCs replaced by Finance Act 2004 regime.

DISCLOSURE AND ACCOUNTING

May 1986	SORP 1 effective.
01.11.86	Disclosure requirements introduced.
15.12.88	FAS 87/8 effective for accounting periods beginning after 15.12.88 (15.12.86 for US plans).
28.09.92	Time limits for disclosure introduced.
06.04.97	New disclosure requirements introduced by Pensions Act 1995.
06.04.97	Financial Reports of Pension Schemes (SORP) replaced SORP 1.
15.12.97	FAS 87/8 disclosure requirements changed for accounting periods beginning after 15.12.97.
22.06.01	FRS 17 accounting procedures to be gradually introduced, starting with company accounts for years ending on or after this date.
31.12.02	New directors' remuneration reporting standards introduced.
01.01.03	Revised SORP issued for scheme years beginning on or after 01.01.03.
06.04.03	Statutory annual benefit projections to be provided to pension scheme members with money purchase benefits.
15.12.03	FAS 87/8 disclosure requirements changed for (in most cases) periods ending after 15.12.03.
20.03.04	DB scheme valuations to include solvency calculations.
01.01.05	Consolidated group accounts of companies listed and regulated in EU Member States generally required to comply with International Accounting Standards (IAS). Full implementation of FRS 17 required by UK companies not adopting IAS.
30.12.05	New requirement for trustees to provide defined benefit members with an annual funding statement.
06.04.07	FRS 17 disclosure requirements brought into line with those of IAS 19.

DIVORCE

01.07.96	Courts in England and Wales required to take pension rights into account when making financial provision orders on petitions for divorce filed on or after this date.
19.08.96	Courts in Scotland required to take pension rights into account when making financial provision orders on actions for divorce filed on or after this date.
01.12.00	Pension sharing provisions in force.
05.12.05	Revised forms and procedures for pension sharing and earmarking introduced.
06.04.09	Legislative restrictions on safeguarded rights abolished.

EQUAL TREATMENT

08.04.76	*Defrenne* judgment in ECJ established (after later clarification) the right of men and women to equal access to pension schemes.
07.11.87	Sex Discrimination Act 1986 came into force: compulsory retirement ages must be the same for men and women.
06.04.88	Protected Rights annuities must be on unisex basis.
17.05.90	*Barber* judgment (as clarified by later cases and Article 119 protocol): occupational pensions are pay, and benefits in respect of service after 17.05.90 must be equal (unless claims lodged before this date). Applicable to survivors' pensions, but not to actuarial factors in funded defined benefit schemes.
23.06.94	Maternity and family leave provisions of Social Security Act 1989 brought into effect. Benefits during periods of paid maternity absence must continue to accrue based on notional full salary.
16.10.94	All employment rights (other than pay) to be maintained during statutory ordinary maternity leave.
02.12.96	Parts of the Disability Discrimination Act 1995 dealing with employment and the supply of services effective.
May 1999	The relevant article (formerly 119) of the Treaty of Rome is renumbered and becomes 'Article 141 of the Treaty of Rome, as amended by the Treaty of Amsterdam'.
01.07.00	Discrimination against part-timers illegal under the terms of the Employment Relations Act 1999 unless objectively justified.
01.10.02	Discrimination against fixed-term workers became illegal unless objectively justified.
06.04.03	Changes to maternity, paternity and adoption rights.
01.12.03	Legislation against discrimination by sexual orientation in force.
02.12.03	Legislation against discrimination by religion or belief in force.

01.10.04	Revised disability discrimination legislation in force.
05.12.05	The Civil Partnership Act 2004 came into force. Civil partners must be given the same benefits, for future service, as those who are married.
01.12.06	Legislation against discrimination by age in force.
01.04.07	Statutory maternity and adoption pay periods increased from 26 to 39 weeks.

HMRC APPROVAL AND LIMITS

06.04.70	New code approval available.
06.04.73	New code compulsory for new schemes and amended existing schemes.
05.04.80	New code for all approved schemes accepting contributions.
17.03.87	Revised limits for new members on or after 17.03.87.
06.04.87	Controls on surplus.
01.07.88	Personal pensions available.
14.03.89 & 01.06.89	1989 Revenue limits regime introduced for members joining newly established schemes on or after 14.03.89 and existing schemes on or after 01.06.89.
27.07.89	Concurrent membership of approved and unapproved schemes permissible.
31.08.91	Changes in Revenue SPSS practices, including 12:1 conversion factor; relaxation of retained benefits tests; other minor changes.
29.11.91	New Practice Notes issued for new schemes.
30.06.95	Deferral of annuity purchase and income withdrawal permitted for personal pensions.
01.01.96	New rules for maintenance and submission to Revenue of pension scheme information.
01.06.96	New basis for spreading tax relief on special contributions if paid in a chargeable period ending on or after 01.06.96.
01.01.97	Reinstatement to pension schemes permitted on special terms for those mis-sold personal pensions.
02.07.97	Tax credits on UK dividend income can no longer be claimed by pension schemes.
30.06.99	Annuity purchase deferral and income drawdown introduced for money purchase occupational schemes and buy-out contracts.
06.04.01	Changes to personal pension tax regime: (i) Contributions of up to £3,600 p.a. permitted irrespective of earnings. (ii) 'Carry forward' facility removed.

       (iii) 'Carry back' facility radically reduced.

       (iv) Contributions for risk benefits, for new entrants, limited to 10% of total contribution paid for year.

       (v) Concurrent membership of occupational and personal pension schemes permitted for those earning under £30,000 p.a.

11.05.01	Rate of tax on refund of surplus reduced from 40% to 35%.
06.04.02	Withdrawal of interim scheme approval option, except for new schemes following sale/purchase.
06.04.06	New tax regime replaces former contribution and benefit limits, permitting all individuals lifetime tax-privileged pension savings up to a standard limit (£1.8m for 2010/11 to 2015/16).
22.04.09	Special annual allowance charge introduced for 2009/10 and 2010/11 as an 'anti-forestalling' measure prior to the abolition of higher-rate tax relief for high earners from 2011.
06.04.10	Increase in the normal minimum pension age from 50 to 55.

PROTECTING MEMBERS

06.04.88	Compulsory membership of occupational schemes prohibited.
29.04.88	Financial Services Act 1986 effective.
17.08.90	No surplus refund to employer unless LPI given.
12.11.90	Independent trustee on insolvency.
02.04.91	Pensions Ombudsman in operation.
May 1991	Pension Schemes Registry established.
31.07.91	First levy due.
09.03.92	Self-investment restrictions effective.
29.06.92	Debt on employer on winding up of pension scheme.
06.10.96	Member-nominated trustees legislation commenced (and became fully effective from 06.04.97).
06.04.97	(i) Minimum Funding Requirement and Statement of Investment Principles introduced.
	(ii) LPI increases compulsory for future benefit accrual.
	(iii) Appointments of scheme actuary and auditor required.
	(iv) Internal Dispute Resolution Procedures required.
	(v) Pensions Compensation Board powers commenced.
	(vi) Opra can remove or suspend trustees and impose civil penalties.
01.06.97	Custody of investments brought within the scope of the Financial Services Act 1986.
03.04.00	Late payment of employees' contributions became a civil rather than a criminal offence.

29.05.00	Protection of pension rights on bankruptcy under approved pension schemes introduced.
06.04.01	Requirement for monitoring contributions to personal pensions introduced.
01.12.01	Most provisions of Financial Services and Markets Act 2000 effective.
19.03.02	Interim MFR changes: lengthened deficit correction periods; partial abolition of annual recertification; changes to wind-up asset allocation priority calculations and debt-on-employer calculations where employer solvent.
15.03.04	For calculation effective dates from this date debt on employer increased for solvent employer scheme wind-ups beginning after 10 June 2003, from MFR to full buy-out shortfall.
06.04.05	First provisions of Pensions Act 2004 came into force, including Pension Protection Fund, new Pensions Regulator and:
	(i) introduction of pension protection on transfer of employment to which TUPE regulations apply, *and*
	(ii) changes to LPI cap from 5% p.a. to 2.5% p.a. for future service. Money purchase benefits exempt from LPI.
01.09.05	Financial Assistance Scheme came into operation.
02.09.05	Debt on employer when leaving multi-employer schemes increases to share of full buy-out deficiency, unless approved withdrawal arrangement put in place.
30.12.05	(i) Introduction of new scheme-specific funding requirement contained in Pensions Act 2004 replacing the MFR.
	(ii) New requirements in force for schemes operating as 'cross-border' within the EU.
06.04.06	Remaining Pensions Act 2004 provisions in force, including:
	(i) new regulations on scheme modifications (section 67)
	(ii) new requirements for member-nominated trustees, including removal of the facility to opt out, *and*
	(iii) new requirements placed on trustees to have specific knowledge and understanding of pension issues.
06.04.08	Revised debt-on-employer provisions give more flexibility in multi-employer schemes.

STAKEHOLDER SCHEMES

01.10.00	Stakeholder schemes may be established.
06.04.01	Members may join stakeholder schemes.
08.10.01	Employer access requirements introduced.
06.04.05	Lifestyle arrangement must be made available by all stakeholder pension providers. Maximum annual management charge increased to 1.5% p.a. for the first ten years and 1% p.a. thereafter.

STATE SCHEMES AND CONTRACTING OUT

06.04.75	Benefits under Graduated Scheme cease to accrue.
06.04.78	Start of SERPS and contracting out.
01.01.85	Anti-franking introduced for leavers on or after 01.01.85.
01.01.86	Transfer Premiums may be paid.
01.11.86	Contracting-out quality test removed.
06.04.87	(i) Contracting out via Personal Pension could be backdated to 06.04.87.
	(ii) Trustees liable for CEPs/LRPs.
06.04.88	(i) SERPS benefits reduced for persons retiring after 2000.
	(ii) GMP accrual rates reduced.
	(iii) GMPs accrued after 06.04.88 must receive increases of up to 3% p.a. from scheme.
	(iv) Fixed rate GMP revaluation for future leavers reduced to 7.5%.
	(v) Widowers' GMPs introduced.
	(vi) Money purchase contracting out introduced.
	(vii) 2% incentive payments introduced.
17.05.90	Protected rights under COMPS may commence at any age between 60 and 65.
06.04.93	(i) Fixed rate GMP revaluation for future leavers reduced to 7%.
	(ii) 2% incentive payments ceased; 1% incentive payments introduced for personal pension contributors aged 30 or over.
06.04.96	Protected rights from COMPS can be secured on winding up by means of appropriate insurance policies.
06.04.97	(i) 1% incentive payments paid to personal pension contributors aged 30 or over ceased.
	(ii) Age-related rebates introduced for COMPS and APPS.
	(iii) Link with SERPS broken.
	(iv) GMP accruals cease and Reference Scheme Test introduced for COSRS.
	(v) Limited Revaluation and State Scheme premium options (other than CEPs) removed.
	(vi) Fixed rate GMP revaluation for future leavers reduced to 6.25%.
	(vii) COMBS permitted.
	(viii) Annuities purchased with post-April 1997 protected rights must in all cases have LPI, fixed 5% p.a. or full RPI increases, but need not include a widow(er)'s pension for single retirees.
01.01.01	Members' protected rights may be commuted in cases of serious ill-health.
06.04.02	(i) State Second Pension (S2P) replaces SERPS.
	(ii) New table of rebates effective from 2002 to 2007, with

	different levels of rebates applying to different tranches of earnings for personal pensions (but not occupational pensions).
	(iii) Fixed rate GMP revaluation for future leavers reduced to 4.5%.
	(iv) New pre-97 protected rights annuities need not include a contingent widow(er)'s pension for retirees who are single.
	(v) Removal of requirement for automatic periodic certification of adequacy of assets of COSRS for contracting out.
06.10.02	Inherited SERPS pension reduced from 100% to 50%, subject to age-related transitional provisions.
06.10.03	Introduction of State Pension Credits which replaces Minimum Income Guarantee scheme.
06.04.05	Higher increases given to individuals deferring state benefits beyond state pension age, and introduction of a new lump sum option.
28.11.05	An amendment to regulations allows the bulk transfer of protected rights from one COMPS to another without the consent of the member.
06.04.07	(i) New table of rebates effective for 2007 to 2012.
	(ii) Fixed rate GMP revaluation for future leavers reduced to 4%.
06.04.09	Trustees, with employer consent, able to convert GMPs into 'normal' scheme pensions.
06.04.10	State pension age for women starts to increase from 60 to 65, over a transitional period to 2020.
06.04.10	Pensions Act 2007 introduces extensive changes to state pensions, including:
	(i) reduction in the number of contributory years needed to qualify for full Basic State Pension (BSP) to 30 for both men and women, *and*
	(ii) phasing-in of reforms to S2P to make it a flat-rate top-up to BSP.
2012	Further changes under Pensions Acts 2007 and 2008 expected to take effect, including:
	(i) abolition of contracting out on a defined contribution basis and removal of all restrictions applying to protected rights funds
	(ii) BSP to increase in line with average earnings *and*
	(iii) Personal Accounts scheme to be introduced.
06.04.2024	State Pension Age for men and women to increase from 65 to 68 over a transitional period to 2046.

TRANSFERS, PRESERVATION AND REVALUATION

06.04.75	Leavers on or after 06.04.75 aged at least 26 and with 5 years' qualifying service entitled to preserved benefits.
01.01.86	(i) Statutory right to cash equivalent for leavers on or after 01.01.86. Non-GMP deferred pensions of such leavers

	accrued from 01.01.85 to be revalued, broadly at lower of 5% p.a. or price inflation.
	(ii) Age 26 requirement for preservation dropped.
06.04.88	Minimum period of qualifying service for entitlement to preserved benefits amended to 2 years, for leavers on or after 06.04.88.
01.01.91	Leavers on or after 01.01.91 receive revaluations on whole non-GMP deferred pension.
29.07.94	Protected rights may be transferred to a contracted-out occupational scheme of which the individual has previously been a member.
19.03.97	Occupational pension scheme members permitted to transfer personal pension benefits into a FSAVC.
06.04.97	(i) Rights to cash equivalent extended to pre-01.01.86 leavers.
	(ii) Three-month guarantee on cash equivalent quotations for salary-related benefits introduced.
	(iii) Cash equivalents subjected to a minimum of the MFR value.
01.12.00	Investment-linked annuity allowed as an alternative to LPI increase for non-protected rights under a money purchase scheme.
06.04.01	Certification requirements for transfers to personal pensions revised.
04.08.03	New transfer legislation allowing trustees to cut back individual transfer values where scheme is underfunded.
06.04.06	Leavers with between 3 and 24 months' pensionable service entitled to a cash transfer sum as an option.
01.10.08	New legislation requiring transfer values to be set by trustees (on a 'best estimate' basis after taking actuarial advice).
06.04.09	Minimum revaluation of non-GMP deferred pensions accrued after 05.04.09 reduced to the lower of 2.5% p.a. or price inflation.

UNAPPROVED BENEFITS

27.07.89	Membership of unapproved schemes permitted to provide benefits on top of those from approved schemes.
01.11.91	Taxation of *ex gratia* lump sum benefits other than on genuine redundancy or as compensation for loss of office.
01.12.93	Taxation of lump sum benefits from offshore FURBS.
06.04.98	National Insurance Contributions payable on contributions to money purchase FURBS.
06.04.99	National Insurance contributions payable on contributions to final salary FURBS.
06.04.06	Special tax treatment of unapproved pension arrangements removed (subject to transitional provisions). Unapproved schemes become Employer-Financed Retirement Benefit Schemes.

UK PENSIONS CASE LAW

This section lists a number of legal cases that we feel have potentially significant importance in the development and understanding of pensions. It is not intended to be an exhaustive list and the comments given are merely an indication of the case content. No reliance should be placed on these summary comments. Legal advice should always be sought for guidance as to the applicability of case law.

The year quoted below for each case usually, but not always, refers to the year of appearance in a published law report. This may be a later year than that in which the judgment was given.

TRUSTEESHIP

Re Whiteley (Court of Appeal) [1886]
The duty of a trustee is to take such care as an ordinary prudent man would take if he were minded to make investment for the benefit of other people for whom he felt bound to provide.

Learoyd v Whiteley (House of Lords) [1887]
A trustee must use ordinary care and caution and is entitled to rely upon skilled persons.

Re Skeats' Settlement (High Court) [1889]
The power of appointment of trustees is fiduciary. The person in whom the power is vested cannot appoint themselves as a trustee.

Re Londonderry's Settlement (Court of Appeal) [1965]
Documents relating to trustees' decision-making on a discretionary matter do not have to be disclosed, in the absence of an action impugning the trustees' good faith.

Re Hastings-Bass (Court of Appeal) [1975]
Where a trustee is given a discretion and acts in good faith, the Court should not normally interfere with his action, provided that the trustee has taken account of the relevant considerations.

Cowan v Scargill (High Court) [1984]
The duty of trustees to act in the best interests of the present and future beneficiaries of the trust is paramount. This almost certainly means best *financial* interests.

Martin v City of Edinburgh District Council (Court of Sessions, Scotland) [1989]
Whilst trustees cannot be expected to set aside completely all personal preferences and conscientiously-held principles, they must exercise fair and impartial judgement on the merits of the issues before them. The investment duty of a trustee is not merely to rubber-stamp the professional advice of financial advisers.

Wilson v Law Debenture (High Court) [1995]
Courts will not compel trustees to disclose the reasons for the exercise of a discretion.

Elliott v Pensions Ombudsman (High Court) [1998]

Trustees can exercise discretion to favour certain categories of members over other categories.

Harding and Others (Trustees of Joy Manufacturing Holdings Ltd Pension and Life Assurance Scheme), petitioners (Court of Session, Inner House, Scotland) [1999]

Trustees in Scotland may not (as in England) surrender the exercise of their discretion to the Court.

Edge v Pensions Ombudsman (Court of Appeal) [2000]

The main purpose of a pension scheme is not served by putting an employer out of business, nor by setting contributions or benefits at levels which deter employees from joining. Trustees are not obliged to put forward proposals on use of surplus that they do not think are fair to the employers.

When exercising discretions, trustees must give proper consideration to all relevant matters, but cannot then be criticised if they reach a decision that appears to favour one interest over others. However, any explanation given may be evaluated critically, and appropriate inferences drawn from a failure to give an explanation when called for.

Allen v TKM Group Pension Scheme (Pensions Ombudsman) [2002]

Trustees may sometimes find themselves judged to have acted with maladministration in circumstances where they would not be regarded as acting unlawfully. As a matter of good administrative practice, trustees should provide reasons for their decisions to those with a legitimate interest in the matter, and should generally make the minutes of their meetings available to scheme members.

The Ombudsman's ruling appears to contradict an established trust law principle that trustees are not obliged to reveal the reasons for their decisions when exercising discretions. An Ombudsman's ruling is, however, not a binding precedent on schemes generally and it may be that a Court would take a different view from the Ombudsman.

Schmitt v Rosewood Trust Ltd (Privy Council) [2003]

It is fundamental to the law of trusts that the courts have jurisdiction to supervise and, if appropriate, to intervene in the administration of a trust. One aspect of this jurisdiction to supervise is the right to seek disclosure of the Trust documents. Therefore it is not necessary for an individual to prove entitlement to benefit from the trust to enable disclosure of trust documentation.

Lawrence Graham Trust Corporation v Trustees of Greenup and Thompson Limited Pension Scheme (Pensions Ombudsman) [2008]

The trustees made a loan to the principal employer, in breach of section 40 of the Pensions Act 1995. The Ombudsman determined that, when the employer went into liquidation, the loan had not been repaid. The trustees were guilty of breach of trust and personally liable for the outstanding amount.

Gregson v HAE Trustees (High Court) [2008]

Beneficiaries cannot bring indirect 'dog-leg' claims against directors of a corporate trustee, as this would circumvent the principle that no direct duty is owed by the directors to the beneficiaries. Although this appears to conflict with a 1997 ruling that an indirect claim could be brought, the difference seems to hinge on the specific circumstances of the case, in particular that the trustee company in the earlier case was the trustee of only one trust and had no other business interest.

EMPLOYERS

Re Courage Group's Pension Schemes, Ryan v Imperial Brewing (High Court) [1987]

The ability to substitute a principal employer is dependent on the purpose for which the intended substitution would be made. A rule-amending power could not be used to change the principal employer to a holding company which had no connection with the previous principal employer and whose purpose was to retain control of a surplus contributed by companies which the holding company had bought.

Imperial Group Pension Trust v Imperial Tobacco (High Court) [1991]

Pension benefits are part of the consideration received by employees for their services. The employer owes his employees a duty of good faith in relation to a pension scheme, and should not act so as to destroy or seriously damage their relationship of confidence and trust.

Hillsdown v Pensions Ombudsman (High Court) [1997]

Under the scheme, the trustees had sole power to deal with a surplus. The employer threatened to bring in employees of new employers to run down the surplus, and persuaded the trustees to agree to an amendment enabling a transfer to another scheme from which a refund to the employer could be made. The Court ruled that the amendment and transfer were for an improper purpose and ordered the refunded surplus to be returned to the scheme. It further ruled that the employer's implied obligation of trust and confidence prevented it from using a power to suspend contributions, whilst at the same time using a power to adhere further employers.

Air Jamaica v Charlton (Privy Council) [1999]

Bearing in mind the employer's obligation to exercise powers in good faith, it was difficult to see how the scheme could be amended in any significant respect once it had discontinued and wind-up was anticipated.

University of Nottingham v Eyett (High Court) [1999]

Where all the relevant information is available to the employee to make his own informed choice, the employer's implied obligation of good faith does not require it to draw the member's attention to the fact that he might have done better financially by changing the timing of his choice.

BENEFITS AND CONTRIBUTIONS

Packwood v APS (Pensions Ombudsman) [1995]

Where trustees failed to consider the use of a power of amendment to increase benefits, this was held to be a breach of trust and maladministration. However, the employer did not breach his implied obligation of good faith by preferring his own interests, having first considered the interests of pensioners.

Buckley v Hudson Forge (High Court) [1999]

Letters to members do not have the effect of a contract and do not override the scheme rules.

Barclays Bank v Holmes (High Court) [2000]

Where a defined contribution section has been added to a defined benefit scheme, the surplus in the defined benefit section may (provided that this is not contrary to the trust deed) be used to meet the defined contributions.

Merchant Navy Ratings Pension Fund Trustees v Chambers (High Court) [2001]

An amendment which allows a pensioner's benefits to be transferred without consent is not automatically prohibited. It is for the actuary to consider whether to give a 'section 67' certificate.

Royal Masonic Hospital v Pensions Ombudsman (High Court) [2001]

Unfunded pension schemes are not subject to the preservation requirements.

Hagen v ICI Chemicals and Polymers Ltd (High Court) [2001]

The Court ruled that the employer had misrepresented the position to employees, when informing them that they would receive broadly similar benefits on transfer to a new scheme following a business transfer. In fact, some individuals' benefits under the new scheme were as much as 5% worse than under the old scheme.

Beckmann v Dynamco Whicheloe Macfarlane Ltd (European Court of Justice) [2002]

Benefits payable from an occupational pension scheme on redundancy, being benefits payable before normal pension age, do not fall under the exemption for occupational pension scheme rights under the TUPE legislation. The 2003 ruling in *Martin and Others v South Bank University* built on this decision, extending it to some other early retirement situations.

Aon Trust Corporation Ltd v KPMG (Court of Appeal) [2005]

The exercise of an express power in the scheme rules (to reduce benefits when the scheme was in deficit) was a power to modify the scheme, coming within the ambit of section 67 of the Pensions Act 1995. Consequently, the power could not be exercised (without member consent) if it would adversely affect accrued rights or entitlements.

The judgment also placed limitations on what could be regarded as a 'money purchase scheme'. The judge ruled that the scheme in question was not such a scheme because it provided 'average salary benefits', and hence it was subject to the MFR and debt-on-the-employer legislation.

Pinsent Curtis v Capital Cranfield Trustees Ltd (Court of Appeal) [2005]

Under a scheme rule which empowered the trustees to determine 'appropriate' contributions, the trustees could seek a lump sum contribution equal to the buy-out deficit during the period for which notice had been given by the employer that he would terminate the scheme.

British Vita Unlimited v British Vita Pension Fund Trustees Ltd (High Court) [2007]

Under the scheme's rules, contributions were set by the trustees without the need for the employer's agreement. This power did not conflict with the transitional

MFR legislation applying prior to the scheme's first valuation under the Pensions Act 2004. It therefore did not prevent the trustees from calling for a higher contribution in accordance with the rules. The position remains unclear for schemes that have put in place a schedule of contributions under the new regime.

WINDING UP

Bridge Trustees Ltd v Yates (High Court) [2008]

Pensions deriving from money purchase assets but paid directly by the scheme are, for the purposes of the statutory winding-up provisions, no longer money purchase benefits once in payment. Money purchase benefits subject to a GMP minimum count as underpin benefits.

Bainbridge v Quarters Trustees Ltd (High Court) [2008]

Unless they are specifically ring-fenced under the rules, money purchase assets will not be ring-fenced on wind-up. The extent to which this applies to schemes entering wind-up after 5 April 2005 is unclear.

NBPF Pension Trustees Ltd v Warnock-Smith (High Court) [2008]

Trustees may use scheme assets on wind-up to purchase insurance to protect themselves against 'run-off' liabilities and claims from overlooked beneficiaries.

MCP v Aon (High Court) [2009]

Trustees are not discharged from liabilities in a scheme wind-up despite giving notice under section 27 of the Trustee Act 1925. The case was brought against the scheme administrators, who had lost records of transferred-in members.

SURPLUS AND DEFICITS

British Coal Corporation v British Coal Staff Superannuation Scheme Trustees (High Court) [1995]

An employer's liability to pay future standard contributions may be set against any scheme surplus.

National Grid Co plc v Laws (Court of Appeal) [1999]

Members have no rights in a surplus, only a reasonable expectation that any dealings with that surplus will pay a fair regard to their interests.

Wrightson Ltd v Fletcher Challenge Nominees Ltd (Privy Council) [2001]

In a balance of cost scheme, any surplus on a final dissolution is generally to be considered as resulting from past overfunding by the employer.

EQUAL TREATMENT

Defrenne v Sabena (No. 2) (European Court of Justice) [1976]

The principle of equal pay, under Article 119 (now Article 141) of the Treaty of Rome, may be relied upon by the national courts. However, this cannot be applied to claims for periods prior to 8 April 1976. (This case has been taken to indicate that *access* to pension schemes should be equal for men and women from 8 April 1976.)

Bilka-Kaufhaus GmbH v Weber von Hartz (European Court of Justice) [1986]

Where the exclusion of part-timers affected a far greater number of women than men, the equal pay requirements of the Treaty of Rome were infringed unless the employer could show that the exclusion was objectively justified.

Barber v GRE (European Court of Justice) [1990]

Benefits under a pension scheme are deferred pay and therefore subject to equal treatment between men and women.

Bullock v Alice Ottley School (Court of Appeal) [1992]

An employer may have a variety of retirement ages so long as there is no direct or indirect discrimination based on gender.

Roberts v Birds Eye Walls (European Court of Justice) [1993]

The principle of equal treatment presupposes that men and women are in identical situations. Therefore, where a 'bridging pension' is paid only to a male member to offset the fact that a woman's State pension starts earlier, this is not direct sex discrimination. [*Note*: a later case in the ECJ, *Bestuur van het Algemeen Burgerlijk Pensioenfonds v Beune*, seemingly contradicts this conclusion, although some arguments have been advanced, distinguishing the circumstances and reconciling the results.]

Ten Oever v Stichting Bedrijfspensioenfonds voor het Glazenwassers (European Court of Justice) [1993]

A survivor's pension falls within the scope of the equal pay requirements. However, equal benefits only had to be provided in respect of benefits earned from 17 May 1990 (the date of the *Barber* judgment), unless a claim had already been started before then.

Coloroll Pension Trustees v Russell (European Court of Justice) [1994]

Equal pension benefits for men and women need only be provided for service from 17 May 1990, except where a claim had been initiated earlier. Unequal benefits must be levelled up for any service after 17 May 1990, but schemes can, in principle, change benefit structures to level down for any subsequent service after the date of change.

Additional benefits stemming from contributions paid by employees on a purely voluntary basis are not pay and therefore not subject to the same equal treatment requirements.

Preston v Wolverhampton (European Court of Justice) [2000]

Part-timers whose exclusion from membership of an occupational pension scheme amounts to indirect sex discrimination can claim retrospective membership as far back as 8 April 1976. However, national courts may impose a time limit on lodging claims after leaving service. The House of Lords later confirmed that, for the UK, this time limit is six months.

Uppingham School v Shillcock (High Court) [2002]

Offsets from pensionable salary without pro-rating for part-timers are not discriminatory where applied equally to all members. The approach adopted was in any case objectively justifiable as a reasonable method of implementing the legitimate objective of integration with the State scheme.

Allonby v Accrington & Rossendale College (European Court of Justice) [2004]

The female claimant did not have to identify a male comparator with the same employer, where the indirect sex discrimination arose from a wider 'single source'. (In this case, the single source was the entry rules to a particular statutory pension scheme.)

Lindorfer v Council of the European Union (European Court of Justice) [2007]

The use of sex-dependent factors in the calculation of transferred-in benefits in this case infringed the principle of non-discrimination on account of sex. However, the implications for UK schemes are unclear.

Bloxham v Freshfields (Employment Tribunal) [2007]

The tribunal held that the treatment suffered by Mr Bloxham when Freshfields introduced new pension arrangements was potentially discriminatory on grounds of age, but that Freshfields' actions were objectively justified as no less discriminatory means were available to them.

Foster Wheeler v Hanley (Court of Appeal) [2009]

Consent to retirement from age 60 could not be withheld from members with service in the *Barber* window (with a Normal Retirement Age of 60). For any part of the benefit due from age 65, an early retirement reduction could be applied. This was consistent with the 2007 judgment in *Cripps v TSL* in relation to the winding-up statutory priority order.

Age UK v Secretary of State for Business, Innovation & Skills (High Court) [2009]

The Court ruled in the 'Heyday' case that the default retirement age of 65 was not unlawful when adopted by the Government in 2006 in the Employment Equality (Age) Regulations. But the judge commented that there was a compelling case for the default to be increased from 65.

ADVISERS AND PROFESSIONALS

Re George Newnes Group Pension Fund (High Court) [1969]

An actuary is an expert. If an actuary acts honestly and does not make an objective mistake, the decision is not open to challenge.

Bartlett v Barclays Trust Co Ltd (No. 1) (High Court) [1980]

A higher duty of care is expected from professional trustees.

Auty v National Coal Board (Court of Appeal) [1985]

Actuarial evidence (relating to loss of value dependent on future economic trends) can be rejected by courts on the grounds that it is based on hearsay and speculative in nature.

Re Imperial Foods Ltd Pension Scheme (High Court) [1986]

An actuarial certificate (relating to a bulk transfer payment) could not be successfully challenged in the absence of a cardinal error of principle or a mathematical error.

Re the Minworth Limited Pension Scheme, Anderson v William M Mercer (Pensions Ombudsman) [1999]

A professional trustee who had failed to give proper thought to risks associated with investment mismatching during a wind-up was 'recklessly indifferent' to the fact that it was in breach of its duties, and was therefore not entitled to be exonerated by a clause exempting trustees from liability other than arising from wilful default or fraud. In addition, the Ombudsman ruled that an actuary was inherently 'concerned with the administration' of the scheme, and so a complaint against the actuary came within his jurisdiction.

Wirral BC v Evans (Court of Appeal) [2000]

Administrators have no general duty to advise present or intending members of the scheme.

Gleave v PPF (High Court) [2008]

Insolvency practitioners cannot dispute section 75 debt claims as calculated by the scheme actuary. The companies went into administration in 2001. The insolvency practitioners had argued that the actuary had overestimated the claim, exercisable by the PPF, by using later mortality tables.

TAXATION

Hillsdown v Commissioners of Inland Revenue (High Court) [1999]

The employer had been obliged to repay a refund of surplus on which tax had been paid. The Inland Revenue had originally refused to reimburse this tax. The Court ruled that a repayment of surplus in which no beneficial interest passed was not a payment for the purposes of section 601 ICTA 1988.

JP Morgan Fleming Claverhouse Investment Trust plc and the Association of Investment Trust Companies v Commissioners of HM Revenue & Customs (European Court of Justice) [2007]

The ECJ has outlined principles for assessing whether Investment Trust Companies (ITC) should be exempt from paying VAT in respect of investment management charges. The particular question has now been referred to the UK courts to make a ruling. The NAPF and Wheels Common Investment Fund have launched a joint challenge against HMRC, on the grounds that any such exemption should also apply to pension schemes.

ERRORS AND DISPUTES

Bradstock v Nabarro Nathanson (High Court) [1996]

In negligence claims, time runs from the date when damage occurred, not from when the negligence of the advice first became known.

Armitage v Nurse (Court of Appeal) [1997]

Trustees can be indemnified under an exoneration clause, even where they have been grossly negligent, provided that they were not reckless.

Hogg Robinson v Pensions Ombudsman (High Court) [1998]

The trustees were not guilty of maladministration by refusing to extend a guarantee period where the member had had problems because of an incorrect quotation. (But the Court's implication, and the Ombudsman's subsequent determination when he revisited the case, was that the failure to produce an accurate quotation in good time was maladministration.)

Derby v Scottish Equitable (Court of Appeal) [2001]

A member who had received a substantial overpayment from a personal pension was obliged to give up the overpayment after the insurer had realised its mistake, except to the limited extent to which he had spent the money irreversibly and could claim a 'change of position'.

Steria v Hutchison (High Court) [2006]

The judge decided against previous precedents which indicated that the trust deed and rules would override mistakes in the scheme booklet and other communications to the member. The judge did, however, indicate that the error here was in a 'relatively simple' area of benefit entitlement, and that the conclusion would have been likely to be different if a more complicated area were involved.

Tyler v Robert Fleming Benefit Consultants and Minet Benefit Consultancy (Pensions Ombudsman) [2008]

The Ombudsman held that Minet (the former administrators) were responsible for the disappearance of data in respect of Mr Tyler. He directed Minet to put Mr Tyler in the position he would have been in had he been included in the subsequent bulk buy out by purchasing a deferred annuity for him.

Colorcon v Huckell (High Court) [2009]

The Court granted an order for rectification of the scheme rules. Evidence showed that the rules relating to the revaluation of deferred pensioners had been amended incorrectly and contrary to the common intention of the employer and trustees.

GENERAL AND MISCELLANEOUS

Mettoy Pension Trustees v Evans (High Court) [1991]

Interpretation of pension scheme documents should be practical and purposive, rather than detailed and literal.

Employers' contribution rates are in practice set by agreement between the employers and trustees, after consultation with the actuaries, even where the power is vested in the trustees. On the other hand, although surplus in a balance of cost scheme is derived from past employer overfunding, it should not necessarily be assumed that any surplus belongs to the employer.

Nuthall v Merrill Lynch (UK) Final Salary Plan trustees (Pensions Ombudsman) [1999]

Trustees can be guilty of maladministration for unnecessary delays in transferring money to individual members' accounts, even if the payments have been made within the maximum timescales permitted by the Pensions Act 1995.

Needler Financial Services v Taber (High Court) [2001]

The windfall bonus arising from an insurer's demutualisation was not to be taken into account in determining the loss resulting from negligent advice to take out a personal pension.

Hoover Ltd v Hetherington (High Court) [2002]

The word 'retires' signifies final withdrawal from some office, without prejudicing the individual's entitlement to work for another office or business.

The Court also held that retirement from service by reason of incapacity included retirement in circumstances where the member was in fact capable of full-time work, albeit not of the kind normally undertaken by him or her.

Durant v Financial Services Authority (Court of Appeal) [2003]

Personal data is information that affects an individual's privacy. Two questions can assist in determining the nature of the information: is the information 'biographical', and who is the focus of the information? The fact that an individual's name appears in a document does not mean it will necessarily be personal data about that individual.

The Data Protection Act applies to manual data held in a 'relevant filing system'. A filing system will only be such if it is of sufficient sophistication to provide 'ready accessibility' broadly equivalent to a computerised filing system.

Bonner v NHS Pension Scheme (Pensions Ombudsman) [2004]

The scheme's inability to deal quickly with a transfer payment was maladministration. (The ruling essentially extended the duty to carry out investment transactions promptly, as seen in *Nuthall v Merrill Lynch* above, to other types of pension scheme transaction and showed that the Ombudsman expects trustees to operate without delay in all cases.)

Robins and others v Secretary of State for Work and Pensions (commonly referred to as the Allied Steel Workers (ASW) case) (European Court of Justice) [2007]

The ECJ ruled that the UK Government had not adequately protected the rights of workers in occupational schemes in the event of insolvency (in particular, an insolvency occurring in April 2003), under the 1980 European Insolvency Directive.

In a related case, shortly after the ECJ's ruling, the UK High Court found in *Bradley and others v Secretary of State* that the Government had provided misleading official information on the security of occupational pension schemes and was guilty of maladministration.

INTERNATIONAL

Introduction

The summaries below have been derived from Hewitt's online eGuides. Necessarily, much detail has been omitted. For example, the 'Recent developments' section contains a single item that we hope will be interest. Readers interested in seeing the fully detailed eGuides should e-mail *InternationalBenefits@Hewitt.Com*.

Countries covered:

- Americas:
  - Brazil
  - Canada
  - United States of America

- Europe:
  - Notes on the European Union
  - Belgium
  - France
  - Germany
  - The Netherlands
  - Russia
  - Spain
  - Switzerland

- Asia Pacific:
  - Australia
  - China
  - India
  - Japan.

The economic indicators and social security information for selected countries *on pages 207 to 211* have been obtained by Economic and Financial Publishing Ltd from the sources indicated.

ECONOMIC INDICATORS AND SOCIAL SECURITY INFORMATION FOR SELECTED COUNTRIES

Notes to the Following Table

(a)   Gradually being raised to 67 m&f by 2029 (Germany) 2023 (Australia) 2022 (USA).

(b)   Flexible retirement age.

(c)   State pension ages are gradually being equalised at 65 m&f.

(d)   Gradually being equalised at 68 m&f by 2046.

(e)   Being equalised at 62 m&f from 2009.

(f)   Under the New Pensions System. A flat-rate National Old Age pension is also provided for poor people aged 65 and over.

(g)   Mostly funded through general taxation.

(h)   On all earnings (in some countries above a minimum amount).

(i)   Up to earnings ceiling.

(j)   • UK: Up to earnings limit, but no contributions are paid on earnings below £5,200. Employee contributes an additional 1% on earnings above the ceiling.

      • USA: 6.2% on earnings up to the ceiling plus 1.45% on all earnings.

(k)   Variable depending on employee level of earnings.

(l)   Small, flat-rate (Denmark: employer DDK1,950, employee DDK975).

(m)   3 times the average wage for the district, city or province.

(n)   The figure shown is the TA ceiling for contributions towards old-age benefits..

(o)   €63,600 for retirement and unemployment insurance; €43,200 for health and long-term care insurance (West Germany).

(p)   There is no earnings ceiling on contributions for those entering the social security system before 1 January 1996.

(q)   Beijing has been used to represent the whole of China.

State pension formula:

   A: not related to earnings

   B: related to earnings below a fixed ceiling

   C: effectively related to all earnings

   D: individual capitalisation system

Sources: *International Financial Statistics* and *World Economic Outlook*, International Monetary Fund, October 2009; *2009 World Population Data Sheet*, Population Reference Bureau; Allianz Global Investors AG pension research: *Central and Eastern European Pensions 2007, Asia–Pacific Pensions 2007, Retirement at Risk: The US Pension System in Transition 2008, Funded Pensions in Western Europe 2008*; and *Social Security Programs Throughout the World: Europe 2008* and *Asia and the Pacific 2008*, US Social Security Administration and International Social Security Association, September 2008 and March 2009.

1. Economic indicators	Australia	Belgium	Canada	China (exc. HK/Macau)	Denmark
Population (2009, million)	21.9	10.8	33.7	1,331.4	5.5
Percentage of population aged 15–64	68	66	69	73	64
Percentage of population aged 65+	13	17	14	8	17
GDP (2009, local currency billion)	1,201.4	336.0	1,523.7	35,528.9	1,674.3
GDP per capita (2009, local currency)	54,822	31,284	45,298	24,379	303,778
GDP per capita (2009, current £ equivalent)	30,357	28,232	25,628	2,171	36,666
Price inflation (third quarter 2009, % pa)	1.6	0.2	0.1	0.0	1.7
Money market/Treasury bill rate (third quarter 2009, %)	3.00	1.29	0.50	2.79	1.70
Government bond yield (third quarter 2009, %)	5.57	3.61	3.43	–	3.65
Exchange rate (£1 as at 2 November 2009)	1.8059	1.1081	1.7675	11.2303	8.285
2. Social Security Information (2008)					
State pension ages	65m 63f (a)	65m & f	65 m&f	60m 50–55f	65 m&f
Contribution to State pension (employer, %)	(g)	8.86 (h)	4.95 (i)	20 (i,q)	(l)
Contribution to State pension (employee, %)	(g)	7.5 (h)	4.95 (i)	8 (i,q)	(l)
Earnings ceiling (local currency)	n/a	n/a	46,300	– (m)	n/a
Earnings ceiling (approx £ equivalent)	n/a	n/a	26,195	–	n/a
Social Security pension type(s)	A	B	A+B	A+D	A
Gross replacement rate, average earner (%)	40	41	27	59	45

Note: In some countries (notably France) the total social security contributions payable are considerably higher than the figures shown above, usually because separate contributions are levied for old-age and other social security and/or regional programmes.

	France	Germany	Hungary	India	Italy
1. Economic indicators					
Population (2009, million)	62.6	82.0	10.0	1,171.0	60.3
Percentage of population aged 15–64	65	66	69	63	66
Percentage of population aged 65+	17	20	16	5	20
GDP (2009, local currency billion)	1,918.5	2,355.9	25,792.7	57,039.0	1,521.5
GDP per capita (2009, local currency)	30,648	28,720	2,571,294	47,403	25,452
GDP per capita (2009, current £ equivalent)	27,658	25,918	8,436	617	22,969
Price inflation (third quarter 2009, % pa)	0.3	0.1	4.5	8.7	0.8
Money market/Treasury bill rate (third quarter 2009, %)	0.40	0.66	6.74	6.00	0.94
Government bond yield (third quarter 2009, %)	3.51	3.22	–	3.25	3.93
Exchange rate (£1 as at 2 November 2009)	1.1081	1.1081	304.800	76.785	1.1081
2. Social Security Information (2008)					
State pension ages	60–65m&f (b)	65 m&f (a)	62m, 61f (e)	60m&f (f)	57–65 m&f (b)
Contribution to State pension (employer, %)	9.9% (i)	9.95% (i)	18% (h)	10% (h)	23.8% (h)
Contribution to State pension (employee, %)	6.65% (i)	9.95% (i)	8.5% (h)	10% (h)	8.9%
Earnings ceiling (local currency)	33,276 (n)	63,600 (o)	5,070,000	78,000	88,669 (p)
Earnings ceiling (approx £ equivalent)	30,030	57,396	16,634	1,016	80,019
Social Security pension type(s)	B	B	B	A+D	C+D
Gross replacement rate, average earner (%)	66	43	90+	50	79

Note: In some countries (notably France) the total social security contributions payable are considerably higher than the figures shown above, usually because separate contributions are levied for old-age and other social security and/or regional programmes.

	Japan	Netherlands	Poland	Russia	Spain
1. Economic indicators					
Population (2009, million)	127.6	16.5	38.1	141.8	46.9
Percentage of population aged 15–64	64	67	71	71	69
Percentage of population aged 65+	23	15	14	14	17
GDP (2009, local currency billion)	479,289.4	575.0	1,332.3	41,103.0	1,047.3
GDP per capita (2009, local currency)	3,456,888	34,253	34,959	290,704	22,675
GDP per capita (2009, current £ equivalent)	23,406	30,911	7,405	6,082	20,463
Price inflation (third quarter 2009, % pa)	–1.1	0.9	3.4	12.3	–0.3
Money market/Treasury bill rate (third quarter 2009, %)	0.50	1.29	3.75	10.00	1.29
Government bond yield (third quarter 2009, %)	1.42	3.49	–	5.5	3.78
Exchange rate (£1 as at 2 November 2009)	147.69	1.1081	4.721	47.795	1.1081
2. Social Security Information (2008)					
State pension ages	60–65 m&f (c)	65 m&f	65 m 60f	60m 55f	65 m&f
Contribution to State pension (employer, %)	7.32 (i)	0	9.75 (i)	26 (k)	23.6 (i)
Contribution to State pension (employee, %)	7.32 (i)	17.9 (i)	9.75 (i)	0	4.7 (i)
Earnings ceiling (local currency)	7,440,000	31,589	90,981	none	36,889.20
Earnings ceiling (approx £ equivalent)	50,376	28,507	19,272	none	33,290
Social Security pension type(s)	A+B	A	D	A+B+D	B
Gross replacement rate, average earner (%)	60	30	n/a	–	91

Note: In some countries (notably France) the total social security contributions payable are considerably higher than the figures shown above, usually because separate contributions are levied for old-age and other social security and/or regional programmes.

	Sweden	Switzerland	UK	USA
1. Economic indicators				
Population (2009, million)	9.3	7.8	61.8	306.8
Percentage of population aged 15–64	65	68	66	67
Percentage of population aged 65+	18	17	16	13
GDP (2009, local currency billion)	3,089.2	535.5	1,401.0	14,266.2
GDP per capita (2009, local currency)	335,144	73,144	22,771	46,423
GDP per capita (2009, current £ equivalent)	29,045	43,720	22,771	28,350
Price inflation (third quarter 2009, % pa)	2.2	-0.4	1.9	-0.4
Money market/Treasury bill rate (third quarter 2009, %)	0.25	0.05	0.50	0.50
Government bond yield (third quarter 2009, %)	3.26	2.05	3.63	3.4
Exchange rate (£1 as at 2 November 2009)	11.539	1.673	1	1.638
2. Social Security Information (2008)				
State pension ages	65 m&f	65-64 m&f (b)	65m 60f (d)	66 m&f (a)
Contribution to State pension (employer, %)	11.91 (h)	4.2 (h)	12.8 (h)	6.2 (i)
Contribution to State pension (employee, %)	7 (i)	4.2 (h)	11 (i)	6.2 (i)
Earnings ceiling (local currency)	359,115	none	40,040	102,000
Earnings ceiling (approx £ equivalent)	31,122	none	40,040	62,290
Social Security pension type(s)	A+B+D	A	A+B	B
Gross replacement rate, average earner (%)	53	58	17	38.5

Note: In some countries (notably France) the total social security contributions payable are considerably higher than the figures shown above, usually because separate contributions are levied for old-age and other social security and/or regional programmes.

AUSTRALIA

Economy and Government

Australia is a constitutional monarchy with a parliamentary government. The Queen is represented in Australia by a governor-general and six state governors.

The national (federal) Parliament consists of the Queen (through the governor-general), the House of Representatives and the Senate. The 150 members of the House of Representatives (each representing an electoral district) are elected for three-year terms. The majority party or group forms the government, selecting a prime minister and the cabinet from its ranks. The current Prime Minister is Kevin Rudd of the Australian Labor Party, which won elections held in November 2007.

Labour relations

Until 2006, when the Howard government passed sweeping industrial relations reforms (WorkChoices), labour relations and employment conditions in Australia were generally determined by statutes that provided for the compulsory arbitration of disputes through a network of arbitration tribunals at the federal and state levels. The federal tribunal (the Australian Industrial Relations Commission (AIRC)) played a central role in the settlement of labour disputes and the determination of wages. The Labor Party election victory promises to bring an end to WorkChoices. Legislation to bring this about is at various stages of development and passage.

Cost of employment

The social security system is financed from general tax revenues. For workers' compensation, employers contribute varying percentages of payroll, depending on the risk category and the state.

Employment terms and conditions

The Workplace Relations Amendment (WorkChoices) Act is intended to eliminate redundant or unnecessary regulation and encourage an industrial relations system based on Australian Workplace Agreements (AWAs) rather than awards. Most of the act's provisions and Workplace Regulations 2006 came into effect from 27 March 2006, based on the federal government's constitutional powers to control and regulate certain corporations on a national basis. It covers all incorporated employers (with a few exceptions).

Social security and other required benefits

The social security system is a combination of universal and social assistance programmes financed from general tax revenues. Benefit payments and customer service are coordinated through Centrelink, which centralises the many services provided by the Departments of Family and Community Services; Education, Training, and Youth Affairs; Health and Family Services; Primary Industries and Energy; and Transport and Regional Services.

Healthcare system

Healthcare is administered at the Commonwealth (federal), state, and local levels and is delivered through a combination of public and private resources.

At the Commonwealth level, the Department of Health and Ageing is responsible for overall health policy (especially in the areas of public health, research, and information management) and is involved in the coordination of healthcare primarily through the national health insurance system known as Medicare. The Commonwealth government also maintains the Medicare fee schedules – the Medicare Benefits Schedule Book and the Schedule of Pharmaceutical Benefits for Approved Pharmacists and Medical Practitioners. Medicare Australia administers Medicare, the Pharmaceutical Benefits Scheme (the national prescription drug programme), and an immunization programme for children, and acts as both claims payer and auditor.

Taxation of compensation and benefits

Australia has a federal tax on personal income, but no state or local income taxes. Residents are taxed on income from all foreign and domestic sources. If tax has been withheld on foreign-source income by the foreign country, a tax credit is granted equal to the lesser of Australian tax or the foreign tax. Tax on employment income is withheld at source. Non-residents are taxed on Australian-source income only. The tax year (like the fiscal year) runs from 1 July to 30 June. Tax returns based on self assessments generally must be filed by the following 31 August.

Recent developments

The Social Security and Other Legislation Amendment (Pension Reform and Other 2009 Budget Measures) Act has received Royal Assent. Beginning 1 July 2017, the retirement age will gradually increase from age 65 to age 67 at a rate of six months every two years. The Act also adjusts the income test taper for pension benefits and introduces the Work Bonus, which allows pensioners to exempt A$500 per fortnight in employment income from the pension income test.

BELGIUM

Economy and Government

Belgium is a constitutional monarchy with a parliamentary democracy. The current king, Albert II, is the head of state. The government is led by the prime minister (appointed by the king on the basis of majority support in the House of Representatives) and the Council of Ministers. Parliament consists of a House of Representatives with 150 members elected through a system of proportional representation and a Senate with 71 members (40 popularly elected, 31 appointed by the Regional Councils). Members of both houses stand for election every four years. The House is the dominant legislative body; the Senate's responsibilities include oversight of constitutional revisions, treaties and relations between the linguistic communities.

Labour relations

Terms of employment and labour relations are governed by statute and through collective agreements signed at the national and inter-industry level, at the industry level, by regions or groups of companies, and at the company level. They are hierarchical – agreements signed at a lower level build on those signed at a higher level – and cumulative – they amend or add to earlier agreements. Employers must use the language of the region in which they are located for all documentation. In Brussels, which is bilingual, employers are required to communicate with an employee in his or her dominant language.

Cost of employment

The social security system is comprehensive in scope and coverage and involves substantial cost, approximately 75% of which is borne by the employer. Contributions are based on the employee's gross salary plus any bonuses and benefits in kind, with no earnings ceiling (except for workers' compensation). All employees and firms employing ten or more persons pay full social security contributions on the vacation bonus.

Employment terms and conditions

Employment law distinguishes between blue- and white-collar workers. While the classifications are ambiguous – blue-collar as 'manual' and white-collar as 'intellectual' – distinct provisions apply to each classification as regards termination procedures, probationary periods, payment intervals and non-competition agreements.

The 1978 Law on Contracts of Employment, as amended, governs contracts for blue- and white-collar workers, commercial representatives, domestic workers and students. Employment contracts may be written or verbal; however, fixed-term, part-time, temporary, replacement and student contracts must be written. In practice, almost all employment contracts are in writing.

Social security and other required benefits

Separate but closely related programmes exist for wage earners, salaried employees, the self-employed, miners and seamen. The first two programmes cover all employees in private industry and commerce, except for some company directors considered self-employed for social security purposes. Benefits for the self-employed are significantly lower than those under the other programmes. Other separately financed and administered statutory systems cover national and local government employees and railway workers.

Healthcare system

The extensive healthcare system, which covers all Belgian residents, includes hospital care, visits to doctors (both general practitioners (GPs) and specialists), dental care, pharmaceuticals and home care. The system includes both private and public elements and is highly regulated. The Ministry of Social Affairs and the Ministry of Public Health share responsibility for health insurance, hospital costs, drugs, medical practice and vaccinations. Some responsibility for public health, institutions and home care has devolved to the regional governments.

The National Institute for Sickness and Invalidity Insurance (INAMI/RIZIV) oversees health insurance. Government-approved 'mutuelle' (sickness fund) groups administer the system. All Belgians must enrol with a *mutuelle* of their choice. The *mutuelles* developed from self-funded, self-help community organisations, although now primarily funded by employee and employer (and self-employed) payroll contributions through the federal government. There are six networks of government-approved *mutuelles*, although the affiliation may not be apparent to the *mutuelle* member.

Taxation of compensation and benefits

A resident is subject to Belgian income taxes on worldwide income. An individual is resident if he or she is living in or has a 'centre of economic interest' in Belgium. Non-residents are taxed only on income produced or received in Belgium. Special rules may apply to expatriates. Income taxes are imposed at the national level. Municipalities may levy a surtax, which varies from 0% to 10%. There is no wealth tax in Belgium and, in general, capital gains are not taxed. The tax year is the calendar year. Individuals must file a tax return by 30 June following the tax year.

Recent developments

The Belgian-Indian social security totalisation agreement is effective 1 September 2009. Under the agreement, employees seconded to either country for a period of up to five years will be subject to their home country's social security regime. This period may be extended by agreement of the two countries. Periods of secondment before 1 September 2009 will not be included in the determination of the five-year period. For the purpose of determining benefit eligibility, contributions paid in both countries, including those paid prior to 1 September 2009, will be considered. In related news, the social security totalisation agreements between Belgium and South Korea, and Belgium and Uruguay, entered into force on 1 July 2009, and 1 August 2009, respectively.

BRAZIL

Economy and Government

Brazil is a democratic republic with a presidential government. The president serves as chief of state and head of government. The president and vice president are elected by direct popular vote for a four-year term and may be re-elected once.

Labour relations

The constitution protects employees' and employers' rights of association and prohibits government intervention in the organization or administration of unions or employers' associations. Most employer–union negotiations occur at the industry or professional level or at the level of the enterprise. National-level negotiations between the social partners (employers, unions and government) are infrequent, generally addressing macropolitical or economic stabilisation issues.

Cost of employment

Employee social security contributions are levied on total earnings according to salary brackets, up to an earnings ceiling of R3,218.90 per month as of 1 February 2009. The employee's contribution is based on 12 months' pay only.

The employer's contribution is levied on total payroll with no ceiling. Employer contributions may vary slightly according to the nature of the business.

Employment terms and conditions

Terms of employment and labour relations are governed by the constitution and legislation. Most employment and labour laws have been consolidated in the CLT – Consolidação das Leis do Trabalho (the labour code).

Employment conditions and labour relations may also be regulated by collective agreement and individual contract. Employees may not waive rights granted to them by law. Employment contracts may be written or oral. In practice, most employment contracts are in writing.

Social security and other required benefits

The National Institute of Social Security (INSS) administers social security benefits for insured persons and their dependants, including the self-employed and foreign residents. Civil servants, military personnel, politicians and rural workers are covered by special legislation.

Social security benefits include old-age pensions, length-of-service pensions, special early retirement pensions for working in a hazardous environment, survivors' pensions, long-term disability pensions, cash sickness benefits, medical care benefits, maternity leave and family allowances. Retraining and professional rehabilitation after work-related accidents are also provided under social security.

Healthcare system

The Ministry of Health is responsible for national policy, regulating the public healthcare system (Sistema Unificado de Saude, SUS), and providing technical and financial assistance to states and municipalities. State ministries of health control regional healthcare networks and provide technical and financial assistance to the municipalities. The municipalities have primary responsibility for local healthcare planning and delivery. Health councils assist the government at all three levels.

Taxation of compensation and benefits

Residents are subject to a graduated federal income tax on worldwide income. An individual is considered resident if he or she has a permanent residence permit, an employment contract in Brazil (even if he or she has a temporary work visa), or lives in Brazil for more than 183 days in a 12-month period. Non-residents pay a flat withholding tax on Brazilian-source income (25% on earned income or 15% on other income). Income source is established by the location of the payer regardless of where work is performed. A resident absent from Brazil for 12 months is taxed as a non-resident.

Recent developments

Effective 1 January 2010, pension fund administrators (EFPCs) in Brazil must adopt International Accounting Standard No. 26 (*Accounting and Reporting Retirement Benefit Plans*) for supplementary pension plans. Pension fund administrators must share information with fund members and third parties, explaining in a clear and concise manner the benefit plans offered and their financial history.

CANADA

Economy and Government

Canada is a constitutional monarchy. The Queen is represented by a governor-general (appointed on the advice of the prime minister) who convenes and dissolves Parliament, assents to bills, and exercises other executive functions. Canada is structured as a confederation of ten provinces and three territories. The federal government consists of an elected House of Commons and an appointed Senate.

Labour relations

Employment standards and human rights legislation in each of the federal, provincial and territorial jurisdictions set the minimum age for industrial employment, maximum work hours, overtime rates of pay, minimum wage rates and statutory vacations with pay. They also regulate employment practices and termination procedures, prohibit discrimination and regulate apprenticeships. Provincial and territorial legislation covers employees working within their borders, except those under federal jurisdiction (generally employees engaged in any work of an interprovincial, national, or international nature).

Terms of employment are also governed by collective agreements, which cannot establish terms less favourable than those provided by legislation.

Cost of employment

Retirement, death and disability benefits under the Old Age Security Act (flat-rate benefit and means-tested supplements) are financed through general revenues. In addition, there are employer and employee payroll deductions to cover the Canada Pension Plan (earnings-related benefits), employment insurance (including cash sickness and maternity), hospital/medical benefits and workers' compensation.

Employment terms and conditions

Full- and part-time permanent employees are not usually covered by a contract other than a collective agreement. However, it is strongly recommended that employers require all employees to enter into written employment contracts. All employees, whether or not they are party to a written employment contract, are protected under employment standards legislation at the federal, provincial, or territorial level. Employment contracts are subject to all applicable employment and tax law in the contract's jurisdiction. If a self-employed person invoices for work done, he or she is treated as an agency or separate company for tax and employment law purposes and is normally liable for income tax, employment insurance, health insurance premiums and other employment costs.

Social security and other required benefits

The social security system is a combination of federal, provincial or territorial, and federal provincial programs, which provide benefits in all the categories generally found in European social security systems. Virtually all residents are covered by social security. Foreign nationals employed in Canada and paid from a Canadian payroll may also be covered. Under specified circumstances, Canadian nationals employed outside Canada may continue to contribute to the Canada Pension Plan.

Healthcare system

Healthcare falls under provincial and territorial rather than federal control. Each province and territory administers a healthcare plan meeting criteria set out in the (federal) Canada Health Act. Healthcare represents a major expenditure and is a highly visible government concern. The ministry of health in each province or territory is responsible for negotiating the pay of health professionals, the distribution and management of hospitals and their services, setting education policies, standards and quotas for health practitioners, and funding and oversight of the agency that pays for services.

Taxation of compensation and benefits

Residents pay personal income tax on worldwide income. Non-residents are taxed only on Canadian-source income. Canadian income taxes are imposed by the federal government and the provincial and territorial governments. In all provinces and territories, except Quebec, provincial and territorial personal income taxes are a fixed percentage of the federal tax, collected by the federal government. Quebec assesses and collects income tax separately. Starting in 2000, the other jurisdictions delinked the provincial or territorial and federal tax calculations and moved to a separate tax on income, although individuals (other than Quebec residents) continue to file a single tax return.

Recent developments

Service Canada has published the Old Age Security (OAS) payment rates for the period April through June 2009. The average monthly OAS benefit is C$489.57, and the average monthly Guaranteed Income Supplement (GIS) benefit is C$451.12. For spouses, the OAS allowance is no longer paid once income reaches C$28,992, while the GIS is no longer paid at C$37,584. Pensioners with an individual net income above C$66,335 must repay part or all of the maximum Old Age Security pension amount.

CHINA

Economy and Government

Formally, the government and the Communist Party are separate, complementary institutions; however, there is considerable cross-membership. Hu Jintao is currently head of state and the General Secretary of the Politburo Standing Committee of the Party. The current leadership is expected to remain in power until 2013 (two five-year terms).

Labour relations

Employment terms are mainly established by the Labour Law, which applies to all types of company. The Labour Contracts Law, effective 1 January 2008, substantially changed a number of terms of employment covered by the Labour Law. Earlier Regulations for Labour Management in Foreign-Invested Enterprises apply only to joint ventures, wholly foreign-owned enterprises and Chinese–foreign joint stock companies. As in some areas of the Labour Law and the Regulations the interpretation may be unclear, the local labour authority should be consulted.

Cost of employment

Contribution rates for social security and other mandatory programmes vary according to city or province. Many cities and provinces have established contribution rates which vary from the national guidelines. City or provincial regulations supersede national guidelines.

Employment terms and conditions

From 1 January 2007, employers are required to register the following employment details at the labour and social security bureau where the business is registered: the name, legal representative, economic type and enterprise code of the employer; and the name, gender and national identification number of the employee, along with the date the contract was signed and its expiry date. Employers are required to file the required information within 30 days of hiring an employee and 7 days after termination of the employment.

Social security and other required benefits

The social security system includes pensions, housing and medical care. Each person is assigned a social security number. Social security and other mandatory programmes are financed through contributions by employers and employees which *(as mentioned above)* vary by city or province.

Healthcare system

The healthcare system has been complicated by the move from a planned to a market economy. Between 1983 and 2003, government and social insurance expenditures fell, respectively, from 37.43% and 31.12% to 16.96% and 27.16%. Out-of-pocket expenditures have become the primary source of healthcare financing, and increased from 31.45% to 55.87% over the same period.

Taxation of compensation and benefits

Individual income tax rates for Chinese citizens and for foreign-national residents are the same, but different monthly allowances apply (C¥2,000 for Chinese citizens and C¥4,800 for foreigners, effective 1 March 2008). Residence is principally based on physical presence, domicile or (in certain cases) the right to reside in China. The length of stay establishing residence is not explicitly defined; however, in practice, individuals who are in China for one full tax year or more are considered to be resident and are subject to tax on worldwide income. Temporary absences not exceeding 30 days at a time or 90 days (in aggregate) over a tax year are included in calculating the period of stay. Chinese nationals who have a domicile in China are considered resident for tax purposes. Foreign individuals resident in China for between one and five years can, with the approval of the tax authorities, be taxed only on China-sourced income. Non-residents are taxed only on China-sourced income.

Recent developments

In China, the Beijing and Shanghai governments released their new city average wage (CAW), which is the basis for social insurance contributions. Effective 1 April 2009, the CAW for Beijing is C¥3,726 per month (increased from C¥3,322). In Shanghai, the CAW increased from C¥2,892 to C¥3,292 per month.

EUROPEAN UNION

Economy and Government

The 27 Member Countries of the EU are: Austria, Belgium, Bulgaria, Cyprus, Czech Republic, Denmark, Estonia, Finland, France, Germany, Greece, Hungary, Ireland, Italy, Latvia, Lithuania, Luxembourg, Malta, Netherlands, Poland, Portugal, Romania, Slovak Republic, Slovenia, Spain, Sweden and the UK.

The 30 countries of the EEA are the 27 Member Countries of the EU plus Iceland, Liechtenstein and Norway. The three additional countries in the EEA do not participate in the development of EU legislation and have no vote on EU matters. Also, the EEA is not a customs union and border controls with Iceland, Liechtenstein and Norway remain.

Labour relations

All EEA members, including Iceland, Liechtenstein and Norway, must observe the labour requirements of the EU, including Directive 93/104 on Working Time, and their nationals have the right of freedom of movement of employees within the EEA. The Directive applies to all public- and private-sector employees, with no exceptions for small firms, but there are numerous exceptions to the provisions for certain types of work. There are also extended transition periods for the provisions on vacation and length of the working week.

Cost of employment

Social security benefits are provided by the programmes of each EEA Member Country. The EU itself provides no social security system. There is no obligation upon Member Countries to have a similar level of contributions or benefits under their social security programmes. However, Resolution 94/C 368/03 on EU Social Policy Objectives notes that the objectives of EU social policy include improving competitiveness, protecting workers' rights through minimum standards, convergence of social security systems rather than the imposition of uniform rules, and reinforcing dialogue among Member Countries. The United Kingdom did not agree to the Resolution, however.

Employment terms and conditions

These vary between countries.

Social security and other required benefits

The EU social security totalisation agreement now extends to the nationals and social security institutions of Iceland, Liechtenstein and Norway. The agreement allows nationals of EEA countries to combine their years of participation under the social security systems of all EEA countries to establish eligibility for benefits. Each country then pays proportionate benefits for the years of coverage under its own social security system. All EU requirements for statutory benefits are extended to Iceland, Liechtenstein and Norway, as EEA members.

Healthcare system

Following several European Court of Justice judgments covering patient reimbursement for healthcare received in another Member Country, the long-awaited draft directive on cross-border care 'aims to clarify how patients can exercise their rights to cross-border health care, while at the same time providing legal certainty for Member States and health care providers'. Among the directive's major provisions:

1. patients would have the right to seek healthcare within the European Union and be reimbursed up to what they would have received at home

2. Member Countries would be responsible for providing healthcare in their territory, *and*

3. the development of European reference networks would be facilitated, that is, specialized centres in different Member Countries.

The directive also would promote activities in e-health and health technology assessment.

Taxation of compensation and benefits

Income tax is levied by each Member Country of the EEA. The EU itself does not levy any taxes, but collects revenues from a percentage of value added taxes levied in each Member Country. There is no obligation to harmonize the income tax systems at present.

Recent developments

The European Council formally adopted a new directive on European Works Councils (EWCs). The changes introduced by the new directive include:

1. fall-back rules where no rules are in place to handle changes in the structure of the company, such as in a merger

2. clarification of the role of EWCs, linking different levels of employee representation, *and*

3. provision of training for employee representatives, who have the duty to report back to employees.

Officials from the European Commission note that EWCs will be 'strengthened to better inform and consult workers during restructuring' under the new directive. EU Member States have two years to pass implementing legislation. Employees have the right to establish an EWC in 'Community-scale undertakings' and 'Community-scale groups of undertakings' that employ at least 1,000 workers across the EU Member States, with at least 150 workers in each of two Member States.

FRANCE

Economy and Government

France has a 'mixed' system of presidential and parliamentary government. The president is the head of state and commander in chief. He or she names the prime minister, formally presides over the cabinet (and may name members), concludes treaties, can dissolve the parliament and call for national referenda. The prime minister is the head of government; he or she is usually the leader of the majority party in parliament and nominates cabinet members. The parliament consists of the National Assembly and the Senate. Representatives to the National Assembly are directly elected for five-year terms. Senators are elected by an electoral college and serve nine-year terms; one-third of the Senate is elected every three years. Two other institutions – the Economic and Social Council and the Constitutional Council – play important roles. The Economic and Social Council (representatives from the trade union confederations, employers' associations, social welfare groups and consumers' organisations) is consulted on long-range economic plans and various bills. The Constitutional Council reviews acts of parliament to determine their constitutionality. It consists of nine members: three are appointed by the president, three by the speaker of the National Assembly, and three by the speaker of the Senate.

Labour relations

Labour relations and the terms of employment are determined by statute, case law and collective agreement. At the national level, trade union confederations and employers' associations meet to study and seek solutions for labour market problems, such as skill development and training and unemployment. Despite collaboration between the 'social partners' (government, labour and employers), workplace conflict persists. Strikes are often called during periods of corporate restructuring, especially if the unions and management cannot reach agreement on a 'job protection plan'. They also are used as a political tool – to protest governmental or EU policies.

Cost of employment

Salary *tranches* are used to determine both contributions and benefits under social security and to express premiums and costs under employer-sponsored benefit plans. The *tranches* are adjusted once a year (in January) in relation to wage and price changes.

Employment terms and conditions

In France, employees may be classified as:

- non-*cadres*: blue-collar and lower-level, white-collar employees
- *cadres*: employees who are primarily managerial or who have special academic qualifications
- *cadres assimilés*: technicians, foremen and senior white-collar employees, *and*
- *cadres supérieurs, cadres dirigeants*: executives, top management.

Employees' rights are established primarily through statute and collective agreement. However, a benefit granted repeatedly over time may become a right, unless the employer explicitly stipulates that the benefit is granted at its discretion.

Social security and other required benefits

Coverage under the social security system is mandatory for all employees in commerce, industry and public works. Pensions are payable in any country with which France has diplomatic relations. The Ministry of Employment and Social Affairs, assisted by a Secretary of State for Health, is responsible for the general supervision of the social security system. Compulsory employee and employer contributions are collected by a joint collection agency and distributed to the National Sickness Insurance Fund, the National Old Age Insurance Fund and the National Family Allowance Fund, from which benefits are paid. The government funds additional pension benefits and allowances, certain health and social services and, under certain circumstances, unemployment benefits.

Healthcare system

Membership in a health insurance fund is compulsory for any person working in Metropolitan France (excluding the overseas *départements* and territories), regardless of nationality, provided that an employment relationship exists and the work is paid. Dependants are covered through the employee's insurance. Coverage is now almost universal. The majority of the population is covered through CNAMTS (the programme for salaried employees).

Taxation of compensation and benefits

Residents are subject to national income tax on worldwide income. In addition to a local property tax which is levied on the occupants of all types of accommodation, taxpayers are also subject to three social taxes – the general social contribution (CSG), the social debt reimbursement (CRDS), and the social levy. Individuals who are physically present for more than 183 days a year, who have a home or primary abode in France, or whose main occupation or centre of economic activities is in France, are considered resident for tax purposes. Non-residents are subject to tax only on France-sourced income. The tax year is the calendar year. Tax returns must generally be filed by the following 1 March. Income tax is not withheld from employee pay for individuals domiciled in France. Income taxes are paid in advance (based on pre-assessments of tax liability) in two instalments equal to one-third of the total liability from the previous year or via monthly instalments. Final settlement is due in September/October or November/December, respectively, based on final assessments issued by the tax authorities.

Recent developments

Effective 1 July 2009, employers covered by the National Interprofessional Agreement (Accord National Interprofessionnel) must provide employer-sponsored health, life and disability benefits to employees who have been dismissed. Article 14 of the Agreement requires employers to maintain coverage for the duration of unemployment, up to a maximum of nine months. To receive this coverage, an employee must: 1) be eligible for unemployment under the social security system; 2) have been terminated for reasons other than just cause; and 3) have been covered by the relevant benefit plans before employment was terminated. To fund the extension of benefits, employers and employees may share the costs under the terms applicable to active employees, or a pooling arrangement may be established via collective agreement. Terminated employees have ten days to opt out of the continuation of benefits. If an employee opts out, he or she must opt out of all benefits; employers must obtain the opt-out in writing. The agreement applies to its signatories. The government may adopt the measures outlined in Article 14, thereby making them applicable to all employers.

GERMANY

Economy and Government

Germany is a parliamentary democracy with a federal system of government. It has a bicameral legislature and an independent judiciary. The president may be elected to two five-year terms, but his or her other duties are largely ceremonial; executive power is exercised by the chancellor.

The Bundestag has 601 deputies, who are elected every four years; one-half of the deputies are elected directly from single-member districts, while the remainder are elected through proportional representation. It is responsible for electing the chancellor and controls the executive branch through its power to call for a vote of no confidence. The Bundesrat (upper house or Federal Council) has 69 members who are delegates of the 16 *Länder* (state governments). Their terms vary in length. The Bundesrat represents the interests of the states at the national level.

Labour relations

Labour relations and terms of employment are determined by statutes, case law and collective bargaining. Traditionally, collective bargaining has been centralised at the industry level. During the past decade, however, some decentralisation has occurred; and the number of agreements signed at the company level has increased. Labour relations in Germany are cooperative. Employees enjoy a dual system of representation: at the industry level, they are represented by trade unions and at the company level by works councils.

Cost of employment

Annual earnings ceilings applicable in the western and eastern *Länder* for sickness, maternity and medical benefits, as well as long-term care insurance, were equalised in 2001. Two different earnings ceilings still exist for contribution to old age, survivors' and disability pensions, as well as employment promotion. As income levels become uniform, these ceiling levels also will be made uniform.

Employment terms and conditions

Employers must provide employees with specified terms of their employment within one month of the start of the employment relationship. Fixed-term contracts may not run for more than two years.

Social security and other required benefits

The social security system covers all German employees and provides old age, survivors' and long-term disability pensions, as well as unemployment insurance. Medical care (routine and long-term) and cash sickness and maternity benefits are administered through health funds. Workers' compensation is maintained through a variety of funds administered by employers' associations, or *Land* or local municipalities. When the West German social security system replaced the East German system on 1 January 1992, transitional regulations and grandfathering provisions were implemented, some of which are still in effect.

Healthcare system

The healthcare system is a hybrid of the managed care model and a centralised system in which the government can intervene. The Law to Strengthen GKV Competition (GKV Wettbewerbsstärkungsgesetz), passed in 2007, will alter the traditional sole reliance on employment taxes for medical care. It restructures the manner in which employer and employees pay for statutory health insurance.

Taxation of compensation and benefits

Residents are taxed on worldwide income. In general, residents are defined as persons living in Germany for more than 183 days per year. Non-residents are taxed only on German-source income at a minimum rate of 25% (though executives of supervisory boards may be taxed at a higher rate). Taxable income is always assessed by calendar year. Married couples who are residents may file separately or jointly.

Recent developments

The German government recently passed a law guaranteeing social security pension levels. Pension benefits are linked to changes in gross wages. The new law guarantees that benefits will not decrease if gross wages decline.

INDIA

Economy and Government

India is a federal republic with a parliamentary government. The 'union executive' consists of a president, vice president, prime minister and the council of ministers. The president serves as head of state while the prime minister serves as head of government. The president and vice president are elected to a five-year term by an electoral college that is composed of members of the national parliament and the state legislative assemblies. The president is empowered to declare a 'state of emergency' if he or she believes the country faces an external threat, and to assume control over state governments if there is a constitutional crisis in a state.

Labour relations

Labour relations and terms of employment are determined primarily by statute. National laws are applicable, except where states have passed amending acts to address local circumstances. At both the national and state levels, employers and employees must comply with omnibus acts, as well as 'sectoral' acts. The most important sectoral acts regulating the terms of employment are the Factories Act, which is a national law covering factories, and various shops and establishments acts, passed by the states and covering shops, offices, and commercial establishments that are not regulated by the Factories Act. Case law and custom also play an important role in guiding labour–management relations and employment issues. The Supreme Court regularly hears appeals of decisions made by industrial tribunals; it has ruled on labour–management disputes, employee terminations, conditions of employment, and wages and benefits. Custom and local practice are significant factors in the establishment of acquired rights.

Cost of employment

Contributions for old age, survivors', disability, cash sickness and maternity benefits are based on monthly basic salary plus 'dearness' allowance (cost of living) and retaining allowance (if any), (both employer and employee contributions) up to a specified ceiling. Employees whose earnings exceed the ceilings are excluded from these programmes.

Employment terms and conditions

Employment contracts can be written or oral. Typically, employers issue an 'appointment letter' that outlines the general terms and conditions of employment. A 'letter of confirmation' is sent to the employee within 30 days of hire. The contents of an appointment letter are not determined by statute, except for employees covered by the Sales Promotion Employees (Conditions of Services) Act. This act requires that the job title, date of appointment, probation period, wage scale, rate of wage increases, total wages and conditions of service be delineated in the appointment letter. The Industrial Employment (Standing Orders) Act requires employers to create a written document, known as 'standing orders', that establishes the terms of employment, and provides a 'model standing orders' for any employer to use. If an employer wishes to develop its own standing orders, it must be certified by the relevant authorities, and it cannot contain terms and conditions that do not meet the standards outlined in the model document.

Social security and other required benefits

The social security system consists of programmes at the national and state levels, including compulsory savings (provident fund), pensions, and insured welfare benefits in the event of sickness, maternity, death and work-related accident or illness. Indemnities are payable by the employer upon termination of employment for any reason except just cause (with some exceptions). Employees covered by Employees' State Insurance are entitled to unemployment and medical benefits in the event of layoffs. Several states have their own unemployment programmes, which are financed from general revenue.

Healthcare system

The states are responsible for the delivery of most healthcare services. The federal (union) government responsibilities include population control, medical education, family welfare and food and drug regulation. Nationally, the Ministry of Health and Family Welfare oversees all aspects of healthcare policy and delivery through the Department of Health and Family Welfare

(DHFW) and the Department of Ayurveda, Yoga and Naturopathy, Unani, Siddha and Homeopathy (AYUSH). The DHFW regulates the manufacture or import, distribution, and sale of drugs and oversees medical education, training, and research standards as well as numerous educational institutions. The Central Government Health Scheme (CGHS), under the DHFW, operates medical facilities for certain groups including active and retired national government employees and members of parliament. The second department (AYUSH) was created in 1995 to develop the Indian Systems of Medicine and integrate them into the general healthcare system.

Taxation of compensation and benefits

Residents are taxed on worldwide income. Non-residents are taxed on Indian-source income only. A person is a resident if he or she spent at least 182 days in the previous tax year in India, or 60 days in the previous tax year plus at least 365 days in the preceding four years. However, an Indian national who leaves India to work abroad is not considered a resident unless he or she has been in India for at least 182 days in that year. Income payable for services rendered in India is considered Indian-source income, irrespective of its place of accrual or payment. Persons 'resident but not ordinarily resident' in India – someone who has not been a resident in India in nine of the ten previous years or who has not been in India a total of 730 days or more during the preceding seven years – generally do not pay tax on income earned outside India, unless it is derived from a business controlled in India. Taxable income includes wages, salaries, allowances, fees, commissions, benefits in kind, annuities or pensions, gratuities in excess of the tax-free portion, dividends, interest and discounts, rent, royalties, technical service fees and lottery or contest winnings. The tax year begins on 1 April and ends on 31 March.

Recent developments

The New Pension Scheme (NPS) is scheduled to open to all individuals on 1 May 2009. The Election Commission has approved the 1 May start date. Contributions will receive tax-favourable treatment. Several observers are urging the government to make NPS withdrawals tax-free to encourage participation.

JAPAN

Economy and Government

Japan is a constitutional monarchy with a parliamentary government. The emperor serves as the symbolic head of state; the prime minister is the head of government and leads the executive branch. The prime minister is elected by the parliament or Diet and must be a member of the Diet at the time of his or her election to the executive branch. The prime minister appoints cabinet members, a majority of whom must also be members of the Diet. The Diet consists of the House of Representatives and the House of Councillors. The House of Representatives has 480 members who are elected to four-year terms. The 247 members of the House of Councillors are elected for six-year terms. Of the two houses, the House of Representatives is more powerful.

Labour relations

Employment terms are defined primarily by employers. The Labour Standards Law stipulates minimum conditions. Wages, on the other hand, are often established through the 'spring labour offensive' or *Shunto*, a system of annual industrial collective bargaining. Given Japan's recent economic difficulties, the impact of the *Shunto* on wage increases has been negligible during the past few years. Historically, labour relations have been cooperative, though recent circumstances have created some distrust between employers and workers. The 2001 Law for Promoting the Resolution of Individual Labour Disputes, aiming to facilitate the prompt resolution of labour disputes by rapid intermediation through 300 general labour consultation desks, has had somewhat limited success, however, so the 2004 Labour Tribunal Law provides a venue for the speedy resolution of labour disputes.

Cost of employment

Social security combines a universal programme providing flat-rate benefits through the National Pension Plan (NPP), with an employment-related programme providing benefits based on earnings through the Employees' Pension Insurance Plan (EPIP). Contributions to the EPIP are based on monthly covered earnings, with 30 earnings grades ranging from J¥98,000 to J¥620,000 per month and seasonal bonuses up to J¥1,500,000 per year. Contributions to the Employee Health Insurance System (EHI) are based on monthly covered earnings, with 47 earnings grades ranging from J¥58,000 to J¥1,210,000 per month and seasonal bonuses up to J¥5,400,000 per year. Contributions to unemployment insurance, workers' compensation insurance, and family allowances are based on total payroll.

Employment terms and conditions

Traditionally, employment law and practices have emphasised homogeneous groups of employees, who are long-serving and receive seniority-based wages. Given this focus, employment law stipulates that employers with ten or more employees must establish a set of work rules that specify the terms of employment. These work rules generally substitute for contracts and collective agreements, even though they are not subject to negotiation.

Social security and other required benefits

The NPP provides flat-rate benefits for all residents. The EPIP provides pay-related benefits that supplement the NPP. The EPIP also provides limited flat-rate benefits. Employers and sole proprietors with five or more full-time employees, and all corporations, including employers (legal directors and auditors) and employees, must participate in the EPIP and the EHI. This includes branches and sales offices of foreign companies which are treated as incorporated businesses and representative offices which are treated as sole proprietorships. (Part-time employees must also be covered if their working hours are 75% or more of the working hours of full-time employees.) However, employers with at least 1,000 employees may contract out of the EPIP under certain conditions, and employers with at least 700 employees may contract out of the EHI. Workers' compensation insurance, unemployment insurance and family allowances are provided under separate programmes.

Healthcare system

The Ministry of Health, Labour, and Welfare (MHLW) develops health care policy and coordinates overall health and welfare administration. In the MHLW, the Department of National Hospitals manages and administers national medical facilities including hospitals, sanatoriums and specialized medical centres. The Health Insurance Bureau handles policy planning and coordination of the health insurance systems which the MHLW oversees. The Social Insurance Agency manages and administers the various health, welfare, and pension plans. While the government administers and/or coordinates health insurance coverage, healthcare providers are almost exclusively private. More than 80% of hospitals and 90% of physicians, dentists, clinics and nursing homes operate on a for-profit basis.

Taxation of compensation and benefits

Japan levies national, prefectural and municipal income taxes on individuals. Permanent residents are taxed on worldwide income. Individuals who are domiciled in Japan or who are present in Japan for one year or more are considered to be resident for tax purposes; domicile is defined as the place in which an individual's life is centred. Individuals who have been resident in Japan for fewer than five of the past ten years are considered to be non-permanent residents and are taxed only on Japanese-source income and on income received in Japan from overseas. Non-residents are taxed on income from services in Japan, even if paid overseas, at a flat 20% rate (without residents' deductions). Individuals present in Japan for fewer than 183 days in a 12-month period are generally exempt from income tax on foreign-sourced income. The tax year is based on the calendar year. Employers are required to withhold taxes from salaries, wages, and bonuses paid to resident employees. Withholding tables are adjusted for the employee's personal and family situation. Employers must make a year-end adjustment to withholding for employees (excluding employees with annual salary income of J¥20,000,000 or more) to account for any overpayment or underpayment of taxes. As a result, many employees do not need to file a tax return.

Recent developments

Effective 1 January 2010, employers will be able to contribute up to J¥51,000 per month into their employees' defined contribution plan. Employers may make a tax-deductible contribution up to J¥51,000 per month (currently J¥46,000) to an employee's defined contribution plan if it is the only pension plan offered. Employers that offer another pension plan in addition to the defined contribution plan will be permitted to contribute up to J¥25,500 per month (currently J¥23,000) to the defined contribution plan. A proposal to allow employee contributions is expected to be reconsidered after the 30 August 2009 elections for the lower house of the Diet.

THE NETHERLANDS

Economy and Government

The Netherlands is a constitutional monarchy with Queen Beatrix as the reigning head of state. Formally, the government is divided into the Crown; the legislature, represented by the States General (parliament); and the judiciary. The States General has two houses: the Upper Chamber with 75 members and the Lower Chamber with 150 members. General elections for both chambers are held at least every four years. Members of both chambers are elected by proportional representation. Members of the Upper Chamber are elected by the members of the provincial governing bodies not more than three months after the election of the members of the provincial councils. Members of the Lower Chamber are elected directly by all Dutch nationals aged 18 and over.

Labour relations

Employment terms are determined through national labour laws, collective bargaining and individual employment contracts. Labour–management relations are cooperative. The government has a statutory obligation to consult with the Social and Economic Council (SER) over proposed changes in labour and employment laws and general decisions affecting employment. SER functions primarily as an advisory board on macro-economic issues. Additionally, the Labour Foundation (STAR), a bipartite body representing employers and unions, is a central forum for consultation and negotiation.

Cost of employment

Employers and employees pay social security contributions to two programmes based on total earnings up to specified ceilings. Rates and ceilings are normally revised in January and July. Cash sickness and maternity benefits (ZW) are funded in full by the government. There is no separate workers' compensation programme. Benefits for work-related accidents are paid under the medical, disability and survivors' benefit plans of social security.

Employment terms and conditions

Employment contracts are required and, unless otherwise stated, are indefinite. The maximum term for a probationary period is two months if the contract is indefinite or for a fixed term exceeding two years. For fixed-term contracts that do not exceed two years, the maximum probationary period is one month. During a probationary period, the contract may be terminated without notice by either party. Only within a Collective Labour Agreement (CAO) can there be different probation periods. If the employer terminates the employment contract during the probation period, the employer must state the reasons for the termination in writing, upon the employee's request.

Social security and other required benefits

The comprehensive social security system provides benefits through the National Insurance System and the Employed Persons Insurance System. Social security programmes do not distinguish between blue- and white-collar employees. The basic National Insurance System is financed through employee contributions and provides flat-rate old age pensions and survivors' benefits, family allowances and special health insurance for the entire population, as well as disability benefits for the self-employed. The Employed Persons Insurance System is financed by employer and employee contributions and provides additional health insurance for lower-paid persons, and disability, cash sickness, maternity and unemployment benefits.

Healthcare system

There is no national health service, but public health policy is primarily the responsibility of the Ministry of Welfare, Health, and Sport Affairs. The Ministry of Social Affairs and Employment is partially responsible for preventive healthcare and works closely with the Ministry of Welfare, Health, and Sport Affairs on this issue. Additionally, the Ministry of the Interior and the Ministry of Housing, Spatial Planning, and the Environment are involved in plans to establish a National Epidemiological Center to improve monitoring and control of contagious diseases.

Taxation of compensation and benefits

Residents are taxed on worldwide income. Non-residents are subject to tax only on Dutch-source income. Dutch tax law does not define residence, which is determined on individual circumstances such as where a person lives regularly, the length of stay in the Netherlands and the taxpayer's centre of interests. The tax year for individuals is the calendar year. Tax returns must generally be filed by 1 April of the following year. Taxes are collected via withholding or advance payment.

Recent developments

The Dutch Accounting Standards Board issued new guidelines for pension accounting leading to a major change in the local accounting requirements. With the new guidelines, the Dutch Standards have ceased to converge on International Financial Reporting Standards (IFRS).

The Board argues that the Dutch pension market contains specific features that lead to severe application problems for defined benefit accounting under IFRS rules. Dutch pension entitlements accrue and are funded in pension funds that operate as independent, autonomous legal entities, while employers contract with insurers to administer company pension plans.

According to the Board, for most Dutch pension plans the plan sponsor is no longer the sole underwriter of risks (actuarial and investment risk). If indexation is conditional, (former) plan participants bear the risk. From the plan sponsor's perspective, a contribution is paid to cover all costs of the annual pension accrual. From then onwards, the pension administrator (pension fund or insurer) takes ownership.

The new accounting guidelines provide defined contribution accounting with extensive disclosure requirements about the local financial position of the pension plan and the funding conditions laid down in the funding agreement. Users of the financial statements should be provided with information that enables them to evaluate the nature and extent of risks arising from the sponsoring relationship with the pension provider. The new guidelines were finalised in April 2009 and are effective for financial statements covering periods beginning on or after 1 January 2010 (early adoption is allowed).

RUSSIA

Economy and Government

The Russian Federation comprises Russia plus 21 autonomous republics and numerous other autonomous territories and regions. The president has extensive powers, nominates the highest governmental officials, including the 'chairman of the government' (prime minister) who must be approved by the legislature, and can pass decrees without consent from the legislature. Presidents are elected for four-year terms and cannot serve more than two consecutive terms. The legislative body has two chambers – the State Duma (lower house) and the Federation Council (upper house). The State Duma consists of 225 members elected from single member districts and 225 members elected from party lists. The Federation Council consists of 178 members – two representatives from each of the country's regions, one from the legislative body and one from the executive body of the region.

Labour relations

An amended Russian Federation Code of Labour Laws (KZOT) came into effect in October 2006. The 2006 amendments primarily affect employment contracts, wage payment, severance and vacation pay. The Ministry of Health and Social Development's Federal Labour Inspectorate and regional and local government inspectorates have the responsibility to enforce the labour and safety laws. These inspectors have free access to all enterprises and companies to conduct inspections and have the power to levy fines for infractions.

Cost of employment

A revised system was implemented in 2001, including the introduction of a graduated scale of of social security contributions, higher for lower-income employees, designed to discourage employers from under-reporting employees' wages. The revision also introduced a partial ceiling on contributions for employees earning RUR600,000 per year and over. Unemployment benefits are now financed through general income tax revenues.

Employment terms and conditions

All employment relationships in Russia, regardless of the location of the employee's legal employer, are subject to the Labour Code. Labour Code amendments enacted in October 2006 added specificity and broadened the definition of employer to include individual entrepreneurs and domestic employers. The Code requires that all employees have a written employment contract (a labour contract). Self-employed persons may be hired under civil law agreements, provided they are registered as entrepreneurs. Civil law agreements are regulated by the Civil Code instead of the Labour Code.

Social security and other required benefits

The administration and assets of the social security system are separated into the Pension Fund and the Social Insurance Fund. Contributions to these funds are collected locally, and the assets are managed by local officials. The Pension Fund administers the old age, survivors', and long-term disability pensions, plus child care allowances. The Fund is an independent body reporting to the State Duma. Cash sickness and maternity benefits, workers' compensation benefits and other social welfare benefits are paid through the Social Insurance Fund. The Fund is run by the government and guarantees benefits to all employees. A workers' compensation system, with risk-related premiums paid by employers, is managed by the Social Insurance Fund. Previously, work injuries were treated as regular death and disability (i.e. Pension Fund) events.

Healthcare system

The healthcare system is still highly inefficient and needs continued reforms. The Ministry of Health and Social Development formulates federal policies and controls their execution. Below the national level the *oblast*, autonomous, or *krai* health departments govern regional healthcare. The degree of independence from the ministry varies for each regional unit. District or *rayon* health authorities have an executive role at the local level. Health insurance foundations administer medical insurance funds. Health insurance foundations have not been established in all parts of the country. The district health authorities manage the public-sector hospitals and clinics in areas without the foundations' presence.

Taxation of compensation and benefits

The Ministry of Taxes and Collections regulates tax matters and issues numerous 'instructions', 'orders' and 'letters' to expand on, clarify or reverse earlier documents, and occasionally they appear to conflict with the tax or other laws. From 1 January 2007, individuals who have been in Russia more than 183 days in a consecutive 12-month period are considered resident for tax purposes. Residents are taxable on worldwide income. Foreign nationals who are resident are taxed in the same manner as local nationals. Non-residents are taxed on income from Russian sources only; payment from offshore companies for work in Russia is counted as Russian-source income. The tax year is the calendar year. Procedures for registration with the tax authorities and filing tax returns, due dates for returns, and penalties for non-compliance change frequently. Therefore, professional tax advice is necessary to ensure up-to-date information and compliance.

Recent developments

The finance ministry has released a draft 15-year fiscal strategy that includes increasing contributions to fund pensions. The government proposes to levy an additional 3% pension contribution on individuals born in or after 1968. The strategy also includes a plan to increase the base rate of the Unified Social Tax paid by employers from 26% to 34% by 2010. Beginning in 2015, the government wants to gradually increase the retirement age to age 60 for women (currently 55) and to age 62.5 for men (currently 60).

SPAIN

Economy and Government

Spain is a parliamentary monarchy; the president of the government is nominated by the monarch and subject to approval by the Congress of Deputies (lower house). The Spanish legislature is bicameral: Senators are elected in each of the provinces, and members of the Congress are elected via proportional representation. The structure of governance is semi-federal, with the powers of the national government shared with 17 'autonomous communities'. Each of these communities, or regional governments, has its own president, parliament and court system. The Basque Country and Catalonia have the strongest regional traditions, marked by their history and separate languages. The revenues of the autonomous communities are derived from personal income taxes (approximately 30% of personal income taxes collected in the autonomous community are returned to it), the wealth tax, estate budget transfers and other minor taxes.

Labour relations

Employment terms and labour relations are governed by statute, national framework agreements and collective agreements. There are mechanisms at the national level and regional or provincial levels – the Economic Social Councils – to promote social dialogue among employers, trade unions, government officials and political parties. Employees have the right to affiliate with the labour union of their choice, elect union representatives and take industrial action.

Cost of employment

The social security system has been subject to several revisions in contribution rates and ceilings in recent years in an attempt to base the contributions on an amount closer to actual salary for each of the applicable wage classes (11 in all). However, the current ceilings are still too low to compensate executives effectively. All social security contributions are paid on earnings within the applicable class's wage range. Contributions are based on 12 monthly salaries (bonuses are spread *pro rata*). A minimum contribution wage base applies to each occupational group (or wage class). The maximum contribution wage base has been the same for all wage groups since 1 January 2002. The minimum wage base for the employer's workers' compensation tax is the same as for wage classes 4–11.

Employment terms and conditions

All employment contracts must be in writing. Spain has implemented the EU directive on proof of employment, which requires an employer to confirm in writing the terms and conditions of employment. There are approximately 20 types of employment contract in Spain – indefinite-term contracts, temporary contracts, 'special relationship' contracts, and the partial retirement contract. The growth in type and number of temporary contracts is a consequence of government policies designed to encourage job creation. Provided there are no collective agreements to the contrary, employers may stipulate a limited trial period during which the employer or the employee may unilaterally terminate the employment contract without notice, cause, or compensation.

Social security and other required benefits

The social security system is a comprehensive programme covering a significant portion of the population and providing a wide range of protection. It is based on a combination of employment-related (contributory) and universal (non-contributory) plans. The General System (*Régimen General*) is compulsory for all employees aged 16 and over, including foreign nationals working for companies that are registered in Spain. Under the *Régimen General*, there are special programmes for employees of specific industries (for example, certain types of employment in market research/public opinion firms and in the hotel and food industries). There are special systems for the self-employed, maritime workers, mining, homemakers and agricultural workers.

Healthcare system

During the 20th century, healthcare services evolved into a true system of national healthcare provision, and almost 100% of the population is covered. All responsibility for purchasing and delivery of healthcare rests with Spain's 17 autonomous regions, aided by the National Institute of Public Health (INGS). The Ministry of Health and Consumer Affairs has overall responsibility for health policy, including establishing minimum healthcare standards and ensuring that national policies are implemented at the regional level. It has direct responsibility for public health policy, immunizations and inspection of meat and animal products imported from other countries (*sanidad exterior*), and legislation on pharmaceutical products.

Taxation of compensation and benefits

Individual income tax (IRPF – *Impuesto sobre la Renta de las Personas Físicas*) is levied by three tiers of government: the central government, the autonomous regional governments and local municipal governments. Central government taxes are administered by the Ministry of Economy and Taxation and are collected at provincial branches across the country. The laws applicable to individual taxpayers were consolidated in a new law (Ley 40/1998) effective for income and capital gains (or losses) arising on or after 1 January 1999. Ley 46/2002 of 18 December 2002 and implementing decrees decreased the tax rates on employment income, introduced a 'motherhood allowance' (tax credit), and extended the level of tax-deductible contributions to pension plans.

Recent developments

Employers' social security contributions may decrease and unemployment benefits may be extended in Spain. Government officials, unions and employers' associations are preparing to begin negotiations over a new social accord to deal with the repercussions of the economic crisis. Two issues on the negotiating table are a decrease in employers' social security contributions of 0.5% to 2.0% and the extension of unemployment benefits from six months to one year.

SWITZERLAND

Economy and Government

Switzerland has a federal system of government with both parliamentary and direct systems of democracy. The federal government (whose official name is the Helvetic Confederation) is composed of 26 cantons (20 of which are 'full' cantons and 6 are 'half' cantons). The federal government is responsible for matters that affect the entire country, for example, foreign policy, national defence, customs and monetary controls. The cantons implement federal laws, and can pass their own legislation on local issues. Each canton has its own parliament and government. In three half cantons, members of the federal government are elected by assemblies of the citizens. In the other cantons, federal and cantonal government members are elected by ballot.

Labour relations

Labour relations and terms of employment are determined by the Federal Constitution, statutes and collective agreements. The cantons are responsible for administering federal laws and providing arbitration courts, labour courts and appeal processes. Labour–management relations are cooperative. The government regularly consults with union confederations and employers' associations over proposed changes in labour and employment laws.

Cost of employment

Contributions to the federal social security system are required of all employed persons over age 17 and of residents aged 20 and older who are not part of a direct employer–employee relationship. Widows/widowers receiving a widow's/widower's pension and spouses who do not reach normal retirement age at the same time are required to contribute to social security during the years prior to reaching normal retirement age. Contribution rates are applied to total earnings, including bonuses, severance pay, and income replacement benefits. For individuals with no earned income, the contribution is based on the individual's assets. Contributions are not required on workers' compensation benefits, special bonuses or awards, or employer-paid insurance premiums.

Employment terms and conditions

Employment contracts may be written or oral. Contracts for special categories of employees – apprentices, 'commercial travellers' and home workers – must be in writing. Employment law does not specify the contents of the employment contract. However, some provisions must be in writing to be valid (for example, non-competition provisions). Employees' rights are established through laws and collective agreements. However, a benefit granted repeatedly over time may become a right unless the employer specifically states that the benefit is granted at its discretion.

Social security and other required benefits

The retirement system is based on the 'three pillars'. The federal social security system is the first pillar, a basic universal pension financed on a pay-as-you-go basis.

Mandatory occupational pension plans under federal law (BVG/LPP) form the second pillar and individual savings and insurance constitute the third. The federal social security system provides old-age and survivors' pensions (AHV/AVS) and long-term disability benefits (IV/AI) as well as short-term income replacement benefits (EO/APG). Workers' compensation, unemployment insurance, and family allowances are provided under separate legislation. Medical care benefits are not provided by social security.

Healthcare system

The role of the federal government is limited to matters such as control of food and drugs, control of communicable diseases, poison control, etc. Healthcare delivery is managed at the level of the 26 cantons. Each canton decides the type and scope of healthcare services to be provided to residents. Services can range from government-run hospitals (at canton- or community-level) to financial support for services provided by private facilities to purchasing services from facilities in other cantons. About half of the cost of these services is covered by the cantons through general revenues and half by patient insurance.

Taxation of compensation and benefits

Taxes are levied by federal, cantonal and municipal authorities on the worldwide income of residents, exclusive of income from foreign real estate and foreign permanent establishments. Criteria for residence, which vary for federal, cantonal and municipal tax purposes, are based on length of domicile, economic activity or ownership of property. The rates of federal tax are common to all cantons, but each canton sets its own basic tax rates and allowances for cantonal and municipal tax purposes. The cantonal and municipal taxes payable in any year are calculated by applying multiples to the basic rates. All cantons levy a wage withholding tax for foreigners who do not have a permit to stay permanently in Switzerland. Each cantonal authority is responsible for the assessment and collection not only of cantonal tax but also of federal and municipal taxes. For federal and cantonal tax purposes, the tax year is the current income year. In general, cantonal tax is payable in instalments. Federal tax bills must be settled by the end of March of the following year. The income of husband and wife is assessed jointly. Different tax tables apply to single and married persons.

Recent developments

Both houses of the Swiss parliament have approved increasing the social security retirement age for women to age 65. Equalizing the social security retirement age for men and women has been planned for several years. Following the votes, the measure is likely to be included in an upcoming package of reforms to the retirement system.

UNITED STATES OF AMERICA

Economy and Government

The United States is a federal republic with powers shared by the national and state governments. The tension between the rights of states and the rights of the federal government plays a crucial role in US politics.

Labour relations

Legal mechanisms exist to impose settlements in disputes in workplaces deemed to be essential to the public good. In addition, minimum wage and maximum work hours are established by law. In general, however, the terms of employment are determined by employers or through collective bargaining. Employers are subject to extensive labour law rules. The Department of Labor is responsible for overseeing employer practices in such areas as hiring, employee benefits and overtime pay. The National Labor Relations Board oversees collective bargaining. In addition, most states also have their own labour laws, which are often different from those of the federal government.

Cost of employment

Social security benefits are financed through contributions paid by employers, employees and the self-employed under the Federal Insurance Contributions Act (FICA) and the Self-Employment Contributions Act (SECA). Employers and employees both contribute an equal percentage of pay up to an annual earnings limit (the taxable wage base).

Employment terms and conditions

The Fair Labor Standards Act (FLSA) governs maximum hours worked and overtime pay. It divides employees into two categories: 'exempt' (salaried employees including executive, professional and administrative [as defined by law]) employees and 'non-exempt' (hourly-paid) employees. The latter are covered by FLSA rules. From 23 August 2004, the determination of employees as exempt or non-exempt under the FLSA changed. Notably, the minimum salary level to qualify for the exemption from the FLSA minimum wage and overtime pay requirements increased to a minimum of US$455 per week (US$23,660 annually). For certain computer-related occupations, employees who earn at least US$27.63 per hour are eligible for the exemption even if they are not paid on a salary basis. In addition, employees must generally meet one of the duties tests to qualify for exemption.

Social security and other required benefits

There are three main programmes in the social security system: old age and survivors' insurance (OASI), disability insurance (DI) and Medicare. Sometimes, they are grouped together and known as OASDHI, or old age, survivors', disability, and hospital insurance. Workers' compensation and unemployment insurance are provided under separate laws. The social security system covers most employees and the self-employed. However, various classes of employee are exempt from coverage, including, for example, certain agricultural, domestic and casual workers as well as certain employees of the federal or state governments. Financing is through contributions (taxes) paid by employers, employees, and the self-employed.

Healthcare system

The USA does not have a comprehensive national health insurance programme. The majority of US families rely on group health insurance plans provided by employers or on insurance that they have purchased individually.

An estimated 40 to 50 million people have no health insurance. The two existing national insurance programmes, Medicare and Medicaid, provide healthcare benefits only to certain segments of the population. Medicare, as a part of the federal social security system, provides medical benefits only for individuals aged 65 or older and for the disabled, while Medicaid helps finance medical care for people with low incomes. Medicaid is primarily funded at the federal level and administered at the state level.

Taxation of compensation and benefits

Citizens and permanent residents are subject to federal income tax on worldwide foreign and domestic income. However, tax relief may be available in the form of unilateral tax credits, double income tax treaty benefits and certain exclusions for specified foreign income. As a result, citizens and permanent residents must file annual tax returns even if they are non-resident for tax purposes for the year in question. Non-resident aliens are taxed only on certain income from sources or businesses in the USA. Most citizens and residents pay federal, state and sometimes local income taxes.

Recent developments

The US Internal Revenue Service (IRS) issued Notice 2009–22, which provides guidance and interim rules regarding the determination of the 'smoothed' value of plan assets permitted for single employer defined benefit pension plan valuations, pursuant to changes made by the Worker, Retiree, and Employer Recovery Act of 2008 (WRERA).

Notice 2009–22 provides automatic approval for a change in asset valuation method for plan years beginning in 2009 to any permissible asset valuation method. The outcome is that for most single employer plans, the 2008 plan year valuation results may now be finalised using previously completed results without requiring additional adjustments. For any plan sponsors that preferred to use a smoothing method as allowed by the WRERA legislation for 2009 valuations but were concerned about the potential retroactive impact on 2008 results, this guidance now provides complete relief since the asset method change for 2009 is granted automatic approval.

While Notice 2009–22 provides needed guidance for the asset valuation methods, there are several other areas where additional guidance is still needed in order for actuaries to complete 2009 valuations (e.g. what expenses are to be included in Target Normal Cost for 2009).

AA	Annual Allowance
ABI	Association of British Insurers
AEI	Average Earnings Index
APP	Appropriate Personal Pension
ARR	Age-related Rebate
ASB	Accounting Standards Board
ASP	Alternatively Secured Pension
AVCs	Additional Voluntary Contributions
AVR	Actuarial Valuation Report
BAS	Board for Actuarial Standards
BCE	Benefit Crystallisation Event
BERR	Department for Business Enterprise & Regulatory Reform
BSP	Basic State Pension
CA	Certified Amount *or* Companies Act
CAPS	BNY Mellon Asset Servicing (formerly Combined Actuarial Performance Services)
CARE	Career Average Revalued Earnings
CEIOPS	Committee of European Insurance and Occupational Pensions Supervisors
CEP	Contributions Equivalent Premium
CETV	Cash Equivalent Transfer Value
CGT	Capital Gains Tax
CIMPS	Contracted-in Money Purchase Scheme
CMI	Continuous Mortality Investigation
COMBS	Contracted-out Mixed Benefit Scheme
COMPS	Contracted-out Money Purchase Scheme
COMPSHP	Stakeholder Contracted-out Money Purchase Scheme
CoP	Code of Practice
COSRS	Contracted-out Salary Related Scheme
CPA	Compulsory Purchase Annuity
CPF	Combined Pension Forecast
CPI	Consumer Prices Index
DB	Defined Benefit
DC	Defined Contribution
DWP	Department for Work and Pensions
ECJ	European Court of Justice

ECON	Employer's Contracting-out Number
EEA	European Economic Area
EFRBS	Employer-financed Retirement Benefit Scheme
EPB	Equivalent Pension Benefit
EPP	Executive Pension Plan
ERF	Early Retirement Factor
ERI	Employer-related Investment
EU	European Union
FA	Finance Act
FAS	Financial Assistance Scheme *or* Financial Accounting Standard
FASB	Financial Accounting Standards Board
FCF	Fraud Compensation Fund
FRC	Financial Reporting Council
FRS	Financial Reporting Standard
FSA	Financial Services Authority
FSCS	Financial Services Compensation Scheme
FSMA	Financial Services and Markets Act
GAD	Government Actuary's Department
GMP	Guaranteed Minimum Pension
GN	Guidance Notes
GPP	Group Personal Pension
GSIPP	Group Self-invested Personal Pension
HMRC	Her Majesty's Revenue & Customs
HMT	Her Majesty's Treasury
IAS	International Accounting Standard
IASB/IASC	International Accounting Standards Board/Committee
ICTA	Income & Corporation Taxes Act
IDR/IDRP	Internal Dispute Resolution (Procedure)
IFRIC	International Financial Reporting Interpretations Committee
IFRS	International Financial Reporting Standard
IHT	Inheritance Tax
ISA	Individual Savings Account
ITEPA	Income Tax (Earnings and Pensions) Act
JWG	Occupational Pension Schemes Joint Working Group
LDI	Liability Driven Investment
LEL	Lower Earnings Limit
LET	Low Earnings Threshold
LPI	Limited Price Indexation

LTA	Lifetime Allowance
MND	Member-nominated Director
MNT	Member-nominated Trustee
MPP	Maximum Permitted Pension
NAPF	National Association of Pension Funds
NI	National Insurance
NICO	National Insurance Contributions Office
NISPI	National Insurance Services to Pensions Industry
NMPA	Normal Minimum Pension Age
NPA/NPD	Normal Pension Age/Normal Pension Date
NPSS	National Pension Savings Scheme
NRA/NRD	Normal Retirement Age/Normal Retirement Date
OECD	Organisation for Economic Co-operation and Development
OEIC	Open-ended Investment Company
OMO	Open Market Option
ONS	Office for National Statistics
OPSI	Office of Public Sector Information
PA	Pensions Act
PAB	Personal Accounts Board
PADA	Personal Accounts Delivery Authority
PAEB	Personal Accounts Earnings Band
PAYE	Pay As You Earn
PAYG	Pay As You Go
PCLS	Pension Commencement Lump Sum
PCS	Professional Conduct Standards
PHI	Permanent Health Insurance
PLA	Purchased Life Annuity *or* Personal Lifetime Allowance
PMI	Pensions Management Institute
PPF	Pension Protection Fund
PPP/PPS	Personal Pension Plan/Scheme
PR	Protected Rights
PRAG	Pensions Research Accountants Group
PSA	Pension Schemes Act
PUP	Paid-up Pension
RAC	Retirement Annuity Contract
RPI	Retail Prices Index
RST	Reference Scheme Test
S2P	State Second Pension
SAA	Special Annual Allowance

SAAC	Special Annual Allowance Charge
SCON	Scheme Contracted-out Number
SERPS	State Earnings-related Pension Scheme
SFO	Statutory Funding Objective
SFP	Statement of Funding Principles
SFS	Summary Funding Statement
SHP	Stakeholder Pension
SI	Statutory Instrument
SIP	Statement of Investment Principles
SIPP	Self-invested Personal Pension
SLA	Standard Lifetime Allowance
SMPI	Statutory Money Purchase Illustration
SORP	Statement of Recommended Practice
SPA	State Pensionable Age
SRI	Socially Responsible Investment
SSA	Social Security Act
SSAS	Small Self-administered Scheme
SSB	Short Service Benefit
SSPA	Social Security Pensions Act
STRGL	Statement of Total Recognised Gains and Losses
TAS	Technical Actuarial Standard
TKU	Trustee Knowledge and Understanding
TPAS	The Pensions Advisory Service (formerly OPAS)
TPR	The Pensions Regulator
TUPE	Transfer of Undertakings (Protection of Employment) Regulations
TV	Transfer Value
UEL	Upper Earnings Limit
WGMP	Widow's/Widower's Guaranteed Minimum Pension
WR&PA	Welfare Reform and Pensions Act

Source: Hewitt.

GLOSSARY OF TERMS

| **Bold Text:** | Cross references that it is felt might improve the understanding of the term concerned. |
| *Italicised Text:* | Terms which, whilst not forming part of the basic definition, provide the reader with additional guidance. |

DEFINITIONS

The definitions in this Glossary are current at the time of going to print.

A DAY 6 April 2006, when the FA 2004 tax regime came into force.

ACCRUAL RATE The rate at which rights build up for each year of **pensionable service** in a **defined benefit scheme**.

ACCRUED BENEFITS The benefits for service up to a given point in time, whether **vested rights** or not. They may be calculated in relation to current earnings or projected earnings.

*Allowance may also be made for **revaluation** and/or **pension increases** required by the scheme rules or legislation.*

ACCRUED RIGHTS The benefits to which a member is entitled, as of right, under an **occupational pension scheme**. These include **accrued benefits**. Depending on the context, accrued rights for an **active member** can be based on benefits as if the member had left service or could include a right to have benefits linked to future salary changes.

*The term is given various specific definitions in PSA 1993 for the purposes of **preservation**, **contracting out** and in the Disclosure Regulations. It is also given a specific meaning in PA 1995, e.g. in relation to scheme amendments.*

ACTIVE MEMBER A member of an **occupational pension scheme** who is at present accruing benefits under that scheme in respect of current service.

ACTUARIAL ASSUMPTIONS The set of assumptions as to rates of return, inflation, increase in earnings, and mortality, etc., used by the **actuary** in an **actuarial valuation** or other actuarial calculations.

ACTUARIAL CERTIFICATE A certificate given by an **actuary** arising out of actuarial work. Actuarial certificates include:

(a) the **reference scheme test** certificate

(b) the calculation of **technical provisions** certificate

...continued

(c)   the **schedule of contributions** certificate *and*

(d)   the **bulk transfer** certificate.

ACTUARIAL EQUIVALENCE   A test of actuarial value which compares benefits immediately before and after a modification. For the test to be satisfied, the total value of the member's subsisting rights immediately after the modification must be no less than the value of those rights immediately before the modification. This term is used in connection with **section 67** of PA 1995.

ACTUARIAL GAINS AND LOSSES   Used in **FRS 17** to mean changes in actuarial deficits or surpluses that arise because:

(a)   events have not coincided with the **actuarial assumptions** made for the last valuation (experience gains and losses) *or*

(b)   the actuarial assumptions have changed.

ACTUARIAL LIABILITY   The value placed on the liability of a pension fund for the outgoings due after the date to which the calculations relate.

ACTUARIAL REDUCTION   A reduction made to a member's **accrued benefits** in order to offset any additional cost arising from their payment in advance of the **normal pension date**.

ACTUARIAL REPORT   A written report, prepared and signed by the **scheme actuary**, on the developments affecting the scheme's **technical provisions** since the last **actuarial valuation** was prepared.

ACTUARIAL SURPLUS   The excess of the value of the assets over the **actuarial liability** on the basis of the funding method and **actuarial assumptions** used.

ACTUARIAL VALUATION

(1)   Commonly refers to an investigation by an **actuary** into the ability of a **defined benefit scheme** to meet its liabilities. This is usually to assess the **funding level** and a recommended contribution rate based on comparing the value of the assets and the **actuarial liability**.

(2)   Under PA 2004, specifically refers to a written report, prepared and signed by the **scheme actuary**, valuing the scheme's assets and calculating its **technical provisions**.

ACTUARY   An adviser on financial questions involving probabilities relating to mortality and other contingencies.

For statutory purposes in the UK, the term automatically includes Fellows of the Institute of Actuaries and Faculty of Actuaries.

Persons with other actuarial qualifications may be approved by the Secretary of State for a specific purpose.

ADDED YEARS The provision of extra benefits by reference to an additional period of **pensionable service** in a **defined benefit scheme**, arising from the receipt of a **transfer payment**, the paying of **AVCs** or by way of **augmentation**.

ADDITIONAL VOLUNTARY CONTRIBUTIONS (AVCs)

Contributions over and above a member's normal contributions if any, which the member elects to pay to an **occupational pension scheme** in order to secure additional benefits.

ADMINISTRATOR

(1) The person or persons notified to HMRC as being responsible for the management of a pension scheme.

(2) The person who is responsible for the day-to-day administration of the pension scheme.

(3) A type of insolvency practitioner in relation to companies under the Insolvency Act 1986.

AGE-RELATED REBATE Payments made by **NICO** to a contracted-out occupational **money purchase scheme**, or an **appropriate personal pension scheme** for members who have **contracted out**. These increase with the age of the member.

ALTERNATIVELY SECURED PENSION A variation on **unsecured pension**, where the recipient of the income is over 75, to accommodate religious objections to risk pooling. There are strict limits on income taken.

AMORTISATION

(1) The spreading of an **actuarial surplus** or deficiency over an appropriate period.

(2) An accountancy term for the reduction in the value of an asset, such as leasehold property, caused by the passage of time. If the cause is not solely related to time, the corresponding term is depreciation.

ANNUAL ALLOWANCE The maximum amount of pension savings that can be built up in any one tax year before liability to an **annual allowance charge**.

ANNUAL ALLOWANCE CHARGE The tax charge levied at 40% on an individual who is a member of one or more **registered pension schemes** in respect of the amount by which the **total pension input amount** for a tax year exceeds the **annual allowance**.

ANNUAL REPORT The means by which the **trustees** of an **occupational pension scheme** communicate financial and other information about the scheme to the members, the employer and other interested parties.

The term is used to describe the specific information that is required to be made available by trustees in relation to each scheme year under the Disclosure Regulations. Subject to certain exemptions, this must include a copy of the audited accounts and other information specified, including an investment report. The detailed content of the audited accounts is described in the Pension Scheme SORP.

Trustees often publish a simplified annual report for members containing the above material suitably summarised.

ANNUITY A series of payments, which may be subject to increases, made at stated intervals until a particular event occurs. This event is most commonly the end of a specified period or the death of the person receiving the annuity.

An annuity may take one of a number of different forms including **compulsory purchase annuity**, *deferred annuity,* **purchased life annuity** *and reversionary annuity.*

ANTI-FRANKING REQUIREMENTS The requirements which ban the process whereby statutory increases in **GMP** e.g. between termination of **contracted-out** employment and **state pensionable age** are offset against other scheme benefits, rather than being added to a member's total benefits.

The requirements are covered in Chapter III of Part IV PSA 1993.

APPROPRIATE PERSONAL PENSION SCHEME (APPS)

A **personal pension scheme** that has received an appropriate scheme certificate enabling members to contract out of **S2P**.

ARRANGEMENT Under FA 2004, a contractual or trust-based arrangement made by or on behalf of a member of a pension scheme under that scheme. A member may have more than one arrangement under a scheme.

ASSESSMENT PERIOD The period of time when a scheme is being assessed to determine if the **Pension Protection Fund** can assume responsibility for it.

ASSET ALLOCATION STRATEGY The splitting of the assets of a pension scheme between the various **asset classes** such as equities, bonds and cash. This will primarily reflect the long-term needs of the fund, the 'strategic view', but may be adjusted to favour particular asset classes or markets which look attractive in the short term, the 'tactical view'.

ASSET AND LIABILITY MATCHING A process of selecting assets which are likely to generate proceeds broadly equal to the cashflow needed to meet the liabilities as they occur under different economic scenarios.

An example of this would be the matching of a level pension with fixed interest securities.

ASSET AND LIABILITY MODELLING A technique used to test the effect of different economic scenarios on the assets and liabilities of an **occupational pension scheme**, the inter-relationship between them, the **funding level** and the contribution rates.

ASSET CLASS A collective term for investments of a similar type. The main asset classes are equities (shares), bonds, cash and property.

ATTAINED AGE METHOD A funding method in which the **actuarial liability** makes allowance for projected earnings. The contribution rate is that necessary to cover the cost of all benefits which will accrue to existing members after the valuation date by reference to total earnings throughout their future working lifetimes projected to the dates on which benefits become payable.

AUDITOR An individual or firm appointed to report on the financial statements of an entity. The results of their examination are incorporated within an auditor's report.

AUGMENTATION The provision of additional benefits in respect of particular members of an **occupational pension scheme**, normally where the cost is borne by the scheme and/or employer.

AUTHORISED PAYMENT A payment made by a **registered pension scheme** to an employer or member which is permitted under the provisions of FA 2004.

BARBER **JUDGMENT** The judgment of the European Court of Justice in the case of *Barber v. Guardian Royal Exchange* on 17 May 1990, which confirmed that pensions count as pay for the purposes of Article 141, and therefore are subject to equal treatment between men and women.

BASIC PENSION The flat-rate (not earnings-related) state pension paid to all who have met the minimum NI contribution requirements. The amount paid is increased if the recipient is married and a spouse or widow(er) may claim on the record of his/her spouse.

BENCHMARK A target or measure against which performance is to be judged.

Commonly used to judge the performance of a fund or portfolio.

BENEFICIARY A person entitled to benefit under a pension scheme or who will become entitled on the happening of a specific event.

BENEFIT CRYSTALLISATION EVENT One of ten events defined in FA 2004 that triggers a test of benefits 'crystallising' at that point against the individual's available **lifetime allowance**.

BENEFITS IN KIND Benefits other than cash provided as remuneration for an employment.

BRIDGING PENSION An additional pension paid from a scheme between retirement and **state pensionable age**, which is usually replaced by the state pension payable from that age.

BULK TRANSFER The transfer of a group of members from one **occupational pension scheme** to another, sometimes with an enhanced transfer payment in comparison with an individual's **cash equivalent**.

BUY-IN The purchase by **trustees** of an **occupational pension scheme** of an insurance policy in the name of the trustees. This remains an asset of the trustees.

BUY-OUT The purchase by **trustees** of an **occupational pension scheme** of an insurance policy in the name of a member or other **beneficiary**, in lieu of entitlement to benefit from the scheme, following termination of the member's **pensionable service**.

CASH BALANCE ARRANGEMENT Under FA 2004, a type of **money purchase arrangement**. An **arrangement** is a cash balance arrangement where the member will be provided with money purchase benefits, but where the amount that will be available to provide those benefits is not calculated purely by reference to payments made under the arrangement by or on behalf of the member. This means that in a cash balance arrangement, the capital amount available to provide benefits (the member's 'pot') will not derive wholly from any actual contributions (or credits or transfers) made year on year.

CASH EQUIVALENT The amount which a member of a pension scheme may, under section 94 PSA 1993, require to be applied as a **transfer payment**.

CASH TRANSFER SUM The amount that a leaver with between 3 and 24 months' **pensionable service** may require to be applied as a **transfer payment**, as an alternative to a refund of contributions.

CODES OF PRACTICE The **Pensions Regulator** issues various codes of practice providing practical guidance on compliance with the requirements of PA 2004.

COMBINED PENSION FORECASTS A statement issued by the current pension arrangement to the member showing the combined benefits at retirement that the member may receive from the pension scheme and the state.

COMMUTATION The forgoing of a part or all of the pension payable from retirement for an immediate lump sum benefit.

COMPULSORY PURCHASE ANNUITY An **annuity** which must be purchased on retirement for a member of an insured pension scheme.

CONTINUOUS SERVICE Treatment by an **occupational pension scheme** of the **pensionable service** of a member as continuous with a previous period of pensionable service (within the same scheme or another scheme).

CONTRACTED OUT/CONTRACTED IN A pension scheme is contracted out where it provides benefits (**GMPs**, **protected rights** or **section 9(2B) rights**) in place of **SERPS** or **S2P** and has been given a **contracting-out certificate** or appropriate scheme certificate by HMRC. Members are contracted out if they are in employment which is contracted out by reference to an **occupational pension scheme** or have elected to contract out via an **appropriate personal pension scheme**.

A pension scheme is commonly called contracted in where it is not contracted out, i.e. it provides benefits in addition to S2P. The term 'contracted in' is not referred to in legislation.

CONTRACTED-OUT REBATE The amount by which the employer's and the employee's NI contributions are reduced or rebated in respect of employees who are **contracted out** by virtue of their membership of an **appropriate personal pension scheme** or an **occupational pension scheme**.

The contracted-out rebate consists of a flat-rate rebate and (for contracted-out money purchase schemes and appropriate personal pension schemes) an age-related rebate.

CONTRACTING-OUT CERTIFICATE The certificate issued by HMRC, in respect of an **occupational pension scheme** which satisfies the conditions for **contracting out**, confirming that the employees in the employments named in the certificate are to be treated as being in contracted-out employment.

CONTROLLING DIRECTOR A director who, on his own or with associates, owns or controls 20% or more of the ordinary shares of the employing company.

CROSS-BORDER SCHEME   If a UK scheme has members working in another EU member state, who are not **seconded employees**, the scheme is operating as a cross-border scheme. Such schemes require regulatory approval to accept contributions in respect of cross-border operations and are subject to additional regulations, for example in relation to the **statutory funding objective**.

DEFERRED MEMBER/PENSIONER   A member entitled to **preserved benefits**.

DEFINED BENEFIT SCHEME   A scheme where the scheme rules define the benefits independently of the contributions payable, and benefits are not directly related to the investments of the scheme. The scheme may be funded or unfunded.

DEFINED CONTRIBUTION SCHEME   A scheme which determines the individual member's benefits by reference to contributions paid into the scheme in respect of that member, usually increased by an amount based on the investment return on those contributions. Sometimes referred to as a **money purchase scheme**.

DEPENDANT   For HMRC purposes, a person who was married to, civil partner of or financially dependent on the member at the date of the member's death is a dependant of the member.

A child of the member is a dependant of the member if the child has not reached the age of 23, or has reached age 23 and, in the opinion of the scheme **administrator**, was at the date of the member's death dependent on the member because of physical or mental impairment.

DISCLOSURE

(1)   A requirement introduced by PSA 1993 (formerly SSPA 1975) and strengthened by PA 1995 for pension schemes to disclose information about the scheme and benefits to interested parties.

(2)   Rules introduced by regulatory bodies to disclose product and commission information to the purchasers of life assurance and insured pension products.

DISCONTINUANCE   The cessation of the liability of the sponsoring employer to pay contributions to a pension scheme.

DISCRETIONARY INCREASE   An increase to a pension in payment or to a **preserved benefit** arising on a discretionary basis, i.e. other than from a system of **escalation** or **indexation**. Such an increase may be of a regular or an ad hoc nature.

EARLY RETIREMENT The retirement of a member with immediate payment of benefits before **normal pension date**.
The benefit may be reduced because of early payment.

EMPLOYER-FINANCED RETIREMENT BENEFIT SCHEME
A scheme which is neither a **registered pension scheme** nor a section 615(3) scheme.

ENHANCED LIFETIME ALLOWANCE This is where the **standard lifetime allowance** has been increased as a result of **primary protection**, or **pension credits**, or transfers from overseas schemes or where the member has not always been a relevant UK individual. This results in a **personal lifetime allowance**.

ENHANCED PROTECTION A form of protection from the **lifetime allowance charge** available for all members under the FA 2004 tax regime, regardless of the amount of their benefits pre-**A Day**.

ESCALATION A system whereby pensions in payment and/or **preserved benefits** are automatically increased at regular intervals and at a fixed percentage rate. The percentage may be restricted to the increase in a specified index.

EXPRESSION OF WISH A means by which a member can indicate a preference as to who should receive any lump sum death benefit.
*The choice is not binding on the **trustees**, and, as a result, inheritance tax is normally avoided.*

FINAL PENSIONABLE EARNINGS/PAY/SALARY The pensionable earnings on which the benefits are calculated in a **defined benefit scheme**. The earnings may be based on the average over a number of consecutive years prior to retirement, death or leaving **pensionable service**.

FINAL SALARY SCHEME A **defined benefit scheme** where the benefit is calculated by reference to the **final pensionable earnings** of the member, usually also based on **pensionable service**.

FINANCIAL ASSISTANCE SCHEME A scheme introduced by the government to help workers who have lost pension rights through company insolvency but do not qualify for the **Pension Protection Fund**.

FIXED RATE REVALUATION A method used by a COSRS to revalue **GMP** between termination of **contracted-out** employment and age 65 (men), 60 (women) as one of the alternatives to applying **section 148 orders**.
The rate is reviewed periodically.

FLEXIBLE RETIREMENT The option to take benefits from 6 April 2006 in stages – the member can also remain in employment with the same employer.

FRAUD COMPENSATION FUND Replaced the Pensions Compensation Scheme, with effect from 6 April 2005. Payments can be made from the fund in cases where the assets of a scheme have been reduced since 6 April 1997 as a result of an offence involving dishonesty, including an intent to defraud.

FRS 17 – RETIREMENT BENEFITS FRS 17 is mainly concerned with **defined benefit schemes**, but applies to all retirement benefits as well as pensions, for example medical care in retirement. Exemptions exist for smaller entities.

It requires the scheme assets and liabilities to be valued on a 'fair value' basis and the resulting surplus (or deficit) to be recognised as an asset (or liability) in the balance sheet of the reporting company. The components in the change in the net asset or liability over time are disclosed in its profit and loss account, with the exception of **actuarial gains and losses**, which are recognised in the **statement of total recognised gains and losses**.

FRS 17 requires extensive disclosures in the company's accounts.

FUNDING LEVEL The relationship at a specified date between the value of the assets and the **actuarial liability**. Normally expressed as a percentage.

The funding level may be calculated separately in respect of different categories of liability, e.g. pensions in payment and AVCs.

GUARANTEED MINIMUM PENSION (GMP) The minimum pension which an **occupational pension scheme** must provide as one of the conditions of **contracting out** for pre-6 April 1997 service (unless it was contracted out through the provision of **protected rights**).

HMRC NATIONAL INSURANCE CONTRIBUTIONS OFFICE (NICO)

This office is responsible for the collection and recording of National Insurance contributions. This involves the following: ensuring compliance with National Insurance-related legislation, the collection of National Insurance contributions, the administration of the contracted-out system, the maintenance of accurate National Insurance accounts and the provision of National Insurance information.

HMRC SAVINGS, PENSIONS, SHARE SCHEMES OFFICE (HMRC SPSS) The office of HMRC which deals with **occupational** and **personal pension schemes** under the relevant tax legislation.

HYBRID ARRANGEMENT Under FA 2004, an **arrangement** where only one type of benefit will ultimately be provided, but the type of benefit that will be provided is not known in advance because it will depend on certain circumstances at the point benefits are drawn.

HYBRID SCHEME

(1) An **occupational pension scheme** in which the benefit is calculated as the better of two alternatives, for example on a final salary and a money purchase basis.

(2) An occupational pension scheme which offers both defined benefit and defined contribution benefits.

INCOME WITHDRAWAL An alternative to buying a **lifetime annuity**. It allows a member of a **money purchase arrangement** to draw an income from their pension fund while the fund remains invested.

INDEPENDENT TRUSTEE An independent trustee must be registered and an 'independent person in relation to the scheme'. This requirement will be satisfied if he or she has no interests in the assets of the employer or scheme and is not connected with the employer, insolvency practitioner or official receiver.

INDEXATION

(1) A system whereby pensions in payment and/or **preserved benefits** are automatically increased at regular intervals by reference to a specified index of prices or earnings.

(2) An investment strategy designed to produce a rate of return in line with a particular index, either by replicating the constituents or by sufficient sampling to give a proxy.

INTERNAL DISPUTE RESOLUTION PROCEDURE (IDRP)

Occupational pension schemes (subject to exceptions) are required by section 50 PA 1995 to have a procedure to deal with disputes between **trustees** on the one hand and members and **beneficiaries** on the other hand.

LATE RETIREMENT The payment of retirement benefits to a member after **normal pension date**.

LEVY

(1) The general levy meets the expenditure of the **Pensions Ombudsman**, the **Pensions Regulator** and grants made by the Pensions Regulator (e.g. to TPAS). It is payable by registrable **occupational pension schemes** and **personal pension schemes**.

(2) The Fraud Compensation Levy is payable by occupational pension schemes to fund the **Fraud Compensation Fund**.

...continued

(3) Schemes that are eligible for future entry to the **PPF** pay a Pension Protection Levy to the PPF which is based on a **section 179 valuation**. A PPF Administration Levy and a PPF Ombudsman Levy are also payable.

LIFESTYLING An **asset allocation strategy** used mainly in **defined contribution schemes** whereby a member's investments are adjusted depending on age and term to retirement. Typically assets are switched from equities into bonds and cash as retirement approaches.

LIFETIME ALLOWANCE The lifetime allowance is an overall ceiling on the amount of tax-privileged savings that any one individual can draw. The exact figure will be the same as the **standard lifetime allowance** for the tax year concerned, or a multiple of this figure where certain circumstances apply.

LIFETIME ALLOWANCE CHARGE The tax charge levied on excess funds, following a **benefit crystallisation event**, for any individual with a benefit value more than their **lifetime allowance** (unless they have **enhanced protection**).

LIFETIME ANNUITY Under FA 2004, an **annuity** contract purchased from an insurance company of the member's choosing that provides the member with an income for life.

LIMITED PRICE INDEXATION (LPI) The requirement under PA 1995 to increase, by 5% pa up to 5 April 2005 and 2.5% thereafter, or RPI if less, pensions in payment under an **occupational pension scheme** (excluding **AVCs** and money purchase benefits) and pensions in payment arising from **protected rights** under an **appropriate personal pension scheme** or an appropriate personal pension stakeholder pension scheme. It applies to pensions accrued in respect of service after 5 April 1997.

LIMITED REVALUATION A method used by COSRS to revalue **GMP** by the lower of 5% per annum and **section 148 orders**, between termination of **contracted-out** employment and age 65 (men), 60 (women). It was withdrawn from 6 April 1997.

LOWER EARNINGS LIMIT (LEL) The minimum amount, approximately equivalent to the single person's **basic pension**, which must be earned in any period in order for an individual to accrue state pension benefits.

MARKET VALUE The price at which an asset might reasonably be expected to be sold in an open market.

MEMBER-NOMINATED TRUSTEE A **trustee** who is nominated and elected to a trustee board by members of the scheme.

MINIMUM CONTRIBUTIONS Contributions payable to an appropriate scheme by **NICO** in respect of a member who has elected to contract out. The contributions consist of the **age-related rebate** and, where payment is to an **APPS** or APPSHP, basic rate tax relief on the employee's share of the rebate.

MINIMUM PAYMENTS The minimum amount which an employer must pay into a COMPS. This minimum amount consists of the flat rate rebate of NI contributions in respect of employees who are **contracted out**.

MONEY PURCHASE ARRANGEMENT Under FA 2004, this is an **arrangement** under which the member is entitled to money purchase benefits. A **cash balance arrangement** is one type of money purchase arrangement.

MONEY PURCHASE SCHEME A **defined contribution scheme** where the benefit is provided from contributions to the scheme, increased by the amount of investment return on those contributions.

NET PAY ARRANGEMENT The procedure whereby contributions to an **occupational pension scheme** are deducted from the member's pay before tax is calculated under PAYE, giving immediate tax relief at the highest applicable rate.

NORMAL MINIMUM PENSION AGE The earliest age at which a member is allowed to draw benefits from a **registered pension scheme**, other than in ill health; currently 50. Schemes must implement the new normal minimum pension age of 55 by 6 April 2010. There are transitional provisions allowing members to protect existing rights at **A Day** to receive their benefits from an earlier age.

NORMAL PENSION AGE (NPA)

(1) Commonly the age by reference to which the **normal pension date** is determined.

(2) The statutory definition (relevant for **preservation** and **contracting-out** purposes) is generally the earliest age at which a member is entitled to receive benefits (other than **GMP**) on his/her retirement from employment to which the scheme relates, ignoring any special provisions as to early retirement on grounds of ill health or otherwise (section 180 PSA 1993). This is commonly interpreted to mean the earliest age at which a member has the right to take benefits without reduction.

*This may be different from definition (1) above or **normal retirement age**.*

NORMAL PENSION DATE (NPD)   The date at which a member of a pension scheme normally becomes entitled to receive his/her retirement benefits.

NORMAL RETIREMENT AGE (NRA)

(1)   For employment purposes the age at which the employees holding a particular position normally retire from service.

*This is often (but not always) the same as **normal pension age** or definition (2) below.*

The statutory term 'normal retiring age' is used in sections 109 (unfair dismissal) and 156 (redundancy) of the Employment Rights Act 1996.

(2)   The age of a member of an **occupational pension scheme** at the **normal retirement date** as specified in the scheme rules.

NORMAL RETIREMENT DATE (NRD)   The date (usually the date of reaching a particular age) specified in the rules of an **occupational pension scheme** at which a member would normally retire.

NOTIFIABLE EVENTS   Certain specified events to be automatically notified to the **Pensions Regulator** under section 69 of PA 2004.

OCCUPATIONAL PENSION SCHEME   A scheme organised by an employer or on behalf of a group of employers to provide pensions and/or other benefits for or in respect of one or more employees on leaving service or on death or on retirement. An occupational pension scheme can be registered with the **Pensions Regulator** as a **stakeholder pension scheme** if the necessary conditions are met.

The statutory definition is in section 1 PSA 1993.

OPEN MARKET OPTION   The option to apply the proceeds of an insurance or investment contract to buy an **annuity** at a current market rate from the same or another insurance company.

OVERSEAS PENSION SCHEME   A pension scheme established outside the UK for local residents of that country or employees of an international organisation, which is subject to local pension scheme and taxation regulations.

PARTICIPATING EMPLOYER   An employer, some or all of whose employees have the right to become members of an **occupational pension scheme**.

Usually applied where more than one employer participates in a single scheme.

PAYMENT SCHEDULE A schedule, required under section 87 PA 1995 for **money purchase occupational pension schemes**, specifying contribution rates to be paid and the due dates for such payments.

PENSION COMMENCEMENT LUMP SUM Under FA 2004, the term for the tax-free cash sum that may be paid to a member on taking pension benefits.

PENSION CREDIT

(1) The amount of benefit rights that an ex-spouse of a scheme member becomes entitled to following a **pension sharing order**.

(2) An income-related (means-tested) benefit that boosts a pensioner's state pension to ensure they have a minimum level of income.

PENSION DEBIT The amount of benefit rights given up by a scheme member when a **pension sharing order** is made in respect of that member.

PENSION GUARANTEE An arrangement whereby, on the early death of a pensioner, the pension scheme pays a further sum or sums to meet a guaranteed total.

This total may be established by relation to, for instance, a multiple of the annual rate of pension or the accumulated contributions of the late member.

PENSION INCREASE An increase to a pension in payment.

*Such an increase may arise as a result of **escalation** or **indexation** or may be a **discretionary increase**.*

PENSION INPUT AMOUNT The amount of contributions paid and increases in value of a member's benefits for **annual allowance** purposes as arrived at in accordance with sections 230–237 FA 2004.

PENSION INPUT PERIOD A period of no more than 12 months over which the **pension input amount** for an **arrangement** is measured.

PENSION PROTECTION FUND (PPF) A fund set up under PA 2004 to provide benefits to members of **defined benefit schemes** that **wind up** due to the employer's insolvency with insufficient assets to pay benefits.

PENSION SCHEMES REGISTRY The register of **occupational pension schemes** and **personal pension schemes**, maintained by the **Pensions Regulator**.

*The registry enables members to trace schemes with which they have lost touch and collects the **levy**.*

PENSION SHARING ORDER   An order made in accordance with the provisions of Chapter I of Part IV of WR&PA 1999 which makes provision for the pension rights of a scheme member to be split on divorce.

PENSION TAX RELIEF AT SOURCE   The procedure whereby member contributions are paid net of basic rate tax and the scheme **administrator** claims the tax from HMRC. Any higher-rate tax is claimed under self assessment.

PENSIONABLE SERVICE   The period of service which is taken into account in calculating benefits.

*PSA 1993 gives the term a statutory definition for the purposes of the **preservation**, **revaluation** and **transfer payment** requirements of the Act. PA 1995 gives a further statutory definition.*

PENSIONS OMBUDSMAN   The Pensions Ombudsman deals with disputes about entitlement and complaints of maladministration from members of **occupational pension schemes** and **personal pension schemes**. The Ombudsman's role also includes investigating complaints or disputes between **trustees** of occupational pension schemes and employers, and between trustees of different occupational pension schemes or between trustees of the same scheme.

PENSIONS REGULATOR, THE (TPR)   An independent body set up under PA 2004 to regulate **occupational pension schemes** from 6 April 2005. Its role is to protect members of occupational pension schemes, to promote good administration of schemes, and to reduce the risk of situations arising 'that may give rise to a claim on the **Pension Protection Fund**'. It has the power to impose orders and fines on **trustees** and employers.

PERSONAL ACCOUNTS   A pension arrangement, to be set up by the Government, effective from 2012, with the intention of providing greater opportunities for individuals to save for retirement.

PERSONAL LIFETIME ALLOWANCE   The **lifetime allowance** applicable to individuals who have registered for **primary protection**. This would be higher than the **standard lifetime allowance** and is indexed in line with changes in the standard lifetime allowance.

*See also **enhanced lifetime allowance**.*

PERSONAL PENSION SCHEME   A scheme provided by an insurance company (or another financial institution) to enable individuals to save for a private retirement income.

A personal pension scheme can be registered with the **Pensions**

Regulator as a **stakeholder pension scheme** if the necessary conditions are met.

The statutory definition is in section 1 PSA 1993.

PRESERVATION The granting by a scheme of **preserved benefits** to a member leaving **pensionable service** before **normal pension age** under an **occupational pension scheme**, in particular in accordance with minimum requirements specified by PSA 1993.

PRESERVED BENEFITS Benefits arising on an individual ceasing to be an **active member** of an **occupational pension scheme**, payable at a later date.

PRIMARY PROTECTION A mechanism by which individuals can register pre-**A Day** rights of more than £1.5m and obtain an increased **personal lifetime allowance**.

PRINCIPAL EMPLOYER Commonly used in scheme documentation for the particular **participating employer** in which is vested special powers or duties in relation to such matters as the appointment of the **trustees**, amendments and **winding up**. Usually this will be the employer which established the scheme or its successor in business.

PRIORITY RULE The provisions contained within the scheme documentation setting out the order of precedence of liabilities to be followed if the scheme is wound up.

Section 73 PA 1995 introduced an overriding statutory order of priorities, which was amended by PA 2004 with effect from 6 April 2005.

PROJECTED UNIT METHOD A funding method in which the **actuarial liability** makes allowance for projected earnings. The contribution rate is that necessary to cover the cost of all benefits which will accrue in the control period following the valuation date by reference to earnings projected to the dates on which the benefits become payable.

Also known as the projected unit credit method.

PROSPECTIVE MEMBER An individual, not currently a member of the pension scheme of his/her employer, who is either entitled to join or will become eligible to join in the future by virtue of continuing in employment with the employer.

PROTECTED RIGHTS The benefits from a scheme **contracted out** on a money purchase basis deriving from at least the **minimum contributions** or **minimum payments**, which are provided in a specified form as a necessary condition of contracting out.

PUBLIC SECTOR PENSION SCHEME An **occupational pension scheme** for employees of central or local government, a nationalised industry or other statutory body.

PUBLIC SECTOR TRANSFER ARRANGEMENTS The arrangements of the **transfer club** to which certain schemes, mainly in the public sector, belong.

PURCHASED LIFE ANNUITY An **annuity** purchased privately by an individual. In accordance with section 656 ICTA 1988, instalments of the annuity are subject to tax in part only.

QUALIFYING RECOGNISED OVERSEAS PENSION SCHEME A **recognised overseas pension scheme** where the scheme manager has advised HMRC of its status and undertaken to provide HMRC with certain information.

QUALIFYING SERVICE The term defined in section 71(7) PSA 1993 denoting the service to be taken into account to entitle the member to short service benefit. The current condition is for at least two years' qualifying service.

RECOGNISED OVERSEAS PENSION SCHEME Under FA 2004, an **overseas pension scheme** which is established and recognised in a prescribed country and satisfies all prescribed requirements.

RECOGNISED TRANSFER Under FA 2004, a transfer representing a member's accrued rights under a **registered pension scheme** to another registered pension scheme (or, in certain circumstances, to an insurance company) or a **qualifying recognised overseas pension scheme**.

RECOVERY PLAN If an **actuarial valuation** shows that the **statutory funding objective** is not met, the **trustees** will have to prepare a 'recovery plan' setting out the steps to be taken (and over what period) to make up the shortfall.

REFERENCE SCHEME TEST The comparison of the benefits provided by a COSR with those under the reference scheme to ensure that they are at least equal, as required under section 12B PSA 1993.

*The **scheme actuary** must certify that the scheme complies with the reference scheme test.*

REGISTERED PENSION SCHEME A pension scheme is a registered pension scheme at any time when, either through having applied for registration and having been registered by HMRC, or through acquiring registered status by virtue of being an approved scheme on 5 April 2006, it is registered under Chapter 2 of Part 4 of FA 2004.

RESTRICTED EMPLOYER-RELATED INVESTMENT The restriction under section 40 PA 1995 and investment regulations of employer-related investment to 5% of scheme assets.

RETIREMENT ANNUITY An **annuity** contract between an insurance company or friendly society and a self-employed individual or a person not in pensionable employment, which was established before 1 July 1988.

REVALUATION

(1) Application, particularly to **preserved benefits**, of **indexation** or **escalation** or the awarding of **discretionary increases**. PSA 1993 imposes a minimum level of revaluation in the calculation of **GMP** and of preserved benefits other than GMP.

(2) An accounting term for the revision of the carrying value of an asset, usually having regard to its **market value**.

SAFEGUARDED RIGHTS The component of a **pension credit** which is attributable to the **contracted-out** benefits of the member. Due to be abolished from 6 April 2009.

SALARY SACRIFICE An agreement between the employer and employee whereby the employee forgoes part of his/her future earnings in return for a corresponding contribution by the employer to a pension scheme.

*This is not the same as an **AVC**.*

SCHEDULE OF CONTRIBUTIONS A schedule specifying the contribution rates and payment dates (normally) agreed between the employer and the **trustees** and certified by the **scheme actuary** as being adequate to satisfy the **statutory funding objective** (or, if still applicable, the MFR).

*Required for most **defined benefit schemes** under section 227 PA 2004.*

SCHEME ACTUARY The named **actuary** appointed by the **trustees** or managers of an **occupational pension scheme** under section 47 PA 1995.

SCHEME ADMINISTRATION MEMBER PAYMENT Under FA 2004, payments made by a **registered pension scheme** to a member, or in respect of a member, for the purposes of administration or management of the scheme.

SCHEME AUDITOR The **auditor** appointed by the **trustees** or managers of an **occupational pension scheme** under section 47 PA 1995.

SCHEME PENSION   Under FA 2004, a pension entitlement provided to a member of a **registered pension scheme**, which is an absolute right to a lifetime pension payable by the scheme.

SCHEME RETURN   A form submitted to the **Pensions Regulator** by schemes containing information that it will use to make sure the information it holds on the register of pension schemes is accurate, calculate **levies** due from pension schemes and regulate pension schemes. The information collected is also used by the **Pension Protection Fund**. Schemes with five or more members must complete an annual scheme return.

SECONDED EMPLOYEE   For the purposes of the legislation on **cross-border schemes**, this is an employee who is sent, by a UK employer, to work overseas for a limited period in another EU member state, is still working under the control of the UK employer and, at the end of that period, intends to return to resume work for that employer in the UK or to retire.

SECTION 9(2B) RIGHTS   Rights to benefits (other than benefits from AVCs) under an **occupational pension scheme** which is **contracted out** on a salary-related basis by virtue of section 9(2B) PSA 1993 and which are attributable to contracted-out employment after 5 April 1997.

*Section 9(2B) rights are benefits payable under the scheme, not just the minimum level of benefits required under the **reference scheme test**.*

SECTION 32 POLICY   Used widely to describe an insurance policy used for **buy-out** purposes.

This term came into use as a result of section 32 FA 1981, which gave prominence to the possibility of effecting such policies.

SECTION 32A POLICY   A policy which under section 32A PSA 1993 enables **protected rights** to be bought out on the **winding-up** of a **contracted-out money purchase scheme**.

SECTION 67   Section 67 of PA 1995 requires that **trustees** obtain members' consents, or a certificate from an **actuary**, before making any modification to an **occupational pension scheme** which would or might affect members' entitlements or **accrued rights** in respect of service before the modification.

SECTION 75 DEBT   A debt due to a pension scheme under PA 1995 from a sponsoring employer if that employer becomes insolvent, or the scheme starts to **wind up**, when the scheme is underfunded.

SECTION 143 VALUATION   A written valuation of a scheme's assets and liabilities for the purposes of enabling the **Pension Protection Fund** to determine whether it must assume responsibility for a scheme.

SECTION 148 ORDERS   Orders issued each year in accordance with section 148 Social Security Administration Act 1992 specifying the rates of increase to be applied to the earnings factors on which **S2P** and **GMPs** are based.

*This **revaluation** is based on the increase in national average earnings. Formerly known as section 21 orders.*

SECTION 179 VALUATION   A written valuation of a scheme's assets and liabilities, prepared and signed by the **scheme actuary**, for the purposes of enabling **Pension Protection Fund levies** to be calculated.

SECURED PENSION   Under FA 2004, a pension either underwritten by an insurance company other than a **short-term annuity** or **income withdrawal**, or provided through an employer-sponsored scheme (other than income withdrawal).

SELF-ADMINISTERED SCHEME   An **occupational pension scheme** where the assets are invested, other than wholly by payment of insurance premiums, by the **trustees**, an in-house investment manager or an external investment manager.

Although on the face of it the term self-administered should refer to the method of administering contributions and benefits, in practice the term has become solely related to the way in which the investments are managed.

SELF INVESTMENT   The investment of the assets of an **occupational pension scheme** in employer-related investments.

A 5% limit is imposed on employer-related investments by PA 1995 (with certain exemptions).

SERIOUS ILL HEALTH COMMUTATION   Full **commutation** of benefits if a member's life expectancy is less than 12 months.

SHORT SERVICE REFUND LUMP SUM   A refund of employee contributions because they have stopped accruing benefits under the scheme and have less than two years of **pensionable service** under the scheme.

SHORT-TERM ANNUITY   Under FA 2004, an **annuity** contract purchased from a member's pension fund held under a **money purchase arrangement** that provides that member with an **unsecured pension** income for a term of no more than five years (not reaching to or beyond their 75th birthday).

SOCIALLY RESPONSIBLE INVESTMENT (SRI)   Investment strategies or restrictions that take account of the social, environmental or other impacts that a company's activities can have on individuals and the environment.

...continued

Pension funds are required to disclose in their **Statement of Investment Principles** the extent to which they take these factors into account.

SPECIAL ANNUAL ALLOWANCE (SAA)   The maximum amount of pension savings that can be built up in the 2009/10 and 2010/11 tax years before liability to a **special annual allowance charge**.

SPECIAL ANNUAL ALLOWANCE CHARGE (SAAC)   The tax charge levied on members with income exceeding £150,000 and **pension input** exceeding the **special annual allowance** in the relevant year.

STAKEHOLDER PENSION SCHEME   A **defined contribution scheme** able to accept contributions from 6 April 2001. A scheme, which in addition to being registered with HMRC, must satisfy the CAT standards necessary to be registered with the **Pensions Regulator** as a stakeholder scheme.

Employers who do not come within one of the employer exemptions must offer their relevant employees access to a stakeholder pension scheme.

STANDARD LIFETIME ALLOWANCE   The maximum amount of tax relievable pension savings that can be built up by an individual who has not registered for **primary protection** or **enhanced protection**.

STATE EARNINGS-RELATED PENSION SCHEME (SERPS)

The additional pension provisions of the state pension scheme. This has been replaced by the **State Second Pension (S2P)** from 6 April 2002.

STATE PENSIONABLE AGE (SPA)   The age from which pensions are normally payable by the state pension scheme as defined in Schedule 4 PA 1995.

PA 1995 raised the state pensionable age for women to 65, bringing it in line with men. This is being phased in over a ten-year period between 2010 and 2020.

STATE SECOND PENSION (S2P)   The state pension scheme introduced with effect from 6 April 2002 to replace **SERPS** and to enhance the **basic pension**.

STATEMENT OF FUNDING PRINCIPLES   Statement by the **trustees** setting out their policy for securing that the **statutory funding objective** is met and recording the decisions as to the basis for calculating the scheme's **technical provisions** and the period within which any shortfall is to be remedied.

STATEMENT OF INVESTMENT PRINCIPLES (SIP) A written statement of principles governing decisions about investment for an **occupational pension scheme**, which **trustees** are required to prepare and maintain. Trustees must have regard to advice from a suitably qualified person and consult with the employer.

STATEMENT OF RECOMMENDED PRACTICE (SORP) Guidance on best accounting practice for the presentation of financial information prepared by the particular industry to which the SORP relates.

STATEMENT OF TOTAL RECOGNISED GAINS AND LOSSES (STRGL) One of the four primary statements in the company financial statements, together with the profit and loss account, balance sheet and statement of cash flows. The statement shows the components as well as the total of realised gains and losses, where these have been earned but not recognised. Where a gain is both earned and recognised it will be disclosed in the profit and loss account.

Under **FRS 17**, **actuarial gains and losses** are disclosed in the STRGL and not in the profit and loss account.

STATUTORY FUNDING OBJECTIVE The requirement that a **defined benefit scheme** 'must have sufficient and appropriate assets to cover its **technical provisions**'.

SUMMARY FUNDING STATEMENT A summary of the scheme's funding position. It must be issued to all scheme members and **beneficiaries** (annually except for small schemes) and is their primary source of information on funding matters. Its content is prescribed by regulations.

TECHNICAL PROVISIONS Under the scheme funding provisions of PA 2004, the amount required on an actuarial calculation to make provision for the scheme's liabilities.

TOTAL PENSION INPUT AMOUNT The aggregate of the **pension input amounts** for a period in respect of each **arrangement** relating to an individual under **registered pension schemes** of which the individual is a member.

TRANSFER CLUB A group of employers and **occupational pension schemes** which has agreed to a common basis of **transfer payments**.

TRANSFER PAYMENT A payment made from a pension scheme to another pension scheme, or to purchase a **buy-out** policy, in lieu of benefits which have accrued to the member or members concerned, to enable the receiving arrangement to provide alternative benefits.

*The transfer payment may be made in accordance with the scheme rules or in exercise of a member's statutory rights under PSA 1993. See also **cash equivalent**.*

TRIVIAL PENSION   A pension which is so small that it can be fully exchanged for cash (**commuted**).

TRUST   A legal concept whereby property is held by one or more persons (the **trustees**) for the benefit of others (the **beneficiaries**) for the purposes specified by the trust instrument. The trustees may also be beneficiaries.

TRUST DEED   A legal document, executed in the form of a deed, which establishes, regulates or amends a **trust**.

TRUSTEE   An individual or company appointed to carry out the purposes of a **trust** in accordance with the provisions of the **trust deed** (or other documents by which a trust is created and governed) and general principles of trust law.

TRUSTEE REPORT   A report by the **trustees** describing various aspects of an **occupational pension scheme**. It may form part of the **annual report**.

UNSECURED PENSION   Under FA 2004, payment of **income withdrawal** direct from a **money purchase arrangement**, or income paid from a **short-term annuity** contract purchased from such an arrangement, to the member (who is aged under 75).

UPPER ACCRUAL POINT (UAP)   The maximum amount of earnings on which **S2P** and **contracted-out rebates** are based. It replaced the **UEL** for this purpose from 6 April 2009.

UPPER BAND EARNINGS   Earnings between the **lower earnings limit** and the **upper earnings limit**. The **State Second Pension** is worked out on these earnings.

UPPER EARNINGS LIMIT (UEL)   The maximum amount of earnings (equal to approximately seven times the **lower earnings limit**) on which full NI contributions are payable by employees.

NI Contributions of 1% are payable by employees above this limit from 6 April 2003.

VESTED RIGHTS

(a)   For **active members**, benefits to which they would unconditionally be entitled on leaving the scheme

(b)   for **deferred pensioners**, their **preserved benefits**, *and*

(c)   for pensioners, pensions to which they are entitled including where appropriate the related benefits for spouses or other **dependants**.

WHISTLE-BLOWING   The statutory duty imposed on **trustees**, employers, **administrators** and advisers by section 70 PA 2004 to advise the **Pensions Regulator** as soon as practicable in writing if they have reasonable cause to believe there is a material problem with an **occupational pension scheme**.

WINDING UP   The process of terminating an **occupational pension scheme** (or less commonly a **personal pension scheme**), usually by applying the assets to the purchase of immediate **annuities** and deferred annuities for the **beneficiaries**, or by transferring the assets and liabilities to another pension scheme, in accordance with the scheme documentation or statute (section 74 PA 1995).

WITH-PROFITS POLICY   An insurance policy under which a share of the surpluses disclosed by **actuarial valuations** of the insurance company's life and pensions business is payable in addition to the guaranteed benefits or in reduction of future premiums.

Many of the definitions used in this Glossary of Terms originate from *Pensions Terminology – A Glossary for Pension Schemes, Revised and Updated, Seventh Edition 2007*, published by The Pensions Management Institute, whose kind permission to reproduce here is gratefully acknowledged.

COMPOUND INTEREST TABLES

How to use the compound interest tables to generate additional factors:

Present value of a payment of
one unit due in n years' time

$$v^n = \frac{1}{(1+i)^n}$$

Present value of an annuity of
one unit per annum payable
annually in arrears for n years

$$a_{\overline{n}|} = \frac{1-v^n}{i}$$

Present value of an annuity of
one unit per annum payable
annually in advance for n years

$$\ddot{a}_{\overline{n}|} = \frac{1-v^n}{d}$$

Present value of an annuity of
one unit per annum payable
continuously for n years

$$\bar{a}_{\overline{n}|} = \frac{1-v^n}{\delta}$$

Present value of an annuity of
one unit per annum payable
in two half-yearly instalments
in arrears for n years

$$a_{\overline{n}|} = \frac{i}{i}\, a_{\overline{n}|}$$

Present value of an annuity of
one unit per annum payable
in four quarterly instalments
in arrears for n years

$$a_{\overline{n}|} = \frac{i}{i}\, a_{\overline{n}|}$$

Present value of an annuity of
one unit per annum payable
in twelve monthly instalments
in arrears for n years

$$a_{\overline{n}|} = \frac{i}{i}\, a_{\overline{n}|}$$

Accumulated value after n years
of an annuity of one unit payable
annually in arrears

$$s_{\overline{n}|} = \frac{(1+i)^n - 1}{i}$$

Accumulated value after n years of a single unit payment $[(1+i)^n]$

n	i=1%	i=2%	i=3%	i=4%	i=5%
1	1.010000	1.020000	1.030000	1.040000	1.050000
2	1.020100	1.040400	1.060900	1.081600	1.102500
3	1.030301	1.061208	1.092727	1.124864	1.157625
4	1.040604	1.082432	1.125509	1.169859	1.215506
5	1.051010	1.104081	1.159274	1.216653	1.276282
6	1.061520	1.126162	1.194052	1.265319	1.340096
7	1.072135	1.148686	1.229874	1.315932	1.407100
8	1.082857	1.171659	1.266770	1.368569	1.477455
9	1.093685	1.195093	1.304773	1.423312	1.551328
10	1.104622	1.218994	1.343916	1.480244	1.628895
11	1.115668	1.243374	1.384234	1.539454	1.710339
12	1.126825	1.268242	1.425761	1.601032	1.795856
13	1.138093	1.293607	1.468534	1.665074	1.885649
14	1.149474	1.319479	1.512590	1.731676	1.979932
15	1.160969	1.345868	1.557967	1.800944	2.078928
16	1.172579	1.372786	1.604706	1.872981	2.182875
17	1.184304	1.400241	1.652848	1.947900	2.292018
18	1.196147	1.428246	1.702433	2.025817	2.406619
19	1.208109	1.456811	1.753506	2.106849	2.526950
20	1.220190	1.485947	1.806111	2.191123	2.653298
21	1.232392	1.515666	1.860295	2.278768	2.785963
22	1.244716	1.545980	1.916103	2.369919	2.925261
23	1.257163	1.576899	1.973587	2.464716	3.071524
24	1.269735	1.608437	2.032794	2.563304	3.225100
25	1.282432	1.640606	2.093778	2.665836	3.386355
26	1.295256	1.673418	2.156591	2.772470	3.555673
27	1.308209	1.706886	2.221289	2.883369	3.733456
28	1.321291	1.741024	2.287928	2.998703	3.920129
29	1.334504	1.775845	2.356566	3.118651	4.116136
30	1.347849	1.811362	2.427262	3.243398	4.321942
31	1.361327	1.847589	2.500080	3.373133	4.538039
32	1.374941	1.884541	2.575083	3.508059	4.764941
33	1.388690	1.922231	2.652335	3.648381	5.003189
34	1.402577	1.960676	2.731905	3.794316	5.253348
35	1.416603	1.999890	2.813862	3.946089	5.516015
36	1.430769	2.039887	2.898278	4.103933	5.791816
37	1.445076	2.080685	2.985227	4.268090	6.081407
38	1.459527	2.122299	3.074783	4.438813	6.385477
39	1.474123	2.164745	3.167027	4.616366	6.704751
40	1.488864	2.208040	3.262038	4.801021	7.039989

	i=1%	i=2%	i=3%	i=4%	i=5%
d	0.009901	0.019608	0.029126	0.038462	0.047619
$i^{(2)}$	0.009975	0.019901	0.029778	0.039608	0.049390
$i^{(4)}$	0.009963	0.019852	0.029668	0.039414	0.049089
$i^{(12)}$	0.009954	0.019819	0.029595	0.039285	0.048889
δ	0.009950	0.019803	0.029559	0.039221	0.048790

Note: For GMP fixed rate revaluation factors *see page 48*.

APPENDIX 3: COMPOUND INTEREST TABLES

Accumulated value after n years of a single unit payment $[(1+i)^n]$

n	i=6%	i=7%	i=8%	i=9%	i=10%
1	1.060000	1.070000	1.080000	1.090000	1.100000
2	1.123600	1.144900	1.166400	1.188100	1.210000
3	1.191016	1.225043	1.259712	1.295029	1.331000
4	1.262477	1.310796	1.360489	1.411582	1.464100
5	1.338226	1.402552	1.469328	1.538624	1.610510
6	1.418519	1.500730	1.586874	1.677100	1.771561
7	1.503630	1.605781	1.713824	1.828039	1.948717
8	1.593848	1.718186	1.850930	1.992563	2.143589
9	1.689479	1.838459	1.999005	2.171893	2.357948
10	1.790848	1.967151	2.158925	2.367364	2.593742
11	1.898299	2.104852	2.331639	2.580426	2.853117
12	2.012196	2.252192	2.518170	2.812665	3.138428
13	2.132928	2.409845	2.719624	3.065805	3.452271
14	2.260904	2.578534	2.937194	3.341727	3.797498
15	2.396558	2.759032	3.172169	3.642482	4.177248
16	2.540352	2.952164	3.425943	3.970306	4.594973
17	2.692773	3.158815	3.700018	4.327633	5.054470
18	2.854339	3.379932	3.996019	4.717120	5.559917
19	3.025600	3.616528	4.315701	5.141661	6.115909
20	3.207135	3.869684	4.660957	5.604411	6.727500
21	3.399564	4.140562	5.033834	6.108808	7.400250
22	3.603537	4.430402	5.436540	6.658600	8.140275
23	3.819750	4.740530	5.871464	7.257874	8.954302
24	4.048935	5.072367	6.341181	7.911083	9.849733
25	4.291871	5.427433	6.848475	8.623081	10.834706
26	4.549383	5.807353	7.396353	9.399158	11.918177
27	4.822346	6.213868	7.988061	10.245082	13.109994
28	5.111687	6.648838	8.627106	11.167140	14.420994
29	5.418388	7.114257	9.317275	12.172182	15.863093
30	5.743491	7.612255	10.062657	13.267678	17.449402
31	6.088101	8.145113	10.867669	14.461770	19.194342
32	6.453387	8.715271	11.737083	15.763329	21.113777
33	6.840550	9.325340	12.676050	17.182028	23.225154
34	7.251025	9.978114	13.690134	18.728411	25.547670
35	7.686087	10.676581	14.785344	20.413968	28.102437
36	8.147252	11.423942	15.968172	22.251225	30.912681
37	8.636087	12.223618	17.245626	24.253835	34.003949
38	9.154252	13.079271	18.625276	26.436680	37.404343
39	9.703507	13.994820	20.115298	28.815982	41.144778
40	10.285718	14.974458	21.724521	31.409420	45.259256

	i=6%	i=7%	i=8%	i=9%	i=10%
d	0.056604	0.065421	0.074074	0.082569	0.090909
$i^{(2)}$	0.059126	0.068816	0.078461	0.088061	0.097618
$i^{(4)}$	0.058695	0.068234	0.077706	0.087113	0.096455
$i^{(12)}$	0.058411	0.067850	0.077208	0.086488	0.095690
δ	0.058269	0.067659	0.076961	0.086178	0.095310

Note: For GMP fixed rate revaluation factors *see page 48*.

MALE LIFE ANNUITIES ON S1PMA (Year of Use=2010) TABLE

With improvements of 1.25% p.a. subject to an overlay of 80% of the long cohort.

Exact age:	50	55	60	65	70	75
Interest						
0%	37.019	31.843	26.815	22.043	17.658	13.684
1%	30.425	26.791	23.083	19.399	15.870	12.546
2%	25.463	22.872	20.101	17.224	14.359	11.558
3%	21.665	19.789	17.690	15.418	13.071	10.694
4%	18.709	17.330	15.719	13.906	11.966	9.937
5%	16.373	15.344	14.091	12.629	11.013	9.268
6%	14.499	13.719	12.734	11.542	10.184	8.675
7%	12.975	12.376	11.590	10.609	9.460	8.147
8%	11.719	11.252	10.619	9.804	8.823	7.675
9%	10.673	10.304	9.788	9.104	8.261	7.251
10%	9.790	9.495	9.070	8.491	7.762	6.869

Note: The columns represent the present value of a life annuity of one unit per year payable continuously to a male from the exact age given subject to the mortality experience of the S1PMA table, adjusted for use in 2010, allowing for long-term projected improvements in life expectancy of 1.25% p.a. subject to an overlay of 80% of the long cohort projection factors, and valued at the rates of interest shown.

FEMALE LIFE ANNUITIES ON S1PFA (Year of Use=2010) TABLE

With improvements of 1.25% p.a. subject to an overlay of 60% of the long cohort.

Exact age:	50	55	60	65	70	75
Interest						
0%	38.742	33.786	28.854	24.010	19.390	15.129
1%	31.574	28.186	24.634	20.966	17.305	13.784
2%	26.236	23.886	21.294	18.486	15.557	12.626
3%	22.188	20.535	18.619	16.445	14.079	11.621
4%	19.065	17.885	16.451	14.749	12.822	10.745
5%	16.616	15.762	14.675	13.327	11.743	9.978
6%	14.665	14.037	13.203	12.126	10.812	9.301
7%	13.088	12.620	11.972	11.102	10.004	8.702
8%	11.795	11.442	10.933	10.222	9.298	8.170
9%	10.723	10.452	10.047	9.462	8.677	7.694
10%	9.822	9.612	9.287	8.800	8.129	7.267

Note: The columns represent the present value of a life annuity of one unit per year payable continuously to a female from the exact age given subject to the mortality experience of the S1PFA table, adjusted for use in 2010, allowing for long-term projected improvements in life expectancy of 1.25% p.a. subject to an overlay of 60% of the long cohort projection factors, and valued at the rates of interest shown.

USEFUL WEBSITES

Accounting Standards Board	*www.frc.org.uk/asb*
Association of British Insurers	*www.abi.org.uk*
Association of Consulting Actuaries	*www.aca.org.uk*
Association of Member-Directed Pension Schemes	*www.ampsonline.co.uk*
Association of Pension Lawyers	*www.apl.org.uk*
Board of Actuarial Standards	*www.frc.org.uk/bas*
Companies House Executive Agency	*www.companieshouse.gov.uk*
Chartered Insurance Institute	*www.cii.co.uk*
Department for Work and Pensions	*www.dwp.gov.uk*
DirectGov	*www.direct.gov.uk*
Equality and Human Rights Commission	*www.equalityhumanrights.com*
Faculty/Institute of Actuaries	*www.actuaries.org.uk*
Financial Ombudsman Service	*www.financial-ombudsman.org.uk*
Financial Services Authority	*www.fsa.gov.uk*
Financial Services Compensation Scheme	*www.fscs.org.uk*
Government Actuary's Department	*www.gad.gov.uk*
HM Revenue & Customs	*www.hmrc.gov.uk*
HM Treasury	*www.hm-treasury.gov.uk*
Information Commissioner's Office	*www.ico.gov.uk*
Law Society	*www.lawsociety.org.uk*
National Association of Pension Funds	*www.napf.co.uk*
Office for National Statistics	*www.statistics.gov.uk*
Office of Public Sector Information	*www.opsi.gov.uk*
Pension Protection Fund	*www.pensionprotectionfund.org.uk*
PPF Ombudsman	*www.ppfo.org.uk*
Pensions Management Institute	*www.pensions-pmi.org.uk*
Pensions Ombudsman	*www.pensions-ombudsman.org.uk*
Pensions Regulator	*www.thepensionsregulator.gov.uk*
Pensions Research Advisory Group	*www.prag.org.uk*
Personal Accounts Delivery Authority	*www.padeliveryauthority.org.uk/*
Society of Pension Consultants	*www.spc.uk.com*
TPAS The Pensions Advisory Service	*www.pensionsadvisoryservice.org.uk*